Oxford Shakespeare Topics

Shakespeare and Literary Theory

OXFORD SHAKESPEARE TOPICS

Published and Forthcoming Titles Include:

Oxford Shakespeare Topics

Shakespeare and Literary Theory

JONATHAN GIL HARRIS

UNIVERSITY PRESS

2010

OXFORD
UNIVERSITY PRESS

Great Clarendon Street, Oxford OX2 6DP

Oxford University Press is a department of the University of Oxford.
It furthers the University's objective of excellence in research, scholarship,
and education by publishing worldwide in

Oxford New York

Auckland   Cape Town Dar es Salaam Hong Kong   Karachi
Kuala Lumpur Madrid Melbourne Mexico City   Nairobi
New Delhi Shanghai Taipei Toronto
With offices in
Argentina Austria Brazil Chile Czech Republic France Greece
Guatemala Hungary Italy Japan South Korea Poland Portugal
Singapore Switzerland Thailand Turkey Ukraine Vietnam

Oxford is a registered trade mark of Oxford University Press
in the UK and in certain other countries

Published in the United States
by Oxford University Press Inc., New York

ISBN 978-0-19-957338-7

Printed and bound in Great Britain by
enham and Eastbourne

For Madhavi Menon,
master–mistress of my theoric

Acknowledgements

While writing this book, I have incurred many debts. I wish to thank in particular Peter Holland and Stanley Wells both for suggesting that I take on the project and for their sage counsel throughout; the Folger Institute and the National Endowment for the Humanities for the award of a fellowship that allowed me to write the book; my fellow fellow, David Schalkwyk, and the editorial team of *Shakespeare Quarterly*—especially Barbara A. Mowat and Gail Kern Paster—for their advice and support; my dean, Peg Barratt, and my chair, Jeffrey Cohen, for granting me leave to complete the book; my teachers at the University of Auckland and the University of Sussex who first introduced me to critical theory a quarter of a century ago; the many students who have taken my Shakespeare and Literary Theory seminar; and Lee Edelman, who generously allowed me to read and write about his essay on *Hamlet* before its publication. I am especially grateful to my research assistant, Jennifer L. Wood, who has worked tirelessly for a year to track down and annotate the many examples of what I call Shakespearian theory; without her efforts, this book would not be what it is. My biggest debt, as always, is to Madhavi Menon. Her presence in my life informs every word of this book.

Contents

viii   *Contents*

Shakespeare and Theory

> ...when he speaks,
> The air, a chartered libertine, is still,
> And the mute wonder lurketh in men's ears
> To steal his sweet and honeyed sentences:
> So that the art and practic part of life
> Must be the mistress to his theoric.

Henry V, 1.1.48–53

What does Shakespeare mean by 'theoric'? As modelled in King Henry's 'sweet and honeyed sentences', it incites wonder and emulation; it brings order to the world, stilling the air in Henry's presence; it holds dominion over the 'art and practic part of life'. By play's end, it rules over far more than air and art: the irresistible power of Henry's theoric is of a piece with his conquests of France and Princess Katherine. This rosy vision of theoric's all-conquering power, however, stands in stark contrast to the jaundiced perspective of *Othello*'s arch-villain Iago, who damns his rival Cassio as a man of 'bookish theoric' given to 'Mere prattle without practice' (1.1.23, 25). Theoric in *Henry V* is future-oriented, increasing the scope of its dominion throughout the play. But for Iago, theoric is every bit as dusty as the antique Salic law that Henry's counsellors invoke to justify the invasion of France. Even the term 'theoric' sounds quaint in his mouth, like the name of a medieval horn-helmeted Saxon chieftain. Theoric the Bookish may have won a few skirmishes in his time. But he is simply not equipped—or so Iago would have us believe—to meet the challenges of today.

Shakespeare's theoric in many ways anticipates the diverse ensemble of critical methods that constitutes literary theory. There are, to be sure, differences between them. Theoric imposes meaning on the world; literary theory often questions meaning. Theoric is announced by metaphors of sexual and imperial domination; literary theory tends to be anti-patriarchal and anti-colonial. Yet both theoric and theory refer, in their root sense, to a mode of analytic thought about the nature of things. Each term derives from the Greek verb *theorein*, meaning to view, look at, contemplate. And inasmuch as they represent forms of contemplative abstraction, both theoric and theory have often been compared negatively with practice. For the Iagos of this world, practice is substantial, comfortingly straightforward, hands-on; theoric or theory is ethereal, pointlessly complex, 'bookish'. Even some 'bookish' people share a version of this prejudice. To its naysayers, literary theory can seem not just difficult but even wilfully obscure and jargon-ridden, inimical to the practical tasks of reading, understanding, and enjoying literature. We might dub this the Iagoist position, according to which literary theory is 'mere prattle without practice', a fad out of touch with reality. As such, Iagoism is at odds with what we might term the Henryist position, which celebrates literary theory for its continuing power to lend shape, from on high, to 'the art and practic part of life'. For Henryism, in other words, all practice is informed—no matter how unselfconsciously—by theory.

Despite their seemingly opposed tendencies, the Iagoist and Henryist positions share a significant assumption: that theory is an autonomous domain, separate from or alien to what it theorizes. This assumption has been especially evident in Shakespeare studies. Literary theory is often seen by both its detractors and its advocates as belonging to an entirely different time and place from Shakespeare. It is not just a modern or postmodern phenomenon that comes well after Shakespeare's historical moment; it also hails from an alien land, deriving its critical energies from the intellectual ferments of post-war France in particular. For the Iagoists, modern 'French' literary theory has performed (in a reversal of theoric's conquest of France in *Henry V*) a scandalous takeover of writing steeped in the world of the English Renaissance. For the Henryists, literary theory can finally explain, from a sophisticated Left Bank perspective, what has been hitherto mysterious or mystified about Shakespeare's texts. Despite the obvious antagonism between Iagoism and Henryism, each under-stands literary theory as a foreign body that infects Shakespeare. The Iagoists see theory as a dangerous virus from which Shakespeare needs to be quarantined; the Henryists see it as an inoculation that makes Shakespeare studies healthier.

Each view mischaracterizes not just literary theory but also the nature of literary theory's relation to Shakespeare. In particular, imagining theory as a foreign body extraneous to Shakespeare ignores a fascinating yet mostly unremarked tendency. All the major theoretical movements of the last century—from formalism and structuralism to deconstruction and actor-network theory, from Freudian and Lacanian psychoanalysis to feminism and queer theory, from Marxism and poststructuralist Marxism to new historicism and postcolonial theory—have developed key aspects of their methods in dialogue with Shakespeare. In other words, when we apply theory to Shakespeare's writing, we are not really exposing it to foreign bodies, whether pathogenic or curative. If theory is a virus that has invaded Shakespeare, its genetic material already contains traces of its host. Theory, then, is not straightforwardly foreign to Shakespeare: it is already Shakespearian.

To name just a few examples: Karl Marx was an avid reader of Shakespeare and used *Timon of Athens* to illustrate aspects of his economic theory; psychoanalytic theorists from Sigmund Freud to Jacques Lacan have explained some of their most axiomatic positions with reference to *Hamlet*; Michel Foucault's early theoretical writing on dreams and madness returns repeatedly to *Macbeth*; Jacques Derrida's deconstructive philosophy is articulated in dialogue with Shakespeare's plays, including *Romeo and Juliet*; French feminism's best-known essay is Hélène Cixous's meditation on *Antony and Cleopatra*; certain strands of queer theory derive their impetus from Eve Kosofsky Sedgwick's reading of the Sonnets; Gilles Deleuze alights on *Richard III* as an exemplary instance of his theory of the war machine; and postcolonial theory owes a large debt to Aimé Césaire's revision of *The Tempest*.

These examples underscore how literary theory is less an external set of ideas imposed on Shakespeare's texts than a mode—or several modes—of critical reflection inspired by, and emerging from, his writing. These modes together constitute what we might call

'Shakespearian theory': theory that is not just *about* Shakespeare but also derives its energy *from* Shakespeare. By reading what theorists have to say about and in concert with Shakespeare, we can begin to get a sense of how much the DNA of contemporary literary theory contains a startling abundance of chromosomes—concepts, preoccupations, ways of using language—that are of Shakespearian provenance. Some of these chromosomes may be immediately familiar to us from Shakespeare's writing; some have mutated almost beyond recognition. But they are omnipresent in literary theory's genome. And if 'Shakespearian theory' suggests how theory has always been Shakespearian, it can equally help us realize that Shakespeare's writing has itself always been theoretical. That is why the British literary theorist Terry Eagleton can say that 'it is difficult to read Shakespeare without feeling that he was almost certainly familiar with the writings of Hegel, Marx, Nietzsche, Freud, Wittgenstein and Derrida' (Eagleton 1986, p. ix–x), or the Slovenian psychoanalytic theorist Slavoj Žižek can observe that 'Shakespeare without doubt had read Lacan' (Žižek 1991, 9). Such pronouncements may be deliberately and provocatively anachronistic. But they also recognize how the relation between Shakespeare and theory is not one of prior host and belated foreign body. Rather, the relation is familial, grounded in resemblance. Shakespeare and theory do not belong to different times and lands; they are instead kissing cousins, speaking a shared tongue.

Here we might note that the Greek *theorein* is etymologically related to the word 'theatre'. The theatre is a theoretical space inasmuch as it is a space of *theorein*, of viewing and contemplation. And it is all the more theoretical for being a public rather than a private space. As Wlad Godzich reminds us, the *theoria* in ancient Athens was the name of a class of people who publicly watched political deliberations and affirmed certain states of affairs as facts (Godzich 1986, p. xiv). The *theoria*'s express power of affirmation presumed also an implicit power of negation; its capacity to produce public order—a capacity that anticipates Henry's theoric—masked a more radical power to dissent from states of affairs and hence from the affairs of the state. As such, the *theoria* also anticipates the critical power of literary theory. Crucially, the *theoria*'s dual functions of affirmation and negation, of ratification and critique, were very much part of Shakespeare's theatre as well. His playhouse not only offered public entertainment: it also repeatedly tested ideas about the world, affirming some and unsettling others. Moreover, it made its spectators *theoria*-like participants in its theatrical deliberations. 'Like or find fault; do as your pleasures are', the Prologue brusquely advises the audience at the beginning of *Troilus and Cressida* (Pr. 30); the Chorus in *Henry V* begs the audience 'Gently to hear, kindly to judge, our play' (Pr. 34). In other words, Shakespeare's theatre not only performed its own theoretical inquiries (speculating about the nature of things), but also asked that it be judged theoretically (watched carefully and affirmed or criticized). As a consequence, when we contemplate Shakespeare's writing—whether by viewing the plays on the stage or by speculating about the texts on the page—we enter into theory, whether or not we know it.

This book outlines a variety of ways in which we might enter more self-consciously into theory when reading Shakespeare's plays and poems. It does so by examining the most influential movements in contemporary literary theory and how its leading practitioners have engaged Shakespeare. The reader will encounter here an extraordinary array of theoretical writings that make Shakespeare their primary interlocutor. Some of these writings are exemplary of 'isms'—feminism, Marxism—with which the reader may be at least partly familiar; others exemplify newer movements such as rhizome theory, which will be explained in due course. More specifically, this book considers representatives of formalism (William Empson on ambiguity and Sonnet 73; Cleanth Brooks on paradox and 'The Phoenix and the Turtle'; Mikhail Bakhtin on the carnivalesque and Shakespeare's festive drama), structuralism (Roland Barthes on mythic speech and *Julius Caesar*; Roman Jakobson on poetic structure and Sonnet 129; René Girard on mimetic desire and *Troilus and Cressida*), deconstruction (J. Hillis Miller on the impossibility of *logos* and *Troilus and Cressida*; Paul de Man on prosopopeia and Milton's 'On Shakespeare'; Jacques Derrida on the proper name and *Romeo and Juliet*), and rhizome and actor-network theory (Gilles Deleuze on minor theatre and *Richard III*; Michel Serres on noise and *Macbeth*; Bruno Latour on *Dingpolitik* and *Coriolanus*). It also examines representatives of Freudian psychoanalysis (Sigmund Freud on death in *Merchant of Venice* and *King Lear*; Ernest Jones on the Oedipus complex and *Hamlet*; Melanie Klein on envy and *Othello*), Lacanian psychoanalysis

(Jacques Lacan on desire in *Hamlet*; Julia Kristeva on maternal bonds and *Romeo and Juliet*; Slavoj Žižek on the Real in *Richard II*), feminism (Virginia Woolf on Shakespeare's sister; Hélène Cixous on feminine writing and *Antony and Cleopatra*; Elaine Showalter on female madness and *Hamlet*), and queer theory (Eve Kosofsky Sedgwick on homosocial desire and the Sonnets; Jonathan Dollimore on the perverse dynamic and *Othello*; Lee Edelman on queer education and *Hamlet*). And it examines representatives of Marxism (Karl Marx on money and *Timon of Athens*; Georg Lukács on feudalism's demise in Shakespeare's histories; Bertolt Brecht on contradiction and *Coriolanus*), poststructuralist Marxism (Terry Eagleton on language and reification in *Macbeth* and *Twelfth Night*; Jacques Derrida on 'hauntology' and *Hamlet*; Fredric Jameson on utopian criticism and Shakespearian romance), new historicism and cultural materialism (Michel Foucault on dreams and madness in *Macbeth*; Stephen Greenblatt on subversion and containment in Shakespeare's second Henriad; Alan Sinfield on sexual dissidence in *A Midsummer Night's Dream* and *The Two Noble Kinsmen*), and postcolonial theory (Wole Soyinka on the authentic Arab *Antony and Cleopatra*; Edward Said on Caribbean adaptations of *The Tempest*; Sara Ahmed on oriental orientations and Shakespeare's books). If Shakespeare is theoretical, then, theory is clearly Shakespearian.

Shakespeare and Literary Theory consists of twelve chapters, each devoted to a different theoretical movement. The chapters are in turn grouped into three larger parts, each of which focuses on an umbrella theme. Part I, 'Language and Structure', pursues a trajectory from formalism, structuralism and deconstruction to rhizome and actor-network theory. Part II, 'Desire and Identity', traces a second trajectory from Freudian and Lacanian psychoanalysis through feminism to queer theory. Part III, 'Culture and Society', picks up on a third trajectory from Marxism and poststructuralist Marxism through new historicism and cultural materialism to postcolonial theory. Even as the book seeks to cover the gamut of contemporary literary theoretical movements, its three parts are also calibrated with three persistent theoretical preoccupations in Shakespeare's poems and plays.

I. Language and Structure

Contemporary literary theory is to a large extent distinguished by its understanding of language. Formalism, structuralism, and deconstruction see language not as a transparent window onto a pre-existing reality so much as a self-contained structure or web within which meaning is always provisional, ambiguous, and slippery. As a poet and playwright, Shakespeare's primary medium is language, and he too is especially attentive to its potential slipperiness. On the one hand, he sees language as the basis of social order; when words are unreliable, social relations suffer. The equivocating witches of *Macbeth*, 'imperfect speakers' (1.3.68) who predict the future in riddles, preside over a world where all order is turned upside down. Similarly, in *All's Well That Ends Well*, Bertram complains that the untrustworthy Paroles 'has deceived me like a double-meaning prophesier' (4.3.96). On the other hand, as Paroles's name (French for 'words') suggests, Shakespeare sees all language as slippery and unreliable. Feste says in *Twelfth Night* that a 'sentence is but a cheverel glove to a good wit, how quickly the wrong side may be turned outward' (3.1.10–12). And it is worth noting that Shakespeare himself is 'a good wit' who delights in any opportunity to turn a word inside out and reveal other, unexpected meanings. He revels in puns and sexual innuendoes: as Samuel Johnson famously said, 'A quibble [or wordplay] was to him the fatal Cleopatra for which he lost the world, and was content to lose it' (Johnson 1969, 68). Yet if Shakespeare sees language as a complex structure in which every word punningly contains the trace of others, he also recognizes that the world he contentedly loses in his quibbles is not confined to language, and that there are other elusive structures beyond the realm of signification. As a theatre practitioner, he seems to have been particularly attuned to the power of music and sound. 'The isle is full of noises', says Caliban in *The Tempest*, made by 'a thousand twangling instruments' (3.2.130, 132); and the play's stage directions call for '*Solemn and strange music*' (3.3.18) and '*a strange, hollow, and confused noise*' (4.1.142). Here Shakespeare intimates how the slippery structure of language is paralleled by other, dynamic assemblages that fluctuate between order and disorder—an intuition that, as we will see, anticipates those of rhizome and actor-network theory.

II. Desire and Identity

One of the most influential tributaries of contemporary literary theory is psychoanalysis. In its Freudian and especially its Lacanian versions, psychoanalysis understands desire in ways that radically destabilize gender and sexual identity, with consequences that have been powerfully teased out by feminism and queer theory. Shakespeare is likewise a theorist of desire and the confusions of identity—gendered and sexual—that desire induces. Despite their conventional endings in actual or anticipated marriage, which seem to suggest a stabilization of sexuality and gender, comedies like *A Midsummer Night's Dream* show how desire is extraordinarily protean, skipping willy-nilly from character to character. Any object of desire is potentially indistinguishable from other objects that substitute for it: 'How easy is a bush supposed a bear' (5.1.22)—or, for that matter, how easily is an ass supposed a beautiful lover, or a Helena a Hermia (provided, of course, you're drugged). In tragedies like *Antony and Cleopatra*, desire's restless movements become more dangerous. Antony always desires what he lacks, with the result that 'The present pleasure, | By revolution low'ring, does become | The opposite of itself' (1.2.113–15): he can never be happy with what he has. Shakespeare depicts the dangerous restlessness of desire most comprehensively in his poems. Sonnet 129 presents 'lust in action' as 'perjured, murd'rous, bloody' (129.2–3), an intimation of the violent passion that leads Tarquin to perform the eponymous act of *The Rape of Lucrece*. In such poems, the desirer is split by his compulsions, becoming a stranger to himself; the object of desire mirrors this splitting, appearing simultaneously as angel and devil, male and female. The repeated gender indeterminacy of the beloved—witness the 'maiden-tongued' youth of *A Lover's Complaint* (100), 'the maiden burning' of Adonis's cheeks in *Venus and Adonis* (50), or the androgynous 'master-mistress of my passion' in Sonnet 20 (2)—suggests the metamorphic world of desire, which transforms everything into its opposite. But this indeterminacy was also the condition of Shakespeare's theatre, where female characters were played by boy-actors. Shakespeare repeatedly asks us to see the boy in the woman, whether by cross-dressing 'her' as male or by drawing attention to the stage convention, as with the Page boy who is instructed on how to play Sly's wife in the Induction scenes of *The Taming of the Shrew*. Depending on one's perspective, such gender play discloses unorthodox sexual possibilities (when Rosalind cross-dresses in *As You Like It*, she takes the sexually ambiguous name Ganymede) or underscores patriarchy's control over representations of women on the all-male stage.

III. Culture and Society

The third powerful current in contemporary literary theory is materialist political philosophy. Insisting that culture is shaped by material conditions (modes of economic production, relations of power and knowledge, projects of colonial and imperial domination), Marxism, new historicism, cultural materialism, and postcolonial theory see any work of literature as riddled with the tensions of its historical moment. Shakespeare is likewise a theorist of the historical cusp he was living in, and he repeatedly considers the ramifications of the transition from feudalism to capitalism. Interestingly, his theorization of social transition differs according to genre. In a history play like *Henry IV Part 1*, Hotspur's obsolete code of feudal honour is eclipsed by Hal's new charismatic creed of calculated risk and profit, which seems shaped by the logic of capitalism. As he tells his father, Hotspur 'is but my factor [merchant's agent] . . . To engross up glorious deeds on my behalf' (3.2.147–8). Comedies like *The Merchant of Venice* fantasize a happy marriage between the old feudal wealth of Portia and Bassanio's (or Antonio's) new merchant capital, which dispatches ships around the globe in search of 'spices' and 'silks' (1.1.33, 34). Shakespeare's tragedies approach the shift with a good deal more trepidation: a play like *King Lear* depicts the catastrophic demise of old feudal values at the hands of a frighteningly rapacious individualism embodied by Edmund the Bastard, who denounces the 'plague of custom' (1.2.3). And the unclassifiable play *Troilus and Cressida* is bilious in its depiction of how market values, fuelled by the 'universal wolf' (1.3.121) of appetite, have supplanted the old codes of heroism. The mixed attitudes of the plays about the new cultural dispensations—cautious celebration of individual risk and versatility, dawning horror at the losses that their ascendancy might spell—are not unconnected to the contradictions of Shakespeare's own theatre company, which embodied the social contradictions of its time. On the one hand, the King's Men—as their very name suggests—owed feudal subservience to their royal patron. On the other hand, they were a joint-stock company seeking to make a financial profit from their labour and their capital assets. With one foot in the feudal world and another in capitalism, Shakespeare was institutionally well positioned to theorize cultural conflict and historical transformation.

As these three theoretical preoccupations suggest, Shakespeare's writing repeatedly asks questions of his world. It also asks questions of ours. His plays and poems theorize language and structure, desire and identity, and culture and society in ways that have provided a continuing stimulus to contemporary literary theory. We might remember, moreover, that Shakespeare also theorizes theory—or, rather, theoric. And his theorization of theoric redounds to his own credit. After all, the passage from *Henry V* with which I began can be read as a homage to Shakespeare himself. Henry's 'sweet and honeyed speech' recalls the soubriquets Shakespeare had recently received from his admirers. In 1598, the year before *Henry V* was first written and performed, he was characterized in print as 'honey-tongued Shakespeare' (Meres 1598, 282) as well as 'Shakespeare…whose honey-flowing vein…Praises doth obtain' (Barnfield 1598, E2ᵛ). And in 1599, he was twice described in the university play *The Return from Parnassus Part 1* as 'Sweete Mr Shakspeare' (Macray 1886, 57). The 'sweet and honeyed speech' of *Henry V*—the hallmark not just of its charismatic king, but also his creator—is presented as an exemplary instance of theoric, of a powerful analytic intelligence that generates order and disorder through language. As the many instances of Shakespearian theory in this book make clear, the complexities of Shakespeare's 'honeyed and sweet speech' continue to stimulate, and reward, contemplation. Despite the obsequies performed by the Iagoists, in other words, Theoric the Bookish is not dead yet.

Part I

Language and Structure

1

Formalism

William Empson, Cleanth Brooks, Mikhail Bakhtin

> ... we can clear these ambiguities,
> And know their spring.
>
> *Romeo and Juliet*, 5.3.216–17

Ambiguity is one of the hallmarks of Shakespeare's poetic and dramatic language. But what is its 'spring'? In *Romeo and Juliet*, the Prince promises that, by attending closely to ambiguities, we can find an explanatory origin underlying their complexity. His promise concerns ambiguities in Verona: the mystery of how Romeo, Juliet, and Paris all died in the Capulet tomb. Practitioners of formalism make a similar promise about the ambiguities of literary language. They proceed from the assumption that the form of a literary work, far from being the decorative wrapping of its more meaningful content, is crucial in producing its meanings. Formalists thus read a literary work not just for what it says but also for the often tricky ways in which it is written. Yet by paying attention to the forms that make literary language so distinctively slippery, formalists—like Shakespeare—maintain that we can also know the 'spring' of 'ambiguities', that we can find an origin behind literature's plurality of meaning. For some, this spring is the poetic imagination; for others, the nature of existence itself.

As this might suggest, formalism is by no means a singular or coherent theoretical movement. In its most extreme—and most caricatured—version, formalism asserts that a work of literature is a self-contained system like a machine or an organism. A literary text, in this view, does not really represent anything outside itself; by drawing attention to its unusual and innovative forms, it refers just to itself. In general, however, 'formalism' simply designates any critical approach that attends to the formal details of a text. These details might include not only grammar and syntax but also literary devices like metaphor and paradox. Such an approach tends to diminish, but doesn't always rule out, the relative importance of a text's historical, biographical, and cultural contexts. By turning away from such contexts, formalists react against two earlier approaches to literature: Romanticism, which focuses on the imaginations of individual author-geniuses more than the formal details of their writing; and historicism, which reads literary texts as reflections of the times and cultures in which they were written.

At least in its British and American incarnations, formalism has also become a near-synonym for apolitical criticism. Yet when it first emerged in the 1920s, it had a subtle political purpose. The Cambridge professor I. A. Richards and his student William Empson departed from the critical orthodoxy of their day, a literary history grounded in source study that presumed considerable leisure time and an access to private estate libraries enjoyed largely by upper-class scholars. Redirecting critical attention to the formal ambiguities of the text and the experience of the reader, Richards's and Empson's democratic approach allowed anyone, regardless of their class, to work simply with the text in front of them. The ability to read ambiguity closely—that is, to wrestle with the formal complexities of a play, poem, or even a single line—took precedence over the size of one's library. Richards's and Empson's embrace of close reading had a huge impact in the United States, specifically in the New Criticism associated, post-Second World War, with John Crowe Ransom, W. K. Wimsatt, and Cleanth Brooks. Yet the American New Critics (so-called to differentiate them from 'older' critics, who practised literary history rather than formalist close reading) diverged from their English counterparts in one crucial respect. They were insistent that a work of art was a self-contained formal system; one should not try to ascertain its meaning, as Empson occasionally did, by appealing to the intention of the author—a procedure that W. K. Wimsatt and Monroe Beardsley damned as 'the intentional fallacy' (Wimsatt and Beardsley 1946, 468).

The Anglo-American formalist emphasis on close reading mirrored the innovations of Russian formalists like Viktor Shklovsky and Boris Eichenbaum, who in the years leading up to and after the Russian Revolution of 1917 also theorized literary language through close attention to its formal properties. Empson and Brooks knew nothing of Russian formalism, and vice versa. Yet like the British and American formalists, the Russians insisted that literary language is distinct from ordinary uses of language, and that what a work of literature says cannot be separated from how the work says it. And just as the Anglo-Americans fetishized ambiguity and paradox, the Russians emphasized literature's powers of defamiliarization—its ability, through innovations of form, to make the familiar strange, ambiguous, or ambivalent. But the Russian formalists differed in fundamental ways from their Anglo-American counterparts. Critics like Empson and Brooks tended to regard ambiguity with serene equanimity; by contrast, the Russians sought to shock and transform. These different affects shaded into the political stances of each: detachment on the part of the New Critic, iconoclasm on the part of the Russian formalist.

Different literary genres appealed to these different strands. Anglo-American formalists favoured the more private and often difficult genre of poetry; by contrast, Russian formalists privileged the more sociable form of the novel. What they share, apart from their attention to formal devices, is an abiding interest in Shakespeare in order to elaborate their basic theoretical assumptions and to identify the 'spring' of 'ambiguity'. Their generic biases are evident, however, in which Shakespeare works they read. Russian formalists, in their embrace of the novel, are more likely to absorb Shakespeare into discussions of Rabelais, Cervantes, and Dostoyevsky; they read his plays as novelistic dialogues rather than as performance pieces. By comparison, the best Anglo-American formalist readings are of Shakespeare's poems; even when they analyse the plays, they tend to read them as extensions of his poetry.

Ambiguity in Sonnet 73: William Empson

Seven Types of Ambiguity, published in 1930, was written by William Empson (1906–84) while he was an undergraduate studying with I. A. Richards at Cambridge. In it he theorized a twofold approach to literature that, with little modification, he was to practise for his entire career. This approach might be summarized as follows. First, complex and multiple meanings can be teased out of particular textual phenomena—a poem, a dramatic speech, a line of verse, even a single word—by close attention to their formal details. And second, these multiple meanings must ultimately be apprehended as having singular points of origin outside the text: the author's personal experience; a traumatic historical event; the reader's attempts to make sense of the text; and so on. Although Empson applied these assumptions in readings of poetry by Chaucer, Donne, Herbert, Milton, Wordsworth, and Keats, the connecting thread in his major publications is Shakespeare. He wrote sensitively about the complex meanings of 'dog' in *Timon of Athens*, 'sense' in *Measure for Measure*, and 'honest' in *Othello* (Empson 1967, 175–84, 218–49, 270–88); he also wrote about *Hamlet* and *Macbeth*. But he was most at home writing about the Sonnets, and largely because of the above twofold approach: the Sonnets lend themselves both to close readings of how their formal devices generate the poems' complex, often refractory meanings and to speculation about their author and his strategies for coping with the vicissitudes of love and ageing.

The title of *Seven Types of Ambiguity* discloses its principle of organization—seven chapters devoted to seven different types of ambiguity in literary writing. The first and most exemplary type is the metaphor, the figure of speech whereby two things that have demonstrably different properties are said to be alike. The other types are mostly variations on the first, such as the ambiguity in which two or more distinct meanings are resolved into one—Empson characterizes this as using two different metaphors at once—or the ambiguity in which two separate ideas, connected through context, can be given in one word simultaneously. Empson also considers ambiguities in which two or more meanings of a statement do not agree with each other, but combine to make clear a complicated state of mind in the author; confusions of meaning caused when the author discovers an idea in the act of writing; ambiguities generated by a statement that, saying nothing, forces readers to improvise an interpretation that is most likely in conflict with the author's meaning; and uncertainties produced by two opposing words that expose a fundamental division in the author's mind.

The first type of ambiguity is, for Empson, the hardest to illustrate with specific examples, yet it is the most capacious and typical. He defines ambiguity as 'any verbal nuance, however slight, which gives room for alternative reactions to the same piece of language' (Empson 1963, 1). Thus almost any statement, Empson concedes, can be ambiguous inasmuch as it can produce different reactions. But metaphor in particular, because it conjoins two different entities in one image, produces deliberately ambiguous effects. And because of its reliance on metaphor, literary language is especially susceptible to such ambiguity. To illustrate his argument, Empson discusses the fourth line of Shakespeare's Sonnet 73. Its first three lines read:

> That time of year thou mayst in me behold
> When yellow leaves, or none, or few, do hang
> Upon those boughs which shake against the cold
>
> (73:1-3)

This is the standard metaphor of old age as the autumn of one's years. But the line that interests Empson is the next. Here the narrator shifts from his autumnal metaphor, with its image of trees losing their leaves, and compares himself to 'Bare ruined choirs, where late the sweet birds sang' (73:4). This new metaphor is ambiguous in several ways. We still have the image of the narrator as a deciduous tree in our minds; the apparition of the 'ruined choirs' where 'birds sang' thus borrows its force from the decrepit tree of the previous lines yet replaces it with an altogether different image. And the 'choirs' them-selves might suggest two distinct (if related) referents: a group of singers and the part of the church where such a group might sing.

But these are not the only ambiguities unleashed by the line. Analysing the speaker's metaphorical identification with those 'bare ruined choirs, where late the sweet birds sang', Empson remarks that

the comparison holds for many reasons; because ruined monastery choirs are places in which to sing, because they involve sitting in a row, because they are made of wood, are carved into knots and so forth, because they used to be surrounded by a sheltering building crystallised out of the likeness of a forest, and coloured with stained glass and painting like flowers and leaves, because they are now abandoned by all but the grey walls coloured like the skies of winter, because the cold and Narcissistic charm suggested by choir-boys suits well with Shakespeare's feeling for the object of the Sonnets, and for various sociological and historical reasons (the protestant destruction of monasteries; fear of Puritanism), which it would be hard to trace out in their proportions; these reasons, and many more relating the simile to its place in the Sonnet, must all combine to give the line its beauty, and there is a sort of ambiguity in not knowing which of them to hold most clearly in mind. Clearly this is involved in all such richness and heightening of effect, and the machinations of ambiguity are among the very roots of poetry. (Empson 1963, 2–3)

Empson teases out a remarkable string of associations from this one line. As a result, ambiguity differs here from its etymological sense of two (Latin *ambi-*, or both) possible meanings. Indeed, as his impossibly long and breathless first sentence suggests, there is potentially no end to the ambiguities of Sonnet 73's fourth line—and hence no end to the line's generation and displacement of meaning. For Empson, this seemingly endless ambiguity is what distinguishes the language of poetry, lending it its 'richness' and heightened 'effect'.

Yet it is worth noting that, in Empson's reading, the myriad ambiguities of line 4 do not entirely open up to endless semantic play. Nor does his discussion seek to confine attention exclusively to the words on the page. Instead, line 4's metaphorical twists and turns lead Empson to consider a) the mind of the author ('Shakespeare's feeling'); b) historical context ('the protestant destruction of the monasteries'); and c) the experience of the reader ('there is a sort of ambiguity in not knowing which [reason for the metaphor] to hold most clearly in mind'). We might call these the unambiguous destinations of Empsonian ambiguity—destinations that lend fixed compass points to the otherwise turbulent slippages and oscillations of poetic meaning. That is, Empson reads the forms of ambiguity in line 4 of Sonnet 73 to discover Shakespeare the man and his world. In this, he differs sharply from the American New Critics.

Paradox in 'The Phoenix and the Turtle': Cleanth Brooks

Cleanth Brooks (1906–94) shares with Empson an investment in the complexities of literary form, particularly ambiguity and paradox. But for Brooks, literary form is independent of authorial intention or historical context. He insists that poetry must be read *sub specie aeternitatis*, as true for all time, 'otherwise the poetry of the past becomes significant merely as cultural anthropology, and the poetry of the present, merely as a political, or religious, or moral instrument' (Brooks 1947, pp. x–xi). Brooks, writing after the pitched ideological as well as military battles of the Second World War, valorizes a domain of the imagination that transcends history and its antagonisms. In this domain, which is for Brooks modelled by poetry, conflict is superseded by paradox, the trope that in his estimation best recognizes the perennial diversity-within-unity and unity-within-diversity of the world. In this he opposes himself not just to history and politics, but also to the certainties of science: 'there is a sense in which paradox is the language appropriate and inevitable to poetry. It is the scientist whose truth requires a language purged of every trace of paradox' (Brooks 1947, 3). Although Brooks's criticism is avowedly secular—he states that literature should not be a surrogate for religion—one might detect an echo of Christianity in his embrace of paradox: the mystery of the three-in-one of the Trinity, or of the Son of Man who is both crucified and resurrected, finds a strong parallel in Brooks's recurrent interest in poetry's paradoxical alignment of multiplicity with singularity and death with rebirth.

The transcendent domain of the poetic imagination is illustrated by Brooks's *Well-Wrought Urn* (1947). The book's title advertises how Brooks regards the object of literary criticism as a self-contained, beautiful artefact. The urn's maker, and the culture in which and for it is made, is parenthesized in order to focus attention on the structure of the poem and its play of paradox (indeed, the subtitle of Brooks's book is 'Studies in the Structure of Poetry'). As typifies the New Critics' fascination with Shakespeare's contemporary, the metaphysical poet John Donne, *The Well-Wrought Urn*'s title is a quotation from a Donne poem—'The Canonization'. In the latter, the speaker likens himself and his lover to a phoenix whose ashes are contained in an urn. The phoenix, Brooks argues, is a particularly apt analogy, since it combines the imagery of birds and of burning candles, and adequately expresses the power of love to preserve even as its passion consumes. By combining the two lovers in one image, the phoenix embodies a paradox (the two-that-is-one), which Brooks views as exemplary of poetic language. In a characteristic move, he also sees the poem as harmonizing form and content—a splicing of traditional opposites that can be seen as a second-order paradox. In his reading the poem is not only *about* a 'well-wrought urn' that canonizes the lovers; it is *itself* such an urn, performing in its consummate artistry the memorial act that it describes. The poem memorializes less the lovers, however, than the transcendent power of the poetic imagination.

But the title of Brooks's book also invokes Shakespeare—specifically, his obscure poem 'The Phoenix and the Turtle', which tells of two birds' union in love and their cremation in an urn reminiscent of that from Donne's 'Canonization'. This heavily allegorical piece has vexed attempts at decipherment. Some have speculated that it is an occasional verse to commemorate a marriage; others have seen it as a treatise on Platonic love. Brooks pounces on the uncertainty of such readings to 'boldly pre-empt the poem for our own purposes' (Brooks 1947, 18) and, divorcing it from its putative historical contexts, reads it entirely as an exercise in the poetic language of paradox. Shakespeare presents the lovebirds as repudiating the rational distinction between one and two:

> So they loved as love in twain
> Had the essence but in one,
> Two distincts, division none.
> Number there in love was slain.
>
> .   .   .   .
>
> Single Nature's double name,
> Neither two nor one was called.
>
> (25–8, 39–40)

To which Brooks responds: 'Precisely! The nature is single, one, unified. But the name is double...If the poet is to be true to his poetry, he must call it neither two nor one: the paradox is his only true solution' (Brooks 1947, 18). This is a solution opposed to the certainties of logic and Brooks's enduring object of scorn, science; indeed, Reason is 'in itself confounded' (41) at the union of Phoenix and Turtle. Confronted with the spectacle of the urn, moreover, Reason can only see 'Beauty, truth, and rarity' (53) as cinders enclosed in it. It is incapable, in other words, of recognizing the mystical power of resurrection that distinguishes the phoenix.

Brooks's reading of the poem insists on this phoenix-quality in the very form of the verse itself:

The urn to which we are summoned, the urn which holds the ashes of the phoenix, is like the well-wrought urn of Donne's 'Canonization' which holds the phoenix-lovers' ashes: it is the poem itself.... But there is a sense in which all such well-wrought urns contain the ashes of a phoenix. The urns are not meant for memorial purposes only, though that often seems to be their chief significance to the professors of literature. The phoenix rises from its ashes; or ought to rise; but it will not arise for all our mere sifting and measuring the ashes, or testing them for their chemical content. We must be prepared to accept the paradox of the imagination itself; else 'Beautie, Truth, and Raritie' remain enclosed in their cinders and we shall end with essential cinders, for all our pains. (Brooks 1947, 19–20)

The urn in 'The Phoenix and the Turtle', like its counterpart in 'The Canonization', is not simply a self-contained system. That would be to relegate it to the domain of empirical objects studied by science. For Brooks, the urn performs an imaginative transcendence of the opposition between life and death: it may be a memorial to the dead, but it grants the dead a new poetic life in the imagination. Once again, we can see the quasi-religious cast of Brooks's theorization of paradox. It is a form of transubstantiation that restores imaginative life to dead matter, just as the mystery of the Eucharist lends life—the life of Christ, the living Word—to an inanimate communion wafer. Brooks's conception of paradox, which thrives on the dissolution of rational oppositions, works ultimately to assert a transcendent unity: the power of the imagination. Like Empson, then, Brooks embraces the proliferation of ambiguity only to arrest it. In Brooks's case, however, ambiguity's singular spring is neither Shakespeare the man nor his world but, rather, a mystical unity that transcends both.

Ambivalence in Shakespeare's Carnivalesque Plays: Mikhail Bakhtin

Empson's and Brooks's divergent theories of ambiguity and paradox find a synthesis of sorts in Mikhail Bakhtin's theory of formal ambivalence, which both opens up to consideration of the material world and performs a redemptive regeneration. Bakhtin (1895–1975) was a complex thinker who confounds easy pigeonholing as formalist. Yet many of his most distinctive critical strategies were shaped by the Russian formalist school of the early twentieth century. In his early works, written before the Second World War, Bakhtin cleaves to a recognizably formalist agenda: he treats the novel—as do many Russian formalists—as the essence of the literary, because of its power to defamiliarize convention. It does so primarily by virtue of its investment in dialogic speech, Bakhtin's term for an open-ended utterance that presumes another—a listener, a second speaker—who transforms and displaces its intended meaning. He theorizes the dialogic potential of Dostoyevsky's writing inasmuch as it subverts singular truths with playful polyphony or heteroglossia (literally, different tongues); in this, Dostoyevsky partakes of a tradition that dates back to Shakespeare, 'in which the early buds of polyphony ripened' (Bakhtin 1984, 34). Bakhtin's theorization of the dialogic, polyphony, and heteroglossia suggests a potential interest in theatre. But whereas Empson and Brooks read Shakespearian drama as a subset of poetry, Bakhtin reads it as a subset of the novel.

Bakhtin's best-known work, *Rabelais and His World* (1965), has been read as a veiled critique of totalitarianism. Written while he was a prisoner in a Soviet gulag in the years after the Second World War, the book considers the formal properties of two different social discourses deployed by the sixteenth-century French writer François Rabelais in his extraordinary novel *Gargantua and Pantagruel*: the official discourse of the church and the subversive discourse of carnival and popular culture. Carnival, for Bakhtin, is not just a name for medieval festive holidays such as May Day or Whitsuntide when hierarchy would be systematically inverted (women would dress as men, children would mock elders, and a Lord of Misrule would preside over the proceedings). It also refers to a folk view of the universe opposed to the official cosmology of church and sovereign. Bakhtin sees the latter as monologic, closed, and serious; by contrast, the discourse of carnival is dialogic, open, and festive. This difference derives from fundamentally different understandings of the body. Church discourse understands the body hierarchically, with the head ruling the lower parts; in this discourse, the body is a singular entity with sealed boundaries. Bakhtin calls this the classical body image, and it contrasts the laughing grotesque body of popular culture. The grotesque body 'is a body in the act of becoming. It is never finished, never completed'. It 'ignores the closed, smooth, and impenetrable surface of the body and retains only its excrescences (sprouts, buds) and orifices, only that which leads beyond the body's limited space or into the body's depths' (Bakhtin 1981, 317–18). The fertile grotesque body is not simply an antithesis of the restrained classical body; it also dialectically transcends the latter, both killing it and resurrecting it with its laughter. Similarly, the carnivalesque is not simply oppositional; it mocks in order to regenerate. That is what gives the carnivalesque and the grotesque body their character-istic power of ambivalence: they are always two-in-one, dying and giving life.

Shakespeare is never granted an entire chapter in *Rabelais and His World*; the book is, after all, about Rabelais. But Shakespeare everywhere haunts its pages as an exemplar of the carnivalesque. Bakhtin sees the witches of *Macbeth*, for example, as ambiguous soothsayers who perform a carnivalesque inversion and regeneration ('fair is foul and foul is fair' [1.1.10]). Shakespeare looms especially large in chapter 3, 'Popular-Festive Forms and Images in Rabelais', in which the laughter and the bodies of Shakespeare's clowns are recur-rent preoccupations:

The analysis we have applied to Rabelais would also help us to discover the essential carnival element in the organization of Shakespeare's drama. This does not merely concern the secondary, clownish motives of his plays. The logic of crownings and uncrownings, in direct or in indirect form, organizes the serious elements also. And first of all this 'belief in the possibility of a complete exit from the present order of life' determines Shakespeare's fearless, sober (yet not cynical) realism and absence of dogmatism. This pathos of radical changes and renewals is the essence of Shakespeare's world consciousness. It made him see the great epoch-making changes taking place around him and yet recognize their limitations. (Bakhtin 1981, 275)

This passage offers a suggestive account of Shakespeare's debts to the festive aspects of Elizabethan English popular culture: it can help explain the clowning characters of holiday comedies like *Twelfth Night* or *A Midsummer Night's Dream* and tragedies like *King Lear* and *Hamlet*; the crowning and uncrowning of Lords of Misrule such as Jack Cade in *Henry VI Part 2* and Stefano in *The Tempest*; the alternative, upside-down worlds of Arden in *As You Like It*, Belmont in *The Merchant of Venice*, and even Egypt in *Antony and Cleopatra*.

It is salutary how Bakhtin's critical practice in the above passage overlaps with those of Empson and Brooks. All three are attracted to ambiguity or paradox; in Bakhtin's case, this ambiguity takes the form of festive ambivalence—carnival's capacity to kill and regenerate, to uncrown and crown, to mock and reassert. Like Brooks, Bakhtin has a quasi-religious investment in the resurrectional power of ambiguity (carnival's 'pathos of radical changes and renewals'). And like Empson, Bakhtin moves from instances of literary ambiguity to the mind of the author (Shakespeare's 'fearless, sober... realism and absence of dogmatism'). But Bakhtin's differences from the Anglo-American formalists are equally instructive. Empson and Brooks tend to work with a word, line, or small passage and draw from it an array of meanings. Bakhtin works with a much broader canvas: he is interested not in local formal details but in the larger 'popular-festive form' that Shakespeare shares with Rabelais and carnivalesque discourse. This makes for some deliberately broad brushstrokes that loosely suggest, rather than closely attend to, specific instances in Shakespeare.

Bakhtin repeatedly alludes to without ever naming the festive antihero of *Henry IV Parts 1* and *2*, the bibulous and appetitive Sir John Falstaff, who epitomizes the carnivalesque body in all its grotesque leakiness. When Bakhtin claims that 'Shakespeare's drama has many outward carnivalesque aspects: images of the material bodily lower stratum, of ambivalent obscenities, and of popular banquet scenes' (Bakhtin 1981, 275), he provides a suitable epithet for Falstaff. Shakespeare's 'fat-guts' knight (*1H4*, 2.2.29), a Lord of Misrule in the night world of London's taverns, is certainly a character straight from the pages of Rabelais. His constantly oozing body (he 'sweats to death, | And lards the lean earth as he walks along' [*1H4*, 2.3.16–17]) typifies the grotesque; his language is full of festively ridiculous swearwords ('whoreson caterpillars, bacon-fed knaves!' [*1H4*, 2.2.78]); and his world seems to revolve around food and drink ('there's a whole merchant's venture of Bordeaux stuff in him; you have not seen a hulk better stuffed in the hold' [*2H4*, 2.4.54–6]). But *Henry IV*, even though it is so vividly suggested, is never anywhere explicitly named. This is typical of Bakhtin's style of analysis, in which he uses Shakespeare less as a textual resource and more as a proper noun to ground the discourse of carnival.

Bakhtin's formalist analysis of the carnivalesque, therefore, is a world away from the microanalysis with which the Anglo-American formalists preoccupy themselves. But the increasingly wide focus of the objects of formalist study in this chapter—a line of a sonnet, a lyric poem, an entire dramatic genre—suggests how formalism is not simply about close reading on a microscopic scale. It recognizes recurrent patterns that contribute to the effects of literary language, and thus its object of analysis can be an entire genre as much as an individual word or line. What unifies all the formalisms surveyed in this chapter is their attitude to ambiguity, which is celebrated as the quintessence of the literary. And a certain moral value attaches to that ambiguity. For Empson, it is the unique power of poetic language in relation to everyday speech. For Brooks, it is the richness of the poetic imagination in relation to the poverty of logic and science. For Bakhtin, it is the life-affirming function of the carnivalesque in opposition to the Lenten austerity of official discourse.

As this suggests, formalism's embrace of ambiguity needn't be apolitical or ahistorical. Bakhtin enlists Shakespeare to theorize an anti-authoritarian politics of form, a transformative conception of language that recognizes the protean nature of being. Although his undoubtedly utopian view of carnival's subversive potential has been disputed—as many have observed, carnival rituals often work to consolidate rather than question hierarchy by serving as a 'safety valve' that allows oppressed peoples to let off steam before resuming their customary places within the social order—it also recognizes the complex relations between authority and transgression that are a feature of literature, drama, and ritual. In this, Bakhtin anticipates much of the work of new historicism and cultural materialism (see Chapter 11). But his emphasis on recurrent structures of binary opposition in literature and culture—the monologic versus the dialogic, the official versus the festive, the classical versus the grotesque—most resonates with the gambits of structuralism, as we will see in the next chapter.

2

Structuralism

Roland Barthes, Roman Jakobson, René Girard

> ...such difference 'twixt wake and sleep
> As is the difference betwixt day and night.
>
> *Henry IV Part 1*, 3.1.214–15

That many of our key concepts and terms are understandable through processes of differentiation is the basis not just of Glyndŵr's remark in *Henry IV Part 1*, but also of structuralism. Structuralist approaches to literature derive primarily from a theoretical understanding of language as a system of differences. In his *Course of General Linguistics* (1916), the Swiss linguist Ferdinand de Saussure proposed that 'in language there are only differences, and no positive terms' (Saussure 1983, 118). By this, he meant that language did not, as common sense might suggest, simply reference ideas or things that pre-exist it (according to this common sense view, the word 'dog' signifies *positively*, i.e. it *posits* something outside itself—a four-legged domestic animal with a tail that wags—that is its referent). Rather, language consists of signs whose meanings are generated through their difference from other signs (that is, 'dog' signifies by *not being* 'wolf' or 'fox' or 'cat'; i.e. its meaning is produced *negatively*).

Saussure saw any linguistic sign as containing two parts, the signifier (the acoustic or written part of the sign) and the signified (the concept). He argued that signs are arbitrary; nothing logically links a signifier to a signified. The two parts of the sign become identified only through differentiation, at the level not just of the signified (the concept of a dog is not the same as the concept of a cat), but also the signifier (the word 'dog' is not 'log' or 'cog,' or 'dig' or 'dot'). In a sentence, meaning is produced syntagmatically, through the syntactical structures—e.g. subject, verb, object—that organize any utterance. But it is also produced paradigmatically, in relation to the other absent signs from which any single present sign conceptually differs. So Juliet's question, 'Art thou not Romeo, and a Montague?' (2.1.102), is not only meaningful syntagmatically—that is, through its syntactical movement from an interrogative subject/verb unit, 'art thou', via negation, 'not', to two proper names—a first name and a patronym—joined by a conjunction: 'Romeo, and a Montague'. It is also meaningful paradigmatically: 'art thou' differs from 'knowest thou' or 'resemblest thou'; these transitive verbs differ from the copula 'art', which presumes identity, not difference, between 'thou' and 'Romeo' and 'Montague'. And those proper names are also significant because of what are not: 'Romeo' is not 'Paris' and 'Montague' is not 'Capulet'—the 'thou' addressed by Juliet is divided from her by the interfamilial tensions of her city, in which the difference between Montague and Capulet is not just merely semantic or conceptual but also deadly.

Saussure's emphasis on contingent structures of differential meaning that vary from language to language carried over into the work of the French cultural anthropologist Claude Lévi-Strauss. He examined 'primitive' non-Western cultures on the model of Saussure's theory of language, with unconventional results: rather than judging cultures for the content of their beliefs, he understood them as organized by fundamental grammars or syntaxes. His groundbreaking study, *The Elementary Structures of Kinship* (1949), argued that, akin to Saussure's notion of linguistic value, families are language systems based on differential structures. Similarly, Lévi-Strauss identified myth as a type of speech through which a universal language or structure of thought could be discovered. Thus he sought to identify the fundamental units of myth, which he termed *mythèmes* (Lévi-Strauss 1958, 227–55).

Structuralism in its linguistic and anthropological guises has had an inbuilt appeal to literary critics because of its emphasis on language and signification. As a literary critical movement, however, structuralism owes as much to formalism as to linguistic and anthropological theory. Indeed, many of its earlier practitioners, such as Roman Jakobson, were first trained as formalists. Structuralism provided those who respected the rigour of close reading but were suspicious of the quasi-religious anti-rationalist tendencies of Cleanth Brooks with a more 'scientific' vocabulary. Yet although structuralist principles of analysis often featured in formalist close readings that eschewed social and historical context, these principles also opened literary criticism up to questions of culture. This is partly because semiology, the structuralist study of signs, emphasizes the larger systems of linguistic, ideological, and cultural signification in which any sign is embedded. One of the pioneering semiological studies, Roland Barthes's *Mythologies*, reads instances of modern French popular culture—wrestling, steak and chips, the Citroën car—as powerful subsets of the overarching signifying system of bourgeois capitalism. And many structuralist literary critics have been influenced by Lévi-Strauss's analyses of universal structures of signification: René Girard, for example, has developed an anthropologically tinged theory of desire through structuralist readings of literary texts that open up into considerations of larger cultural rituals of sacred violence.

Shakespeare has played a small yet not insignificant role in these literary critical adaptations of structuralism. This is no doubt partly because his writing employs a wide array of binary structuring devices (cities versus pastoral spaces, hierarchical societies versus topsy-turvy carnivalesque worlds, Fair Youths versus Dark Ladies) ripe for structuralist analysis. It is also because of his intuition—evidenced in Glyndŵr's remark from *Henry IV Part 1*—that words often mean what they do because of what they are not. Fundamentally, however, Shakespeare is fascinated with signs, understood as meaningful marks in the world-as-text, and how to read them. Plays like *Titus Andronicus*, *Much Ado about Nothing*, *Othello*, and *Cymbeline* are all about how to construe and misconstrue signs, especially signs of feminine intention and fidelity. But the task of reading signs is fundamental to the project of theory in general.

Mythic Signs in Mankiewicz's *Julius Caesar*: Roland Barthes

Structuralist literary theory is very much associated with Roland Barthes (1915–80) and his essay 'The Death of the Author'. Like the American New Critics, he regards as fallacious all appeals to authorial intention in determining the meanings of a text. But he does so for slightly different reasons. Whereas the New Critics see the work of literary art as a beautiful self-contained system that is detached from the author at its birth, Barthes argues that meaning originates not in the work of art itself but in larger systems of signification. He expounds on these systems in his influential work *Mythologies* (1957). This book examines the sign systems not of literature, however, but of modern French popular culture. Barthes's title suggests a debt to structuralist anthropology; 'mythologies' might evoke the stories and fables of alien or long-ago cultures analyzed by Lévi-Strauss. But Barthes reapplies the term to the ideological structures of French popular culture that mystify themselves as 'natural'. In other words, he adapts Lévi-Strauss's tools of analysis in order to read his own culture.

To do so, he also adopts Saussure's terminology. In the long theoretical essay that concludes the book, Barthes defines 'mythic speech' as a form of language in which signs function not only at a primary level—as signifiers attached to signifieds—but also as signifiers at a secondary level of mythological signification. One example is a phrase from a Latin textbook, *quia ego nominor leo* (Barthes 1972, 115). The phrase literally means 'because I am named lion'; at a second-order level, however, it has an additional, timeless meaning, one that for the purposes of the textbook illustrates the principle of subject/predicate agreement. The second-order level of timeless mythic signification is often more politically loaded than this otherwise innocuous example would suggest. Barthes's ultimate illustration of mythic speech is the image, on a French magazine cover, of an African soldier saluting the French flag. A simple sign—the photographic image—is co-opted by the magazine editors to signify, at a second-order mythic level, the perennial benevolence of French imperialism. As this suggests, Barthes's analysis of mythology is at root a demystification of ideology. In his view, ideology is what happens when a historically contingent system of signification (mis)represents itself as the timeless truth: 'any semiological system is a system of values; now the myth-consumer takes the signification for a system of facts: myth is read as a factual system, whereas it is but a semiological system' (Barthes 1972, 131).

One of the mythic sign systems Barthes reads, 'Romans in Film', has a Shakespeare connection. In this short essay, he considers the semiology of 'Romanness' in Charles Mankiewicz's 1955 film adaptation of *Julius Caesar*, starring Marlon Brando as Mark Antony. As

Barthes notes, all the male actors sport fringes, which he sees as a mythic sign:

What then is associated with these insistent fringes? Quite simply the label of Roman-ness. We therefore see here the mainspring of the Spectacle—the *sign*—operating in the open. The frontal lock overwhelms one with evidence, no one can doubt that he is in Ancient Rome. And this certainty is permanent: the actors speak, act, torment themselves, debate 'questions of universal import', without losing, thanks to this little flag displayed on their foreheads, any of their historical plausibility. Their general representativeness can even expand in complete safety, cross the ocean and the centuries, and merge into the Yankee mugs of Hollywood extras: no matter, everyone is reassured, installed in the quiet certainty of a universe without duplicity, where Romans are Romans thanks to the most legible of signs: hair on the forehead. (Barthes 1972, 26)

If Barthes reads the fringe as a single mythic sign—it is not only a visual representation of hair, but also of Roman-ness—he also, in structuralist fashion, locates this mythic sign within a larger signifying system of Roman hair. He notes the 'sub-sign' of Portia's and Calpurnia's locks. Both are disordered: Portia's flowing and uncombed tresses represent 'nocturnal distress', and Calpurnia's plait, resting on her right shoulder, functions as 'the traditional sign of disorder, asymmetry' (Barthes 1972, 27). Both are historically contingent signs, conventions of the visual grammar of twentieth-century Hollywood. Yet both are endowed with the timeless aura of 'natural' sense.

The innocuous mythic signifier of Roman hair is accompanied by another that functions more subtly. Whenever Romans in *Julius Caesar* are thinking about a difficult course of action, they sweat: 'to sweat is to think—which evidently rests on the postulate, appropriate to a nation of businessmen, that thought is a violent, cataclysmic operation, of which sweat is only the most benign symptom' (Barthes 1972, 27–8). For Barthes, in other words, sweat-as-sign demonstrates how the capitalist American culture in and for which the film was made transforms thought into labour. It thus betrays an anti-intellectualism that also conceals the far more oppressive forms of labour on which capitalism depends. In other words, mythic signs are themselves conscripted by Barthes as signifiers of bourgeois American ideology. But for Barthes, what is particularly offensive is how the mythic signs in Mankiewicz's film are patently artificial yet nonetheless function as shorthand for Roman 'reality'. This typifies how 'bourgeois art' thrives on what Barthes calls a 'hybrid' sign—both artificial yet masquerading as true—'which is pompously christened *nature*' (Barthes 1972, 28).

Shakespeare's text is not reflected on here; it is simply Mankiewicz's film adaptation, and its relation to mythic speech, that concerns Barthes. Still, we might consider how *Julius Caesar* is itself concerned with the decoding of signs, and a debunking of delusion grounded in skilful decoding, similar to Barthes's own discourse. In a thunderstorm, Casca tells Cicero about his visions of burning images that he regards as ominous signs; Cassius tells Cicero the storm is a good sign of the evil he and his other cohorts plan to do to Caesar; Calpurnia likewise interprets her foreboding dream about Caesar as a sign of impending danger; holy priests pluck the entrails of an animal and, finding no heart in it, read it as a dangerous sign. Reading the ambiguous signs of 'nature' in order to avoid disaster, therefore, is one of the abiding preoccupations of *Julius Caesar*. In its reading of signs and their relation to 'nature', Barthes's essay arguably repeats that preoccupation.

That Barthes does not reflect on 'Shakespeare' as mythic signifier is surprising; it is precisely because Shakespeare has such cultural capital that a director like Mankiewicz could raise the financial capital to make his adaptation of *Julius Caesar*. Indeed, Barthes's analysis of mythic signification has been immensely useful for popular cultural Shakespeare studies, particularly of the modern Shakespeare industry. Graham Holderness's edited collection *The Shakespeare Myth* (1989) begins with an epigraph from Barthes's *Mythologies* before providing analyses of the image of Shakespeare on the twenty-pound note, on a beer mug advertising Flowers Best Bitter, and in the tourism mecca-cum-theme park that is Stratford-upon-Avon. In literary as opposed to cultural criticism of Shakespeare, however, it is structuralism refracted through formalism that has proved to be far more influential.

The Structures of Sonnet 129: Roman Jakobson

The Russian-born literary critic Roman Jakobson (1896–1982) first trained with the Moscow formalists but moved to Czechoslovakia in the 1920s, where he joined a group working on linguistic theory and studied Saussure. He relocated after the war to the United States, where he met and briefly worked with Lévi-Strauss. Not surprisingly, then, Jakobson's work marries elements of formalist and structuralist analysis. He derives from the Russian formalists the conviction that poetic language is distinguished by its capacity to defamiliarize or make strange everyday speech; but he also associates that capacity with the skilful deployment of signs that function in either a metaphorical register (which he sees as the predominant mode of lyric poetry) or a metonymic register (which he associates with the epic and the novel). Each represents a fundamentally different way of processing thought. Metaphor works by assuming similarity between two concepts: Romeo compares Juliet to the sun, because both dazzle his eyes. By contrast, metonymy depends not on similarity but on the contiguity of two concepts: in *All's Well That Ends Well*, Paroles is called 'Tom Drum' (5.3.318) because of the drum he carries (and loses). For Jakobson, metaphor and metonymy closely parallel Saussure's distinction between the paradigmatic and syntagmatic aspects of an utterance; the paradigmatic presumes a chain of signs related by similarity, whereas the syntagmatic presumes a chain related by contiguity. Jakobson's analyses of literature often turn on variations of this binary distinction.

In his early influential essay 'Linguistics and Poetics', Jakobson suggests that literary critics have focused on metaphor more than on metonymy. Shakespeare's poetic drama, however, employs both, and to that end he offers a short yet compelling close reading of Antony's 'Friends, Romans, countrymen' funeral exordium in *Julius Caesar*. Jakobson reads the speech as a complex illustration of 'the poetry of grammar and its literary product, the grammar of poetry', in which Antony performs a series of deft linguistic substitutions that undermine the authority of Brutus's defence of Caesar's assassination, culminating in the 'daringly realized metonymy' of Antony's claim that 'My heart is in the coffin there with Caesar' (Jakobson 1987, 91). Jakobson's is, tellingly, a very different structuralist analysis of *Julius Caesar* from Barthes's. Whereas the latter expansively moves from items in Mankiewicz's film to consideration of larger semiological and ideological systems (Hollywood, bourgeois capitalism), Jakobson's reading resolutely sticks with the speech itself as a self-contained system.

Jakobson's most comprehensive engagement with Shakespeare is in his essay 'Shakespeare's Verbal Art in "Th'Expence of Spirit"' (1970), co-written with L. G. Jones. The essay develops many of Jakobson's trademark insights into literary language through a model structuralist reading of Shakespeare's Sonnet 129. It resembles a formalist analysis of the kind Cleanth Brooks would recognize inasmuch as it reads the poem closely, attentive to moments of semantic ambiguity and paradox. But it does not seek to use such moments to perform a transcendent synthesis; there is no veneration of paradox as an alternative to scientific rationality, and indeed, the impetus of the reading is to represent the sonnet, with almost scientific precision, as a complex yet entirely logical signifying system. Jakobson and Jones begin by reproducing sonnet 129 in its 1609 Quarto spelling and punctuation (with some variations). But they add to the text a series of diacritical marks that divide it up on structural grounds:

I $_1$Th'expence of Spirit | in a waste of shame
    $_2$ Is lust in action, | and till action, lust
    $_3$ Is perjurd, murderous, | blouddy full of blame,
    $_4$ Savage, extreame, rude, | cruel, not to trust,
II $_1$ Injoyd no sooner | but dispised straight
    $_2$ Past reason hunted, | and no sooner had
    $_3$ Past reason hated | as a swallowed bayt,
    $_4$ On purpose layd | to make | the taker mad.
III $_1$ Made[e] In pursut | and in possession so,
    $_2$ Had, having, and in quest, | to have extreame,
    $_3$ A blisse in proofe | and provd | a[nd] very wo,
    $_4$ Before a joy proposd | behind a dreame,
IV $_1$ All this the world | well knowes | yet none knows well,
    $_2$ To shun the heaven | that leads | men to this hell.

(Jakobson 1987, 198)

The diacritical remarks fall into three categories that work to divide the sonnet into various parts: first, the Roman numerals in the left-hand margin divide the sonnet into four strophes or sub-units of three quatrains and a final couplet; second, the Arabic numerals immediately before each line divide these sub-units into numbered lines; and third, each line is divided by one or more vertical slashes. These divisions are crucial to the structural analysis that follows, which consists initially of teasing out patterns across the divisions: rhyme schemes, repetition of rhymed words elsewhere in the Sonnets, metrical patterns and divergences within lines and across the sonnet. Jakobson and Jones then supplement this initial patterning with some comments on spelling and punctuation, a paraphrase that takes note of puns and semantic ambiguities ('spirit', which means both a life-giving vital power and semen, and 'waste', which puns on 'waist' or genitalia), as well as pervasive grammatical and phonic features (it is the only sonnet in the entire sequence to contain no personal pronouns; the widely alliterative and/or repetitive textures of sound within each line). Crucial to this analysis, and typical of structuralist literary criticism, is their teasing out of binary differences throughout the sonnet. And it is the play of these differences that, in Jakobson and Jones's reading, generates the sonnet's meanings.

In their subsection on 'Odd against Even', Jakobson and Jones consider the first of four interstrophic patterns in the sonnet. Contrasting the odd-numbered strophes (the first and third quatrains) with the even-numbered ones (the second quatrain and the final couplet), they notice a cluster of significant differences: the odd strophes confront the different stages of lust, whereas the even ones present the metamorphoses wrought by lust; the odd strophes abound in abstract substantives and adjectives, whereas the even strophes contain concrete substantives; the odd strophes feature rhymes that end in 'm' ('shame'/'blame', 'extreame'/'dreame'), while the even strophes do not. These odd/even symmetries are not the only interstrophic pattern legible in the sonnet, however. In their subsection on the second interstrophic pattern, 'Outer against Inner', Jakobson and Jones note how the first quatrain and the final couplet share certain features that distinguish them from the second and the third quatrain: whereas the outer strophes have repeating finite, i.e. conjugated, verbs ('is', 'is', 'knowes', 'knowes'), the inner strophes are full of participles ('Injoyed', 'dispised', 'hunted', 'had', 'hated', 'layd', 'had', 'having', 'proposd'). The third interstrophic pattern, 'Anterior against Posterior', entails correspondences between the first two strophes (which alternate definite and indefinite articles) and between the last two strophes (which employ only indefinite articles). And the fourth interstrophic pattern, 'Couplet against Quatrain', notes how the last two lines differ from the rest of the sonnet (in particular, its exclusive use of monosyllables).

This fourfold interstrophic structural analysis (which is accompanied by speculation on how the poem's first line and final couplet might contain some punning allusions to Shakespeare's name) lays the platform for their concluding claim that Sonnet 129 demonstrates an 'amazing external and internal structuration palpable to any responsive and unprejudiced reader' (Jakobson 1987, 214). Their claim to objectivity both evokes and pointedly diverges from the interpretive methodology of American formalists. The New Critic John Crowe Ransom had pronounced Sonnet 129 as devoid of any 'logical organization at all' (Ransom 1938, 535). By contrast, Jakobson and Jones believe that the 'unprejudiced reader', a figure repeatedly conjured by New Criticism, would not only recognize the sonnet's 'organization' but also its fundamental 'logic'. This leads them to strongly counter the anti-logical stance of much formalism:

The research of the last two decades has shown the significant role of fanciful ambiguities in the work of Shakespeare, but there is a far-reaching distance from his puns and double meanings to the surmise of the free and infinite multiplicity of semantic load attributed to Sonnet 129.... An objective scrutiny of Shakespeare's language and verbal art, with particular reference to this poem, reveals the cogent and mandatory unity of its thematic and compositional framework. (Jakobson 1987, 215)

Shakespeare's 'fanciful ambiguities' are no longer those of Empson or Brooks. They are not correctives to but rather instantiations of logic, controlled thought experiments that conduce to a 'cogent and mandatory unity'. As this suggests, Jakobson and Jones diverge from crucial aspects of formalist analysis even as they read closely. They treat Sonnet 129 less as a well-wrought urn containing dead ashes that paradoxically regenerate life than as a well-wrought machine containing many interlocking parts. They want to know not how the poem redeems the reader through its use of formal devices, so much as how the poem functions as a more or less self-contained structure that produces a wide but ultimately finite array of effects.

Jakobson and Jones reject 'the surmise of the free and infinite multiplicity' attributed to this or any other sonnet; but their analysis, with its myriad interstrophic patterns, potentially tugs against this circumscription. What arrests the proliferation of correspondences—and what determines which correspondences are genuine or arbitrary? In their invocation of 'Shakespeare's language and verbal art', there is implicit recourse to an author who controls the play of words. This is suggested also by their speculation that Shakespeare leaves his signature in the poem through the use of sounds ('shame'... 'spirit') that evoke his name. But the desire to find the sonic signature of the author who controls the flow of language it itself potentially swamped by that flow. Sounds can potentially evoke an endless chain of signs. By insisting on the paradigmatic chains of signifieds and signifiers that any sign is embedded in, structuralism shows not just how meaning is produced but also potentially displaced. For all the structuralists' insistence on science, then, the logic and certainty for which they yearn are precarious. The infinite substitutability of signs generates potential crises of meaning, crises that many structuralist literary critics overlook.

Mimetic Desire in *Troilus and Cressida*: René Girard

One exception is René Girard (1923–), who notes how Shakespeare is well attuned to the breakdown of meaning that haunts language and its capacity for infinite substitutability. Although he trained as a medieval historian in France, Girard spent most of his academic career as a professor of French literature in the United States. Girard's eclectic and eccentric body of work locates itself at the interface of cultural anthropology and literary criticism. Throughout his writing, he is interested in how cultures practise rituals of scapegoating. Though these rituals are often horrifically violent, not least in their arbitrary selection of the scapegoat, he sees them as authorizing a violence that is necessary for the creation of social order. Scapegoating, in his view, asserts a fundamental distinction between the inside and outside of the social body that becomes the basis of all other social differences. Girard's analysis is recognizably structuralist inasmuch as he insists, as Saussure does in relation to signs and Lévi-Strauss does in relation to kinship, that it is not the positive identity of the scapegoat that is important. Rather, what is significant is the differential structure that the scapegoat enables. Also recognizably structuralist is Girard's insistence that scapegoating rituals are a corrective to a semiological crisis. This crisis is the spectre of undifferentiated meaning, a spectre that he sees as the product of a universal tendency: mimetic desire.

In Girard's analysis, one's desire is never entirely authentic or original, no matter how much we believe it to be provoked by the object of desire alone. Rather, it is quietly informed by envy and jealousy—a desire to copy and appropriate other's desires. This necessarily generates a triangulated structure: A and B are friends; A desires C; hence B, envying and copying A's desire, also desires C; the difference between A and B is thus blurred, generating a crisis of undifferentiated identity and meaning. This is a problem in a triangulated situation, but it becomes even more so in a social body where everyone enviously desires the same thing. Once again, the object itself does not determine the collective desire; rather, it is humanity's mimetic tendency that results in the endless duplication—and duplicity—of desire. In such a situation, where everyone desires the same thing (e.g. wealth or power), and the spectre of undifferentiation looms, difference must be reasserted. This is often done through an act of arbitrary violence against a scapegoat who is blamed for the undifferentiation, and who is made to carry its burden by being killed or banished. For Girard, this is an almost universal phenomenon intuited by great writers, especially Shakespeare.

Girard has written on many of Shakespeare's plays. But he returns repeatedly to *Troilus and Cressida*—most notably in several chapters of his book *A Theatre of Envy: William Shakespeare* (1991). His earliest essay on the play, 'The Plague in Literature' (1974), from his collection *To Double Business Bound*, most clearly articulates his interpretation of *Troilus and Cressida* as a theorization of the dangers of mimetic desire. Unlike Jakobson and Jones's structuralist reading of Sonnet 129, Girard does not focus simply on Shakespeare's text. Just as Barthes reads Mankiewicz's film adaptation of *Julius Caesar* in relation to a larger system of mythic signification, Girard reads *Troilus and Cressida* as an instance of a deeper, universal structure of signification in Western literature from the Greeks to the twentieth century.

Girard's point of departure is the pervasiveness of plague as metaphor from Homer's *Iliad* and Sophocles's *Oedipus Rex* through Boccaccio's *Decameron* and Defoe's *Journal of the Plague Year* to

Dostoyevsky's *Crime and Punishment* and Camus's *La Peste*. Though these present the plague in different ways, 'the differences, at close range, turn out to be minor... The plague is universally presented as a process of undifferentiation, a destruction of specificities' (Girard 1978, 136). Not only does the plague bring death; it also figures the inversion of social order, turning honest men into thieves, virtuous women into lechers, prostitutes into saints. These are not the utopian inversions that characterize Mikhail Bakhtin's celebration of carnival ritual, but rather figures for an absolute death that permits no regeneration. Girard cites the nightmare about epidemic illness dreamed by Raskolnikov, the central character in Dostoyevsky's *Crime and Punishment*, to expose the deeper determinants of the equation of plague with social anarchy and undifferentiation. In the dream, which reflects Raskolnikov's megalomania, those infected by the illness believe themselves to be in sole possession of the truth, and regard with contempt others who believe they have access to the truth; as they confront others suffering from the same illness, they come into conflict, fight to the death, and the infection spreads. For Girard, Raskolnikov's megalomaniacal desire to be in sole possession of the truth 'implies a contradiction; it aims at a near-divine self-sufficiency, and yet it is *imitative*' (Girard 1978, 139). Raskolnikov worships Napoleon, and this kind of imitative worship both turns someone else into a rival as well as a model. (One might think here also of John Lennon's murderer Mark David Chapman, who both mimicked Lennon's appearance and harboured murderous feelings towards him.)

For Girard, the dangers of imitative desire and the crisis of undifferentiation it unleashes is best illustrated by Ulysses' speech on 'degree'—i.e. the differences of social hierarchy—in *Troilus and Cressida*. Speaking to the Greek leaders about the ten-year war against Troy, Ulysses argues that their failure to make progress is due to mimetic desire: 'Achilles imitates Agamemnon, both in the sense that he seriously aspires to his position (he wants to become the supreme ruler of the Greeks) and in the sense that he derisively mimics and parodies the commander-in-chief' (Girard 1978, 140). Achilles's imitation snowballs into a collective crisis of imitation, in which everyone aspires to the same desire as he, and all 'degree' or rank is disregarded. As Ulysses says of 'degree', 'untune that string, | And hark what discord follows' (1.3.109–10). Tellingly, Ulysses represents the crisis of undifferentiation brought on by mimetic rivalry in the familiar terms of illness:

> So every step
> Exampled by the first pace that is sick
> Of his superior, grows to an envious fever
> Of pale and bloodless emulation.

> (1.3.131–4)

Everyone partakes of that 'universal wolf, appetite', meaning everyone imitates everyone else. It is not just the Greeks, but also the Trojans who succumb to this plague: Girard asserts that the title characters may claim to be authentic and original in their desires for each other, but they are constantly emulating others. This imitative desire to be different is, paradoxically, what ensures the wholesale undifferentiation of the Greeks.

What Girard doesn't mention is that Ulysses's solution to the crisis of undifferentiation is to punish Achilles in a way that replicates rather than banishes the problem of mimetic desire. Having derided Achilles for his theatrics, Ulysses proceeds to play-act himself, pretending that Ajax is a better warrior. It is unclear whether this is designed to goad Achilles into action or to humiliate—and even make a scapegoat of—him. On the one hand, we know that Achilles does leave his tent and takes up arms again, allowing the Greeks ultimate victory against the Trojans (though it is not because of Ulysses' goading: it is because of the death of Achilles' lover Patroclus). On the other hand, the play seems to suggest that the crisis of pathological undifferentiation is potentially unending. Not only does Ulysses become like Achilles (play-actors both), Diomedes like Troilus (suitors of Cressida both), and Cressida like Helen (trophy wives exchanged across national borders both), with no restoration of 'degree' or differentiated autonomous identity. The play also ends with Pandarus bequeathing the audience his diseases—in this case, presumably syphilis—and, with it, the promise of no end of infection.

It is perhaps no surprise that Girard, who wishes to insist on the curative power of rituals of scapegoating and sacrifice, ignores the pathological end of *Troilus and Cressida* and turns instead to the play that it in some way mimetically doubles, though with a difference—*Romeo and Juliet*. Girard notes that Mercutio's 'plague o' both your houses' (3.1.87, 101) is not an idle wish but is enacted in the poisonous rivalry between the Montagues and the Capulets. In this play, however, a sacrificial death does seem to end the crisis; Montague tells Capulet that Romeo and Juliet are 'poor sacrifices of our enmity' (5.3.303), about which Girard concludes: 'a scapegoat mechanism is clearly defined as the solution to the tragic crisis, the catharsis inside the play that parallels the catharsis produced by that play' (Girard 1978, 152–3). Searching for an end not just to his essay but to the endlessness of undifferentiation in *Troilus and Cressida*, Girard pounces on another play that wills an end to mimetic rivalry, and makes Shakespeare the spokesman for this supposedly universal truth. Yet Shakespeare's other dramas of mimetic rivalry—and there are many; think of Proteus and Valentine's competition for Silvia in *Two Gentlemen of Verona*, or Harry Bolingbroke and Harry Hotspur's competition for ascendancy in *Henry IV Part 1*—do not always end so happily. Girard's universalism is most expressed in his claim that 'all drama is a mimetic reenactment of a scapegoat process' (Girard 1978, 153), one that he sees as serving an ultimately cathartic function. But that claim founders on the rocks of other Shakespeare plays, particularly those generic hybrids that do not move to tragic catharsis—not just the problem comedy/tragedy/history *Troilus and Cressida*, but also the tragicomedy (co-written with John Fletcher) *The Two Noble Kinsmen*. In this play, the kinsmen Palamon and Arcite battle to the death for Emilia, in a perfect display of mimetic desire and rivalry; the final resolution, however, in which Arcite first defeats Palamon but is then abruptly killed by his horse, seems less like a reassertion of order than an underlining of the arbitrary violence that purchases it.

Girard emerges from structuralism, but pushes it in unexpected directions. Like Saussure, he insists that meaning is generated within systems of difference. Yet he also intuits that such difference is always provisional and slippery: reassertions of difference often amplify rather than solve crises of undifferentiation. Girard shares this intuition with Shakespeare. As a play like *Macbeth* shows, 'nothing is | But what is not' (1.3.140–1). Not only is everything structured by opposition; such oppositions also unravel inasmuch as each term contains the trace of the other. *Macbeth*'s playworld, in which what 'is' simultaneously 'is not', suggests the unstable terrain that deconstruction takes as its object.

3

Deconstruction

J. Hillis Miller, Paul de Man, Jacques Derrida

> 'Merry' *and* 'tragical'? 'Tedious' *and* 'brief'?—
> That is, hot ice and wondrous strange black snow.
>
> *A Midsummer Night's Dream*, 5.1.58–9

How to think two logically contradictory things at once? This is a problem repeatedly broached by Shakespeare—and by deconstruction. Associated primarily with the name of Jacques Derrida, the French theorist, deconstruction criticizes the metaphysical assumptions of philosophy—that is, the assumptions about principles of reality that are supposedly prior to the physical world. Derrida's critique takes the form of a thoroughgoing questioning of what he calls logocentrism. *Logos* is Greek for 'word', but in the specific sense of a pure meaning that precedes language. This realm of pure meaning is also the realm of logic, which derives from *logos*. Derrida does not so much debunk logic and logocentrism as demonstrate, in often very difficult and punning language, what they conceal. In particular, logocentrism depends on a covert linguistic operation that posits a domain of meaning prior to language and, in turn, prioritizes thought over utterance, speech over writing, and origin over copy.

Derrida's interest to literary scholars was initially a product of his critique, in the 1960s, of Saussure's theory of linguistics, which he regarded as both invested in and as troubling the project of logocentrism. Derrida's critique is less adversarial than it is a teasing out of a counter-logic already legible in Saussure. Structuralist linguistics is logocentric inasmuch as it posits in the sign a one-on-one relation between signified and signifier; despite their simultaneity, the signified arguably takes precedence over the signifier, inasmuch as the latter simply names the former. The counter-logic consists in Saussure's twofold insistence on the arbitrariness of the sign and the negativity of meaning—that is, his understanding of language as a system of differences without positive referents. If the condition of a signifier is that it points to something else, then for Derrida even signifieds in Saussure's system are signifiers, pointing to other concepts from which they differentially derive their meaning. For black to signify, it presumes white. It does not just refer to blackness, then, but also contains the trace of something else that it is not. Pure, self-identical *logos* is thus perpetually deferred by language's potentially endless slippages of signification. To describe this phenomenon, Derrida coined the term *différance*—a pun on *différence*, which in French means both difference and deferral. *Différance* thus lexically performs the phenomenon it describes, inasmuch as it contains the trace of something different that defers any self-identical, singular meaning. Likewise with Derrida's other famous neologism 'deconstruction', a portmanteau term that combines destruction and construction.

Binary pairs of terms disguise the process of *différance* by presuming the priority and completeness of one term. The pair 'man/woman' assigns meaning differentially to both its terms so that each contains the trace of the other; but patriarchal ideology presumes that 'man' comes first. Hence 'woman' is understood differentially as lack, as an absence of the (phallic) completeness of the man, who is understood as the originary whole. That is why, in Genesis, Eve is created from Adam, and not vice versa. Similarly, Adam is created from God. Genesis prescribes the basic pattern: in the beginning is the Word (*logos* in Greek), a realm of pure meaning associated with God; the creator-Word generates copies, and increasingly imperfect copies of copies—Adam then Eve, speech then writing—each of which seems to refer back to this pure, self-present origin. Yet for Derrida, the originary *logos* cannot help but bear the trace of the *différance* that constitutes it as originary; it is de-centred, and its pure meaning deferred, by the trace of what it is not. Thus, in a deconstructive reversal, the second, 'lacking' term in each of the above binary hier-archies—woman, writing—models the insufficiency that haunts not just the supposedly 'whole' first term—man, speech—but also *logos* (self-identical meaning, God) in general. Writing, for Derrida, is not a secondary copy of a whole, prior meaning represented by speech. It is primary, inasmuch as meaning is itself afflicted by the self-divisions and deferrals, the endless slippages of signifiers, which constitute writing. That is why Derrida asserts that 'il n'y a pas de hors-texte' (Derrida 1967, 227), there is nothing outside the text or outside writing.

Derrida often elaborated his deconstructive theory in relation to the complexities of literature: Rousseau's *Confessions*, Mallarmé's poetry, Joyce's *Ulysses*. With its slippery language, literature demonstrated for Derrida the deferrals of *logos*. His ruminations on literature resonated with American critics in the early 1970s, particularly those trained in formalism and drawn to the vagaries of ambiguity and paradox. The work of American-based critics like Paul de Man and J. Hillis Miller, who helped popularize Derrida, is in some ways close to formalism, though with certain crucial differences. Indeed, the relation to formalism is one of the vexed subtexts of deconstruction's critical fortunes. Miller developed Derrida's critique of logocentrism in essays that treated literary works as formal systems, albeit systems riven by contradiction or deferral rather than redemptive paradox or ambiguity. And even as de Man critiqued the logocentric tendencies of formalism, he also teased out its deconstructive potential—so much so that he was criticized for practising an apolitical neo-formalism deaf to the pressing political questions of the 1970s.

There was thus an element of glee on the part of deconstruction's detractors when it was revealed that de Man had written some anti-Semitic articles while working as a journalist in Belgium during the Second World War. This revelation was used to smear de Man's literary criticism in particular, and deconstruction in general, as an irresponsible mode of reading that both refused political commitment and performed a sinister erasure, after the fact, of Nazi sympathies. Derrida, himself a Jew, fiercely defended de Man's reading practices as a literary critic. Yet Derrida also insisted on the anti-authoritarian political implications of deconstruction; and in his later work (as we will see in Chapter 10), he increasingly turned to questions of religion, ethics, and politics that demonstrated deconstruction's potential to move beyond celebrating the impossibility of logic and the endless play of linguistic *différance*.

Shakespeare's texts lend themselves to deconstructive reading, and not just because of their famous open-endedness that allows one to think two different things at once. It's also because of their language. Dr Samuel Johnson derided Shakespeare for his love of quibbles or puns, the 'fatal Cleopatra' (Johnson 1969, 68) to which he was forever attracted. But the Shakespearian pun is not merely an indulgent tic; it discloses the properties of language and the social realities it produces and unsettles. Think of the flood of puns that begins the first scene *Romeo and Juliet*: Gregory and Samson slip from 'colliers' to 'choler' to 'collar' (1.1.2, 3, 4), highlighting the instability of words in a world that nonetheless insists on the absolute power of names (Montague and Capulet) to describe inviolable identities. It is less that Shakespeare's texts can be deconstructed by the anti-logocentric critic, then, than that they are already gleefully self-deconstructing artefacts.

The Impossibility of *Logos* in *Troilus and Cressida*: J. Hillis Miller

The sequence of deconstructive critics examined in this chapter—first J. Hillis Miller, then his colleague and mentor Paul de Man, and finally the movement's foundational figure Jacques Derrida—is, in some ways, back-to-front. My principle of organization is prompted partly by the level of difficulty of each critic in relation to the others: Miller is certainly an easier read than de Man, who is in turn less difficult than Derrida. More whimsically, perhaps, this sequence typifies deconstructive interpretation, which defers origins and insists on the priority of copies and supplements. Indeed, it is certainly the case that Derrida became known in the United States as deconstruction's originator precisely because of his prior mediation by Miller and de Man.

In his early published work, J. Hillis Miller (1928–) often associated himself with the Geneva School of literary criticism—a Swiss offshoot of formalism and structuralism that treated the literary text as an organic whole possessed of its own distinctive structures of consciousness. But Miller's work underwent a transformation after he moved to Yale University in 1972. Influenced there by Paul de Man, his criticism from this period departs from the organic formalism of his earlier work, emphasizing instead the ways in which a literary text is in contradiction with itself, and how a reading 'against the grain' of what that text seems to be saying can reveal the contradictions of Western metaphysics in general. In this, Miller not only adapted the philosophical ideas of Derrida for an American audience; he also shaped the distinctive reading strategies of what came to be known as Yale deconstruction, a literary critical movement associated with Miller, de Man, Geoffrey Hartman, and Harold Bloom. One of Miller's most compelling illustrations of his deconstructive reading practice is his essay 'Ariachne's Broken Woof' (1977), on a single word from Shakespeare's *Troilus and Cressida*. Miller expansively moves from the challenge posed by this word to read the instabilities of the passage in which it appears and of Western metaphysics in general.

Miller starts with the sequence in which Troilus, having spied his lover Cressida dallying with the Greek prince Diomedes, expresses both his profound hurt and his mental confusion. The Cressida whom Troilus knows would never betray him. And so Troilus asks:

> This, she? No, this is Diomed's Cressida.
> If beauty have a soul, this is not she.
> If souls guide vows, if vows be sanctimonies,
> If sanctimony be the gods' delight,
> If there be rule in unity itself,
> This is not she. O madness of discourse,
> That cause sets up with and against thyself!
> Bifold authority, where reason can revolt
> Without perdition, and loss assume all reason
> Without revolt! This is and is not Cressid.
> Within my soul there doth conduce a fight
> Of this strange nature, that a thing inseparate
> Divides more wider than the sky and earth,
> And yet the spacious breadth of this division
> Admits no orifex for a point as subtle
> As Ariachne's broken woof to enter.

> (5.2.137–52)

One word in this speech attracts Miller's particular attention: 'Ariachne'. Editors over the centuries, sniffing an authorial or printing mistake, have sometimes emended this to 'Ariadne', the lover of Theseus who led him by a thread through the Cretan labyrinth, and sometimes to 'Arachne', the woman-weaver who hanged herself and was turned into a spider after the gods destroyed her weaving. These are, for Miller, assumptions that 'can entertain only the hypothesis of an either/or: either Ariadne, *or* Arachne, not both; or on the other hand, the hypothesis of some meaningless error on the part of Shakespeare, a copyist, or a printer' (Miller 1986, 636). Miller seeks not to 'correct' the word by assigning it a monologic, i.e. single, meaning, but rather to respect its dialogic doubleness. In this, he illustrates the deconstructive principle of undecidability—that is, the impossibility of deciding on a single meaning without committing violence against a simultaneous, and opposite, meaning. He invokes I. A. Richards's observation that 'Ariachne' functions as a perfect portmanteau term reminiscent of Empson's third type of ambiguity, bringing together two ideas in one receptacle. But unlike the formalist conception of ambiguity, which harmoniously combines different yet compatible ideas, Miller insists that 'Ariachne' brings together two stories that do not fit. And by conflating two incongruent myths, 'Ariachne' effectively condenses the force of Troilus's 'anguished confrontation with the subversive possibility of dialogue, reason divided hopelessly against itself by submission to "bifold authority" ' (Miller 1986, 636).

This 'bifold authority' refers, in Miller's reading, not just to the competing claims of Troilus' knowledge of Cressida in the past and his experience of her in the present. It designates also the doubling intrinsic to signifying systems, which simultaneously presume and displace the singular logic of logocentrism. As Miller notes, the speech is full of key words and figures that imply a logocentric understanding of the world: 'unity', 'discourse', 'cause', 'authority', 'reason'. Yet all these terms are vexed by the simultaneous presence in Troilus's speech of two different language systems—one in which Cressida is faithful to him, and the other in which she is Diomedes' lover. Because both these systems are enclosed in Troilus' single mind, they double his mind against itself. There is unity and discourse for Troilus, but in two separate spheres; cause, authority, and reason thus become plural—and self-contradictory. This is the 'madness of discourse' to which Troilus refers, a madness that makes it impossible to speak with absolute truth or falsity. For Miller, madness is a model of narrative, demonstrating how any story can be two different and incompatible stories; at the level of character, this madness renders

Troilus 'simultaneously one and two, his soul at civil war, inseparably one mind, and yet at the same time cleft by an unbridgeable gap which is yet no gap at all, not even the tiniest hole or "orifex" ' (Miller 1986, 637). Whether as a model of narrative or as an index of character, madness is not so much *opposed* to logic as it is its (il)logical outcome. It is precisely Troilus's commitment to reason, evidenced in his logical arguments and logocentric terminology, which leads him to the realization that madness is always already intrinsic to reason.

The self-contradictory doubleness of 'Ariachne' thus models the doubleness of Troilus's speech and of logocentrism in general. For Miller, this doubleness is the pervasive structuring principle of language, from its most macroscopic (Western metaphysics) to its most microscopic (a single sign)—a pervasiveness that he characterizes with the French term *mise en abime*, which means both 'thrown into an abyss' and 'made from nothing'. Language points to something, but it also diverts to nothing. Miller sees this quality as exemplified by the rhetorical trope known as anacoluthon, which etymologically means 'not following the same path or track': 'it describes a syntactical pattern in which there is a shift in tense, number or person in the midst of a sentence, so that the words do not hang together grammatically. An anacoluthon is not governed by a single *logos*, in the sense of a unified meaning' (Miller 1986, 637). Miller's evocation of anacoluthon might recall structuralist literary critics' interest in tropes; but unlike Roman Jakobson, who reads metaphor and metonymy for the determinate meanings they produce, Miller is interested here in anacoluthon as a trope that resists the project of meaning-making.

Troilus' speech is full of grammatical anacoluthons: it is difficult, for example, to keep hold of the syntactical thread that twists through 'there doth conduce a fight | Of this strange nature, that a thing inseparate | Divides more wider than the sky and earth' (5.2.147–9). But Miller also sees the speech as performing a powerful conceptual anacoluthon, one that involves a doubling and incoherence of gender. When Troilus mentions how 'the spacious breath of this division'— the division in his mind, the division between the two Cressidas who are yet one—'Admits no orifex for a point as subtle | As Ariachne's broken woof' (5.2.150–2), he criss-crosses the attributes of masculinity and feminity: 'The web, the thread, or the woof—feminine images par excellence—are transformed into the instruments of a forced male entry. Ariachne's broken woof, figure of a torn or deflowered virginity, becomes, in a mind-twisting reversal of the sexes, itself a "point" which might tear, though it can find in this case no orifex to penetrate' (Miller 1986, 638). Not only is this conceptual anacoluthon a figure for Troilus' mental state; it hints also at the gender indeterminacy underwriting logocentrism, imaged here simultaneously (and undecidably) as a generative feminine gathering and a violent masculine dividing—a neat illustration of the construction and destruction conflated in the very term 'deconstruction'.

This indeterminacy is not the redemptive paradox of Brooks's formalism, but rather, a profound disruption: 'the harmony is broken, the string untuned' (Miller 1986, 636). Miller's words evoke those of *Troilus and Cressida*'s Ulysses, who says of degree: 'untune that string, | And hark what discord follows' (1.3.109–10). With these lines, which are so crucial to René Girard's reading of the play, we can also recognize how different Miller's reading of *Troilus and Cressida* is from Girard's. Whereas Girard reads the play as producing a crisis of undifferentiation that can be resolved only by the reassertion of 'degree' or order—i.e. meaninglessness transformed into *logos*—Miller shows how the play moves from monologue to dialogue, from coherence to contradiction, from meaningfulness to deferral. He concludes that 'the meaning of Ariachne . . . lies in the labyrinth of branching incongruous relations it sets up, vibrating resonances which can never be stilled in a single monological narrative line'. This has implications not just for the drama in the play, but also for the drama of reading itself: the reader is reduced 'to the same state of exasperated madness of discourse that tears Troilus in two' (Miller 1986, 638).

The Impossibility of Autobiography in 'On Shakespeare': Paul de Man

This tearing of the self also typifies the deconstructive criticism of Paul de Man (1919–83). Along with Miller, de Man was the preeminent popularizer of deconstruction in the American academy. Yet even as his work helped introduce Derrida to American students and literary critics, he practised a less overtly philosophical and more rhetorical brand of deconstruction than Derrida's. Like Derrida, de Man emphasized the slipperiness of language—its failure to mean what it says and to say what it means. Like Miller, he did so by focusing on how rhetorical tropes not only produce but also turn away from meaning ('trope' derives from the Greek for 'turn'). De Man grounded much of his reading practice in the rhetoric of Romantic poets. But Shakespeare also is an important figure in de Man's writing—albeit as an elusive vanishing point, a marker of a beyond that is by definition never fully present. In this, the signifier 'Shakespeare' arguably exemplifies for de Man the tropological twisting and turning of language, which never quite arrives at its supposed referent.

Long before Derrida's critique of logocentrism, and even before the rise of structuralist analysis, de Man wrote 'The Dead-End of Formalist Criticism', an essay that anticipated many of the tenets of his version of deconstruction. In particular, the essay exemplifies de Man's deconstructive hallmark of reading against the grain—that is, teasing out possibilities from a text that seem to contradict its explicit positions. Arguing against the poverty of formalist analysis as modeled by I. A. Richards, de Man suggests that formalism stumbles because it presumes that meaning is fixed and knowable. But he shows how formalism also confronts the impossibility of this presumption. Turning to Empson's reading of line 4 of Sonnet 73 in *Seven Types of Ambiguity*, de Man notes how Empson tries to control its ambiguities but cannot—if anything, they control him. As the proliferating associations Empson teases out of the line makes clear, Shakespeare's language slips endlessly, 'in the manner of a vibration spreading in infinitude from its center' (de Man 1983, 235).

This typifies the strategy of deconstructive reversal that is the hallmark of the later de Man. One of his most powerful essays, 'Autobiography as De-Facement' (published in *The Rhetoric of Romanticism* in 1979), is a meditation on Wordsworth and the genre of autobiography. Here de Man posits the impossibility of autobiography, or at least the impossibility of separating it from other genres of fiction on the grounds that it has a 'real' referent. He does so through a reading of Wordsworth's *Essays upon Epitaphs*, in which Wordsworth makes a claim for 'restoration in the face of death' that he sees as the redemptive power of autobiography—its ability to give the dead author a voice from beyond the grave (de Man 1984, 74). But de Man seeks to reverse this procedure and show how death haunts such assertions of autobiographical life. In the process, he not only deconstructs Wordsworth, but also performs a veiled criticism of the quasi-religious tendency of formalists such as Brooks to regard paradox as revivifying. De Man teases out of Wordsworth a counter-logic to the redemptive or restorative life of autobiography. Just as Miller seizes on one word in *Troilus and Cressida* to knock down the logocentric houses of cards that are Troilus' mind and the whole system of Western metaphysics, so too does de Man find one line with which to deconstruct Wordsworth and the genre of autobiography. And that line points to Shakespeare.

The line appears in Wordsworth's *Essays on Epitaphs*; it is a quotation from John Milton's 'Epitaph on the Admirable Dramatic Poet W. Shakespeare': 'What need'st thou such a weak witness of thy *name*?' (de Man 1984, 75). Wordsworth cites Milton's address to Shakespeare as he reads the epitaphs on graves and considers their power to restore life to the dead. As de Man notes, this power is ultimately figural or rhetorical:

In the case of poets such as Shakespeare, Milton, or Wordsworth himself, the epitaph can consist only of what he calls 'the naked name' . . . as it is read by the eye of the sun. At this point, it can be said of 'the language of the senseless stone' that it acquires a 'voice', the *speaking* stone counterbalancing the *seeing* sun. The system passes from sun to eye to language as name and as voice. We can identify the figure that completes the central metaphor of the sun and thus completes the tropological spectrum that the sun engenders: it is the figure of prosopopeia, the fiction of an apostrophe to an absent, deceased, or voiceless entity, which posits the possibility of the latter's reply and confers upon it the power of speech. Voice assumes mouth, eye, and finally face, a chain that is manifest in the etymology of the trope's name, *prosopon poien*, to confer a mask or a face (*prosopon*). Prosopopeia is the trope of autobiography, by which one's name, as in the Milton poem, is made as intelligible and memorable as a face. (de Man 1984, 75–6)

In Milton's poem, Shakespeare comes to life not because of his epitaph, but because of his 'easy numbers'—his verse—which makes such an impression on its readers. Yet that impression produces a remarkable effect in Milton; as Shakespeare comes to life through prosopopeia, so does Milton—in lines not quoted by

Wordsworth—undergo a reverse transformation: 'Then thou our fancy of itself bereaving, | Dost make us marble with too much conceiving' (de Man 1984, 78). That is, Milton is struck dumb even as he speaks the words that give Shakespeare life. Milton repeats here a Shakespearian motif: in *The Winter's Tale*, Leontes says of Hermione's statue (soon to be transformed into living flesh): 'does not the stone rebuke me | For being more stone than it?' (5.3.37–8). De Man regards this reversal as intrinsic to prosopopeia, and hence to autobiography: the act of conferring face, and hence life, on something inanimate simultaneously produces death in the narrating 'I'. If prosopopeia is the trope of face-ment, of giving face, it is simultaneously the trope of de-facement, of stripping identity from the autobiographical subject.

Of course, de Man's insistence on the impossibility of autobiography has been interpreted by some of his critics as a devious refusal to own his controversial life story. Yet one cannot help but wonder whether, in his insistence on the impossibility of the self, the supremely self-conscious de Man has autobiographically inscribed and defaced his own signature in the title of 'Autobiography as De-Facement'. That 'De' both invokes 'de Man' and deviates from the proper name—in other words, defaces it. The essay is a particularly powerful meditation on the divisions of the authorial self, de Man's included, and it has peculiar resonance for readers of Shakespeare. Flurries of biography notwithstanding, Shakespeare remains a shadowy figure. And this is so nowhere more than in his most autobiographical writing, the Sonnets. He repeatedly signs his name, 'Will', in the Dark Lady sequence. Yet in its punning swerves ('Will' simultaneously means desire, last will and testament, the future auxiliary verb, and genitals), that name also remains divided from Shakespeare and from itself—like the 'de' that survives in, and de-faces, the title of de Man's essay.

The Impossibility of the Proper Name in *Romeo and Juliet*: Jacques Derrida

The conundrum of the proper name, and the authorial signature that both asserts identity and shatters it, is a primary concern also of Jacques Derrida (1930–2004). Throughout his work, Derrida is fascinated by Shakespeare. As he remarked in an interview with Derek Attridge, 'I would very much like to read and write in the space or heritage of Shakespeare, in relation to whom I have infinite admiration and gratitude; I would like to become (alas, it's pretty late) a "Shakespeare expert"; I know that everything is in Shakespeare: everything and the rest, so everything or nearly' (Derrida 1992, 67). This is both far more and less than the standard homage to Shakespeare's supposedly 'infinite variety'. As Derrida's characterization of Shakespeare's 'everything' suggests, he sees in Shakespeare's writing the play of *différance*. 'Everything and the rest' registers a supplement, the trace of an excess, which both differs from the totality posited by that phrase yet also, by structurally enabling it, defers it. And hence that 'everything and the rest', i.e. everything and its supplement, is simultaneously 'everything or nearly', i.e. not quite everything. Thus Derrida sees 'the space or heritage of Shakespeare' less as one to be deconstructed than as itself a model of deconstructive thought. This is a view that he sharpened in his two sustained reflections on Shakespeare plays: *Hamlet* in *Specters of Marx* (to which I shall return in the chapter on Poststructuralist Marxisms) and *Romeo and Juliet* in his essay 'Aphorism Countertime' (1986).

'Countertime' is the literal translation of the French *contretemps*, which can also mean 'mishap' or 'accident'; the phrase *à contretemps* means both 'inopportunely' and, in a musical sense, 'out of time' or 'offbeat'. Derrida's essay on *Romeo and Juliet* is, in a sense, an accidental and offbeat piece, written out of time; he hadn't planned to study the play, and did so only because he was commissioned to write a short essay to accompany a 1986 production of *Romeo and Juliet* in Paris. But the play, which is itself so much about mishaps and untimely accidents, provided Derrida with an opportunity to reflect on contretemps and its peculiar relation to the proper name. In the process, he developed some of the theoretical themes he had limned in his earlier essay, 'Signature Event Context'. This essay elaborates Derrida's theory of the iterability or citationality of the sign: that is, its capacity to become detached from its original context and be redeployed in another. Derrida focuses particular attention on the 'signature' as the inscription that ties together a text, a signatory, and a specific moment in time. The signature thus conjoins multiple contexts: discursive, biographical, and historical. But in its very repetition, which would seem to presume recognition of a fixed referent, the signature can also become dissociated from the contextual conjuncture it seals and signifies; the signature can survive the death of the author, be attached to different texts, or be made to signify differently in different moments. Perhaps the best example is the very name 'Shakespeare'. Shakespeare's signature, affixed to his will, designates the dying man William Shakespeare. Yet the name 'Shakespeare' has come to signify differently, long after that man's death, within a variety of contexts: as the name of a poet-playwright, as shorthand for a body of work central to the literary canon, as the title of the most widely taught course in English departments. Shakespeare's signature is thus continually countersigning itself. To this extent, it discloses the contretemps that lurks in *all* proper names, which are forever diverted from the contexts that supposedly ground them and their referents in space and time. And that is why Derrida chooses to read *Romeo and Juliet* independent of its sixteenth-century contexts.

Derrida's reading of *Romeo and Juliet* takes as its starting point a close cousin of the signature: the aphorism—a pithy quote lent authority by its contexts (the text from which it is excerpted, the author who coined it), yet capable of being endlessly repeated and given a new life long after its initial iteration. Shakespeare's plays provide a good case in point: they have been strip-mined for aphorisms such as 'the better part of valour is discretion' (*Henry IV Part 1*, 5.4.117–18), 'all the world's a stage' (*As You Like It*, 2.7.138), or 'how sharper than a serpent's tooth it is to have a thankless child!' (*King Lear*, 1.4.266–7); and *Romeo and Juliet* has supplied more than its share of aphoristic nuggets—'parting is such sweet sorrow' (2.1.229), 'violent delights have violent ends' (2.5.9), 'a plague o' both your houses' (3.1.87, 101). On the one hand, the aphorism presumes a specificity of context. But because it can be detached from that context and used elsewhere, Derrida also sees the aphorism as occasioning 'an exposure to contretemps' (Derrida 1992, 416). Like a letter that strays from its intended course—an appropriate analogy, given the mishaps occasioned by *Romeo and Juliet*'s mislaid letter—the aphorism opens up to the possibility of accidental diversion and countersigning even as it seeks to deliver a fixed meaning.

In this, the aphorism embodies also the ambivalent power of the proper name. Like the aphorism, the proper name is *both* bound by context—it presumes a referent that belongs to a specific 'moment'—*and* suggests the possibility of its iteration in another time:

I am not my name. One might as well say that I should be able to survive it. But firstly it is destined to survive me. In this way it announces my death. Non-coincidence and contretemps between my name and me, between the experience according to which I am named or hear myself named and my 'living present.' Rendezvous with my name. *Untimely,* bad timing, at the wrong moment. (Derrida 1992, 432)

It should be stressed that, for Derrida, the untimely dimension of the proper name is not occasioned just by the mortal blow that will end life, which would be to make contretemps simply the future mishap that afflicts, and hence comes *after,* the fullness of being. Rather, contretemps is the very condition of the ordering of being implied by naming; any person is always already divided from herself by virtue of her relation to the proper name that confirms her identity. For if a person is, by definition, separate from his name, he nonetheless could not be what he is—a person separate from his name—without that name to separate from. Hence the proper name is undecidably independent of *and* intrinsic to the condition of being human: 'the contretemps presupposes this inhuman, too human, inadequation which always dislocates a proper name' (Derrida 1992, 430). And for Derrida, *Romeo and Juliet* provides an exemplary illustration of the force of contretemps unleashed by the aphoristic proper name.

Pointedly resorting to an aphoristic style himself (he writes in numbered, often terse paragraphs), Derrida focuses on an episode from the play that has become, more than any other, a cultural cliché: the balcony scene. It is itself a kind of aphorism, detached from the play and reiterated over and over again on stage, in the classroom, and in countless textual and cinematic adaptations. But as Derrida notes, the power of this scene has much to do with Juliet's searching analysis of the aphoristic properties of proper names:

> O Romeo, Romeo, wherefore art thou Romeo?
> Deny thy father and refuse thy name.

> Or if thou wilt not, be but sworn my love,
> And I'll no longer be a Capulet.
>
> .   .   .   .
>
> 'Tis but thy name that is my enemy.
> Thou art thyself, though not a Montague,
> What's Montague? It is nor hand, nor foot,
> Nor arm, nor face, nor any part
> Belonging to a man. O, be some other name.
> What's in a name? That which we call a rose
> By any other word would smell as sweet.
> So Romeo would, were he not Romeo call'd,
> Retain that dear perfection which he owes
> Without that title. Romeo, doff thy name,
> And for thy name—which is no part of thee—
> Take all myself.
>
> (2.1.75–8, 80–91)

Juliet insists here on the detachability of names from things—of 'rose' from the flower that would smell as sweet, and of 'Romeo' from the man she loves. Names, she says, are not physically part of the things they label; they are impositions of linguistic convention and, in the case of the proper name, impositions of patriarchal convention, decided by the father. Hence names can be jettisoned without any loss to what they describe (indeed, the cutting of the patronym can't amount even to a symbolic castration, for the proper name is not 'any part | Belonging to a man'). Yet Juliet's speech also discloses a powerful paradox: as she peers from her balcony into the darkness of the night, begging her (supposedly) absent lover to relinquish his name, she does so in his name: 'Romeo, doff thy name'. The proper name in this line is *both* the detachable name *and* the person it describes. Romeo can't escape his name; it is simultaneously separable and inseparable from him, and as Derrida says of Juliet, 'she knows it: detachable and dissociable, aphoristic though it may be, his name is his essence . . . Romeo would not be what he is, a stranger to his name, without his name' (Derrida 1992, 426–7). In Juliet's speech, then, Romeo lives as his name even as she imagines him as separate from it. His mishap, his contretemps, is that he has no being prior to or purified of that name. 'Romeo' was written before and for him, by the patronymic order into which he was born. And his name, like an aphorism, lives on in his absence—his supposed absence in the dark beyond the balcony, his absence from life once he has killed himself in the Capulet tomb, and his absence from the 'real' world by virtue of his being a fictional character. Hence for Derrida, the contretemps—the untimely mishap—of the tension between Romeo and 'Romeo' discloses 'the law of misidentification, the implacable necessity, the machine of the proper name that obliges me to live through precisely that, in other words my name, of which I am dying' (Derrida 1992, 431–2).

Yet even if one's proper name is a 'machine' that presumes the death or absence of what it attaches to, it is also the creative engine of survival. Romeo and Juliet die, but they survive in the title of the play, and in countless performances and adaptations. The reiterations of their proper names illustrate the principle of repetition that is paradoxically necessary for asserting their singular identities. But such reiterations are also always repetitions with a difference. Just as each theatrical production of *Romeo and Juliet* is a singular counter-signing of Shakespeare's play, a staging that transforms it, so too is Derrida's essay another unique countersigning—a transformative re-staging—of *Romeo and Juliet*. That is why deconstruction is not just a *destruction* of logocentric articles of faith (the meaning that is prior to language, the whole self that comes before the proper name). It is simultaneously a *construction*, a creative rewriting and reordering, of that which has been written before and for us. In this at least, it resembles the agenda of rhizome and actor-network theory, which is the topic of the next chapter.

4

Rhizome and Actor–Network Theory

Gilles Deleuze, Michel Serres, Bruno Latour

speechless song being many, seeming one...

Sonnet 8, line 13

An entity beyond language ('speechless') that may seem like 'one' but is irreducibly 'many': this theme is contemplated by both Shakespeare in Sonnet 8 and a group of French thinkers interested in questions of multiplicity. They share deconstruction's suspicion of singular or pure origins. But they also challenge some of deconstruction's assumptions, particularly Derrida's insistence that 'il n'y a pas de hors-texte', there is nothing outside the text. In contrast to Derrida, these thinkers insist that we do have access to a world unmediated by the play of signification. But they do not advocate a return to a positivist reality comprised of singular objects. The philosophers of multiplicity instead theorize structures—the rhizome, the actor-network—that presume diffuse connections rather than individual things. They depart from deconstruction in another way. Structuralism fetishizes a static order; although deconstruction problematizes that order, its dominant metaphors—the trace, the grain—still presume immobile structures, albeit structures marked by *différance*. The philosophers of multiplicity, by contrast, insist not on stasis but on flux, not on being (or its deferral) but on becoming. With their emphasis on movement, they not only reconceptualize form and structure as constantly changing. They also assume that the very act of interpretation both moves and is moved by what it interprets.

In their disciplinary allegiances and activities, these philosophers themselves embody the principle of multiplicity. Gilles Deleuze analyses impersonal and mobile fragments across a variety of fields, including philosophy, film, literature, and even metallurgy. Michel Serres writes about turbulent formations in literature, religion, science, and philosophy in the allusive style of a poet. And Bruno Latour theorizes assemblages that stray across the boundaries between the human and the non-human, the cultural and the natural, the social and the scientific. These three thinkers by no means constitute a movement, but their thought is connected through its very emphasis on movement. Indeed, Deleuze has theorized what he calls 'nomadology', a study of movement that is itself in motion. And each of the three has theorized movement as much as multiplicity with a model that shapes both the object and the mode of their criticism.

For Gilles Deleuze and his collaborator Félix Guattari, that model is the rhizome. In botany, the rhizome is a sprawling, constantly changing, subterranean plant system—the potato tuber is the most familiar specimen—without a singular root; it functions by establishing connections between multiple nodes. In Deleuze and Guattari's work, the rhizome is a suggestive metaphor for any symbiotic system comprising supposedly disparate elements that act in concert. A wasp and an orchid constitute a rhizome, as do a human and her viruses. Deleuze and Guattari use the rhizome primarily to critique hierarchy and identity: unlike arborescent models of development such as the family tree, rooted in a single origin, the rhizome's connections are multiple rather than singular, horizontal rather than vertical. The rhizome is also metamorphic, in a constant state of becoming. It deterritorializes and reterritorializes, changing its form and its limits. As such, the rhizome parallels Deleuze's conception of 'minor' literature. A 'major' literature is one that attempts to root a tradition and solidify it. By contrast, 'minor' literature pluralizes and deterritorializes tradition from within, making new connections and suggesting new becomings. Even subtracting elements from a major literary text can generate new rhizomatic multiplicities.

For Michel Serres, the model is turbulence. Serres has scandalized some intellectual historians by reading *De Rerum Natura*, written by the Roman poet Lucretius in the first century AD, as nothing less than 'a treatise on physics' (Serres 1982, 98). Justifying his conjunction of classical poet and modern scientific discipline, Serres refutes the chronological view of time as linear and entailing stable, quantifiable periods and temporal distances. Serres turns instead to a variety of liquid metaphors—an eddying river that flows upstream as well as down, a percolation whereby one flux passes through a filter but another does not—to suggest ways in which the seemingly distant past and present may come into unexpected contact. These liquid metaphors are consistent with Serres's reading of Lucretius as not just a poet of the atom, but also a scientist of fluid mechanics. What particularly attracts Serres to Lucretius is his insistence on turbulence: the classical Roman poet saw the world as composed of atoms endlessly falling through a void, yet making deviations or swerves that resist the rigid, linear trains of cause and effect. Serres teases out parallels between Lucretius and modern chaos theory in order to reimagine the world's protean forms. He is interested in how philosophy and literature might represent non-signifying, turbulent multiplicities—morphing clouds, noisy crowds, buzzing flocks of birds—that cannot be reduced to any singular essence and that are constantly transforming.

For Bruno Latour, the model is the actor-network. He sees society as consisting of human and non-human 'actors' bonded in complex relations with each other; their heterogeneous association constitutes networks that acquire their own agency. For Latour, an actor-network does not presume prior actors that proceed to work in tandem. Rather, the network is primary; connection precedes identity. This connection is material as much as semiotic. The interactions in a library, for example, involve people, books, and technologies, yet together they form a single network. Such a network is potentially transient, necessitating constant making and remaking even as it is prone to recalibration and dispersal. And if a network assumes a multiplicity of elements, those elements are themselves irreducibly multiple. Any actor is itself a network comprising other, smaller actors from diverse spheres. A toolbox that combines the antique technology of the hammer and the modern technology of the electric drill, or a greenhouse gas that is equally a natural and a cultural event, forms connections between 'different periods, ontologies or genres' (Latour 1993, 73).

Shakespeare too can be seen as a thinker of multiplicity and movement who mixes up different periods and ontologies. Think, for example, of the handkerchief in *Othello*. On the one hand, it is a singular object. On the other, it is a ceaselessly mobile actor in a network that conjoins many people, many narratives, and many times. The handkerchief forms rhizomatic connections with the play's characters: people use it to bandage an aching head (3.3.290–1) and 'wipe [a] beard' (3.3.444), or blow a nose, clean an ear, and dab a pair of lips. But it enters also into networks that transform the world through which it moves—and in the process, it too is transformed. As the handkerchief is passed from person to person, its meanings keep changing. Desdemona and handkerchief is, if only for Othello, a network performing matrimonial chastity and honour; Iago and handkerchief is a network that induces a seizure in Othello; Bianca and handkerchief, spied by Othello and egged on by Iago, is a network performing 'ocular proof' of Desdemona's guilt (3.3.365). Yet the handkerchief is itself a network that conjoins different times: it is simultaneously antique Egyptian token (3.4.54) and fashionable European 'trifle' (5.2.235), obsolete emblem of true love and present marker of promiscuity. Interestingly, Serres himself theorizes time as a crumpled handkerchief, in which two seemingly distant points 'suddenly are close, even superimposed' (Serres and Latour 1995, 60). The Serres-like properties of Othello's handkerchief suggest why the philosophers of multiplicity might regard Shakespeare as a thinker of the many rather than the one. But they also use his plays to produce dynamic, hybrid assemblages of their own, performing modes of interpretation that are different from what we have seen thus far in formalism, structuralism, and deconstruction.

Subtractive Multiplicity in *Richard III*: Gilles Deleuze

In his reading of *Romeo and Juliet*, Derrida invokes the 'machine of the proper name' (Derrida 1992, 431) to think about the inescapability of Romeo and Juliet's deaths. Yet this machine, by allowing the proper name to survive its referent and resignify in a new context, also works to create new Romeos and Juliets on the stage. Gilles Deleuze (1925–95) similarly invokes the machine to theorize creative possibilities for the staging of Shakespeare. In his essay 'One Less

Manifesto' (1979), he turns to Carmelo Bene, the innovative Italian theatre 'operator' (Deleuze rejects the terms playwright, director, and actor), who has rewritten and staged unusual versions of *Romeo and Juliet*, *Hamlet*, and *Richard III*. These versions subtract or amputate, in the manner of a surgical procedure or operation, what we might regard as crucial elements from each play. In his treatment of *Romeo and Juliet*, for example, Bene excises the character of Romeo. And in his rewriting of *Richard III*, he cuts virtually all the male characters and any reference to the apparatus of state power. With these subtractions, however, Bene liberates potentialities within Shakespeare's drama: the irresistible energy of Mercutio, the transgressive creativity of Richard. Like Derrida, Deleuze understands the creative potential of Shakespeare's drama—and of Bene's rewritings and restagings—as the work of a certain kind of machine. Yet for all their affinities, Deleuze's Shakespearian machine is rather different from Derrida's.

For Derrida, the machine of the proper name is propelled by the endless iterability of the signature. Deleuze, by contrast, sees the machine as less a property of language than a principle of creativity immanent to life in general. Life is, for Deleuze, an ongoing process of producing new connections that presume no organizing centre or final goal. Rather, life begins in the middle, producing simply for the sake of producing. This is what makes life machine-like: whereas monotheism, humanism, and logocentrism all presuppose a singular origin (God, consciousness, the Word) and a singular endpoint (salvation, self-awareness, full meaning), a machine is nothing but the variable sum of the changing connections it makes (and unmakes) with others. As a result, the machine models a creative process of becoming-other that is at odds with the singularity and stasis of being. This becoming-other has not just philosophical but also political implications. In *A Thousand Plateaus*, Deleuze and Guattari oppose the war machine of Shakespeare's Richard III, a force that works towards heterogeneity, to the state apparatus, which strives towards homogenization (Deleuze and Guattari 1987, 125–6). The war machine is rhizomatic rather than singular: it consists of many human and inhuman parts—the warrior, his horse, his sword—and by disrupting fixed boundaries of space, time, and thought, it forms new connections that expand life's horizon of possibilities.

For Deleuze, Shakespeare's Richard III is a war machine possessed of a creative power: 'Richard, for his part, is less interested in power than in reintroducing or reinventing a war machine, even if it means the destruction of the apparent balance or peace of the state (what Shakespeare calls Richard's secret, the "secret close intent")' (Deleuze 1997, 240). Indeed, we never find out what exactly Richard's 'secret close intent' (1.1.158) is; but in its very inscrutability, it provides a formula for his objectless energy, which ceaselessly remakes him and the world around him. Bene's subtractive transformation of Shakespeare's play makes Richard's machine-like tendencies explicit. Richard fashions himself on stage out of prostheses, arbitrarily selecting objects that he discards or adds to his body: 'He will make himself, or rather unmake himself, according to a line of continuous variation' (Deleuze 1997, 240). Crooked Richard is thus Bene's doppelgänger, who likewise makes deformity—the overturning of fixed form—the ground of his innovation. Deleuze attends to Bene's deforming variation on Richard's own deformities not to reproduce Bene faithfully, however, but to create his own variation. Bene calls his subtractive version of *Hamlet* 'one less *Hamlet*'. So too does Deleuze title his essay 'One Less Manifesto': he gives us only fragments of Bene's play, just as Bene gives us only fragments of Shakespeare, in order to transpose both into another key—a manifesto on the difference between 'major' and 'minor' consciousness.

For Deleuze, a major language strives for constancy and homogeneity. Insisting on rules, it becomes a medium of power, which Deleuze understands as the movement to reproduce a structure as an invariable form. By contrast, a minor language breaks rules, transforming (or deterritorializing) the language it speaks. By language, Deleuze does not mean a national tongue: any language can be put to major and minor uses. As the language of imperial power, English is major. But the English of African-American subcultures, in its many colloquial variations, is a minor language, as is the unorthodox German written by Franz Kafka, a Czech Jew. Deleuze's distinction between the major and the minor is reminiscent of Bakhtin's oppositions between the classical and the grotesque, the monologic and the dialogic. But whereas Bakhtin uses these oppositions to theorize forms of signification, Deleuze derives his distinction from music, a non-signifying form that depends on changing connections between notes. A major key is normative; a minor key messes things up slightly, introducing a variation. By extension, a major literature is canonical; minor literature is heterodox and transformative.

In conventional productions of Shakespeare, theatre tends to the major, faithfully reproducing not just his play-texts but also audience assumptions about them. Yet theatre has the potential to be minor in its use of voice, gesture, and stage materials. Deleuze noted the heterodox power of theatre in his early work *Difference and Repetition*, where he proposed a 'new theatre or a new (non-Aristotelian) inter-pretation of the theatre; a theatre of multiplicities opposed in every respect to the theatre of representation, which leaves intact neither the identity of the thing represented, nor author, nor spectator, nor character, nor representation which, through vicissitudes of the play, can become the object of a production of knowledge or final recog-nition' (Deleuze 2004, 241). If the production of 'final recognition' is the hallmark of major theatre, Bene's subtractive theatre is minor in its refusal of any such singularity. His plays amputate elements from their Shakespearian sources to disturb existing arrangements of theatrical power. And they do so with multiple variations on language and gesture: Bene's performers stammer, lose their balance, wear ill-fitting costumes, and so on.

These variations are apparent in Bene's adaptation of *Richard III*. His staging techniques draw on Shakespeare's own variations of meaning, which give language 'the slip from all constancy' (Deleuze 1997, 246). The sense of Lady Anne's declamations against Richard in the seduction scene, for example, is as difficult to pin down as his 'secret close intent'. What exactly does she mean when she says 'Thou dost infect mine eyes' (1.2.148)? Deleuze hypothesizes that such an utterance is hardly the same 'when uttered by a woman at war, a child facing a toad, or a young girl feeling a pity that is already consenting and loving' (Deleuze 1997, 246). A major production will fasten on one of these options in order to present Lady Anne's 'true' character; for Bene, by contrast, 'Lady Anne will have to move through all these variables. She will have to stand erect like a woman warrior, regress to a childlike state, and return as a young girl—as quickly as possible on a line of continuous variation' (Deleuze 1997, 246). Deleuze, resorting again to a musical analogy, compares such variation to the genre of the *Sprechgesang*, a type of sung speech in which the singer varies pitch by using ascending and descending notes. Bene's characters are not allowed to coalesce into anything fixed; he insists that his performers amplify their characters' variations through sliding gestures and vocal effects. For example, his play-text insists that Richard's gestures must keep changing forms, and his mother's voice must keep changing tonalities.

In Bene's treatment of the seduction scene, variation is not simply a theatrical experiment but, more specifically, the creative engine of Richard's war machine. As Deleuze notes, this 'sublime scene of Shakespeare [is] often accused of excess and lack of verisimilitude' (Deleuze 1997, 250). But it is precisely these qualities that Bene values. Bene's Richard sports his casts and prostheses triumphantly, flaunting 'his deformities, his war machine' (Deleuze 1997, 251). In response, Bene's Lady Anne creates herself anew, measuring the variation of her character in relation to Richard's; continually undressing and dressing herself, she consents to 'marry a war machine instead of remaining in the shadow and power of a state apparatus' (Deleuze 1997, 251). In each case, Bene presumes not a unified character but rather a machine, a rhizomatic network of variations, through which Richard and Lady Anne are continually becoming-other. And these two beings-that-are-not, as their variations of voice and gesture increasingly intersect and acquire the same rhythm, constitute a larger creative assemblage. Bene, then, does not dramatize who Richard or Anne *are*, but instead locates them on a 'continuum in which the words and gestures play the roles of variables in transformation' (Deleuze 1997, 251).

For Deleuze, Bene's subtractive Shakespeare makes for a moving theatre, in a literal rather than a sentimental sense. By modelling processes of becoming-other (Richard's, Lady Anne's, Shakespeare's play-text's), Bene's adaptation of *Richard III* moves audience consciousness in new directions. This is a movement towards what Deleuze calls 'minority consciousness', according to which 'everyone creates his or her variation of the unity of despotic measure and escapes...from the system of power that is part of the majority' (Deleuze 1977, 255). In this more overtly politicized variation on the major/minor distinction, theatre plays a crucial role: 'Theatre will surge forward as something representing nothing but what presents and creates a minority consciousness as a universal-becoming'

(Deleuze 1997, 256). This 'surge' is instructive: it suggests how Deleuze celebrates non-humanist figures of movement and multiplicity, for a surge is a dynamic action performed not by a single agent but by a collective (like Bene's Richard and his prostheses) that blurs the boundary between the human and the inhuman.

Noisy Multiplicity in *Macbeth*: Michel Serres

It is in precisely this guise that the surge reappears as a shaping figure in Michel Serres's reading of noisy multiplicity in *Macbeth*. In *Genesis* (1982), Serres (1930–) attempts to theorize an object ignored by philosophy—a multiplicity outside of meaning. This object he terms, using an archaic French word, *noise*. The meanings of *noise* overlap with but also exceed those of the English 'noise', as its sense also includes fury, trouble, or ruckus. Yet it is also a creative force. In poetic language, Serres attempts to capture the generative power of this allusive *noise*:

We are immersed in sound just as we are immersed in air and light, we are caught up willy-nilly in its hurly-burly. We breathe background noise, the taut and tenuous agitation at the bottom of the world, through all our pores and papillae, we collect within us the noise of organization, a hot flame and a dance of integers . . . It is the residue and the cesspool of our messages. No life without heat, no matter, neither; no warmth without air, no logos without noise, either. Noise is the basic element of the software of all our logic, or it is to the logos what matter used to be to form. Noise is the background of information, the material of that form. (Serres 1995, 7)

The creativity of this chaotic *noise*, Serres argues, is best captured by Honoré de Balzac in his 1831 short story 'The Unknown Masterpiece'. Here the old master Fremhofer, using the young Poussin's lover Gillette as a model, finishes a painting intended to depict his own mistress, which he entitles *La Belle Noiseuse* (The Beautiful Trouble-maker). However, when Poussin and his mentor Porbus see the painting, they discover that it is a whirl of formless brushstrokes and chaotic colours out of which—to their dismay—they can extract nothing intelligible, save for one exquisitely rendered foot. For Serres, the canvas depicts the birth of form from *noise*: *La Belle Noiseuse* is 'the *noise* of beauty, the naked multiple, the numerous sea, from which a beautiful Aphrodite is born . . . Formed phenomenal information gets free from the chaotic background noise, the knowable and the known are born from that unknown' (Serres 1995, 18).

It is this generative relation of *noise* to form, of non-signifying multiplicity to legible singularity, that Serres explores throughout his study. *Noise* cannot make itself known to reason, but its creative impact can be felt in a variety of ways—the thrum of the ocean, the whirl of the gymnast, the rhythms of music. He also finds intimations of it in myth and literature, from the tales of Irish Cúchulainn to Georges Dumézil's writing. One of Serres's most extended meditations on literary *noise* and its relation to form is his allusive and poetic discussion of *Macbeth*, which he subtitles 'Forest Surge'. Serres focuses on the play's last act, in which Macbeth's enemies adopt an unusual strategy: 'The forest is moving, it is coming forward, the forest of Birnam is rising on Dunsinane Castle' (Serres 1995, 55). Accompanying this surging multiplicity, however, is another irruption of *noise*—what Serres describes as a 'forest of women [that] blows, moans, advances and threatens' (Serres 1995, 56). This prompts Macbeth to ask: 'What is that noise?' (5.5.8). His servant, Seyton, tells him it is the cry of women. But then Macbeth hears a singular shriek and asks, 'Wherfore was that cry?' (5.5.15).

He is soon answered:

SEYTON   The Queen, my lord, is dead.
MACBETH   She should have died hereafter.
    There would have been a time for such a word.
    Tomorrow, and tomorrow, and tomorrow
    Creeps in this petty pace from day to day
    To the last syllable of recorded time,
    And all our yesterdays have lighted fools
    The way to dusty death. Out, out, brief candle!
    Life's but a walking shadow, a poor player
    That struts and frets his hour upon the stage,
    And then is heard no more. It is a tale
    Told by an idiot, full of sound and fury,
    Signifying nothing.

(5.5.16–28)

We might pause here to think about how practitioners of other critical practices would read this speech. A structuralist like Roman Jakobson might note the metronomic power of Macbeth's iambs and spondees ('Tomorrow, and tomorrow, and tomorrow, | Creeps in this petty pace from day to day') and how these are disrupted by the trochees of the last line ('Signifying nothing'), suggesting a powerful distinction between life's forward trajectory and the death to which it leads. A deconstructionist might focus on how Macbeth's speech is organized according to a sustainedly ironic understanding of language, whereby the movement from one signifying unit to another, up to 'the last syllable of recorded time', leads not to a fullness of meaning but to its failure. In each case, then, Macbeth's speech is understood to be preoccupied with language and problems of meaning.

Serres approaches the speech differently. He is interested in how Macbeth's exchange with Seyton is framed by *noise*—the opening question, 'What is that noise', is echoed in the concluding observation that life is 'sound and fury, | Signifying nothing'. Whereas a deconstructionist might approach this 'nothing' as a mark of *différance*, Serres hears in its void something else: 'The *noise* is on the canvas, the *noise* is on the stage . . . The sound and the fury, the clinking of arms and the words in the marketplace' (Serres 1995, 56). Because *noise* signifies nothing, Macbeth concludes that life is pointless, opposed to human endeavour and not worth the living. But for Serres, *noise* is not simply an inhuman enemy to the human; it is always already present within the human—indeed, it is the very creative condition of human life. As Serres notes, 'Shakespeare saw and shows' what others conceal: that behind each surge of *noise* 'there was also a man' (Serres 1995, 55–6), that behind each tree branch in the surging forest was an English soldier, that humans are not opposed to but rather generated out of the same element as *noise*. Serres insists that human life, like Macbeth's, will 'fall into the sere' (5.3.24) only if we insist on retaining exclusive ties to an orderly or meaningful world. Instead, life thrives when it adapts to *noise* and *belles noiseuses*, from which beautiful forms (like the foot in Fremhofer's painting) might be born: 'Health is not silence, health is not harmony; health deals with every appeal, every cry, the caterwauling . . . Health negotiates the *noise*' (Serres 1995, 135). The health of individual life, in other words, necessitates embracing human/inhuman multiplicities beyond signification.

Democratic Multiplicity and *Coriolanus*: Bruno Latour

Bruno Latour (1947–) argues that the health of political life similarly necessitates embracing assemblages of people and things. In 2005, Latour co-curated (with Peter Weibel) an unusual exhibition, *Making Things Public*, at the ZKM Centre for Art and Media in Karlsruhe, Germany. The project assembled more than a hundred writers, artists, and philosophers, who were asked to consider how politics is not just a sphere or a system but a concern for things. This concern forms the basis of Latour's call for a *Dingpolitik*, which would attend to public assemblies of people and things normally considered outside the sphere of the political: scientific laboratories, supermarket aisles, fashion catwalks, Internet forums, even natural phenomena such as rivers. In his introduction to the catalogue accompanying the exhibition, *Making Things Public: Atmospheres of Democracy* (2008), Latour theorizes the *Ding* (or Thing) of *Dingpolitik* in ways that develop his earlier accounts of actor-network theory. This provides the framework for an unorthodox engagement of Shakespeare's *Coriolanus*, not as an object of literary interpretation so much as a participant in a public assembly that conjoins numerous actors.

For Latour, things are not simply individual physical objects (or facts) but also matters of concern that entangle numerous other actors in larger networks, assemblages, or assemblies. He points out that the word 'thing' is, in many Nordic and Saxon languages, a name for a parliament or public assembly: 'Norwegian congressmen assemble in the *Storting*; Icelandic deputies called the equivalent of "thingmen" gather in the *Althing*; Isle of Man seniors used to gather around the *Ting*; the German landscape is dotted with *Thingstätten* and you can see in many places the circles of stones where the Thing used to stand' (Latour 2008, 23). In all these instances, the 'thing' is not just the name for a parliament; it is, more specifically, the issue that brings people together to consider their divisions. In Iceland, the ancient 'thingmen' of the *Althing* met on a desolate spot that happened to rest on the fault line dividing the European and American tectonic plates. Latour similarly advocates reimagining the 'political' as an assemblage of assemblies convened on fault lines: 'we don't assemble because we agree, look alike, feel good, are socially compatible or wish to fuse together but because we are brought by divisive matters of concern into some neutral, isolated place in order to come to some sort of provisional makeshift (dis)agreement' (Latour 2008, 23).

The difficulty is how institutionally to implement this reimagined sense of the political. Latour sees the problem as stemming partly from our conventions of representation—legal, scientific, and artistic—that have not only worked to exclude things from the political but also fantasized it as a unified totality. For example, the political has been understood often on the model of the human body: a singular collective of 'members' that are themselves human. The problem is not just that there are many kinds of bodies, and hence many ways of organizing the political, but also that nature is less organized and unitary than the metaphor of the body politic has presumed. Latour prefers the nine-teenth-century phrase 'Phantom Public', inasmuch as it recognizes the provisional and self-contradictory nature of the political. In the exhib-ition, however, he and his collaborators 'try the impossible feat of *giving flesh* to the Phantom of the Public' (Latour 2008, 38) by tackling the problem of how to produce public assemblies that conjoin people and things in a variety of means and media. The exhibition and the cata-logue are themselves assemblies convened over fault lines, bringing together articles, photographs, and installations on a huge variety of topics pertaining to *Dingpolitik*: a Maori cultural property claim, an election in Papua New Guinea, military photography, virtual laborator-ies, obelisks from Stockholm, assemblies of humans with shells and gods, water parliaments, blogs, and many others.

Included in the catalogue is an extended two-page excerpt from Shakespeare's *Coriolanus*, entitled 'William Shakespeare on the Par-able of the Members and the Belly'. The excerpt concerns the scene in which the Roman patrician Menenius Agrippa attempts to quell the citizens' rebellion. The citizens are suffering from starvation, and accuse the patricians of hoarding all the grain. Menenius responds with a fable of the body politic:

> There was a time when all the body's members,
> Rebelled against the belly, thus accused it:
> That only like a gulf it did remain
> I' th' midst o' th' body, idle and unactive,
> Still cupboarding the viand, never bearing

Like labour with the rest; where th' other instruments
Did see and hear, devise, instruct, walk, feel,
And, mutually participate, did minister
Unto the appetite and affection common
Of the whole body.

(1.1.85–94)

A lengthy argument ensues between Menenius and the First Citizen about what the Belly might say in response to the accusation of the other members. According to Menenius, the Belly digests all the food in order to distribute it throughout the body. For the First Citizen, the Belly's vision of a body politic grounded in a trickle-down theory of resources is simply 'an answer' (1.1.136) that does not settle the immediate problem of the plebeians' hunger. Menenius then pushes his interpretation of the fable:

The senators of Rome are this good belly,
And you the mutinous members. For examine
Their counsels and their cares, digest things rightly
Touching the weal o' th' common, you shall find
No public benefit which you receive
But it proceeds or comes from them to you,
And no way from yourselves. What do you think,
You, the great toe of this assembly?

(1.1.137–44)

The First Citizen disputes Menenius's characterization of him as the body politic's 'toe'. But their conflict is quickly swept under the carpet with the news that the enemy Volscians are preparing to go to war with the Romans. At this point, the excerpt comes to an end.

In his introduction to *Making Things Public*, Latour directs the reader to Menenius' 'Fable of the Members and the Stomach' (Latour 2008, 37). But he does not offer a reading of either the scene in particular or *Coriolanus* in general. Nor is any explicit gloss offered for the excerpt. It performs a function in the catalogue nonetheless, included as it is in the assembly of meditations on assemblies. What work does the excerpt do? Does Menenius' fable of the belly typify a failed way of thinking the political by trying to 'fasten the poor assemblies of humans to the solid reality of nature' (Latour 2008, 37)? Or does it exemplify how the political is grounded in shared 'things' or matters of concern—in this case, grain—that bring together different factions so that they may contemplate their divisions? The answer, surely, is that it does both. The excerpt thus functions less as a unit within an aggregate (whether Shakespeare's play, the exhibition, or the catalogue) than as its own multiplicity, convened on a fault line. Like the other contributions it is less an answer to the question, 'how do we make things public?', than one attempt to pose that question.

As such, Latour's treatment of *Coriolanus* not only models a critical procedure whereby the Phantom Public foregrounds its divisions. It also suggests a way of thinking with Shakespeare that works less to arrive at the true meaning of *Coriolanus* than to grant its divided 'assembly' (1.1.144) a critical agency in the context of a larger, second-order assembly—the exhibition catalogue. In other words, Shakespeare's text is not simply the passive object of criticism; it is itself an actor, albeit a non-self-identical and plural one. In this, Latour's theoretical practice recalls those of Deleuze and Serres. All three theorists resist 'reading' Shakespeare, at least in the sense of reproducing a singular meaning that is supposed to reside already in the text. Instead, they each unleash in the Shakespearian text a power of protean multiplicity that unsettles the very protocols of reading. One might say, with Deleuze, that they each transform Shakespeare's text into a desiring machine. For Deleuze, desire is the very principle of life; it begins by making connections with entities outside itself, connections that produce ever-shifting assemblages and networks. The creative deformity of *Richard III*, the sound and fury of *Macbeth*, the divided assembly of *Coriolanus*, all invite critical activity that goes beyond identifying any pure meaning of the text. Instead, Deleuze, Serres, and Latour transform each into a desiring machine that engenders as much as it embodies multiplicity, making unexpected if temporary connections with other actors (Bene, Balzac, Latour's collaborators). To add desire to his theoretical apparatus, however, Deleuze makes a guerilla raid on the citadel of psychoanalysis. And entering that citadel, we will see in the following chapters, spells a subtle transformation of critical priorities. If the first four chapters constitute a divided assembly convened on the fault lines of language and structure, the next four chapters meet on the equally quake-prone space of desire and identity.

Part II

Desire and Identity

5

Freudian Psychoanalysis

Sigmund Freud, Ernest Jones, Melanie Klein

I have that within which passeth show—

Hamlet, 1.2.85

Hamlet refers here not just to elements of his personality that outsiders cannot see. As the play unfolds, it becomes clear that he is in the grip of compulsions invisible even to himself. Shakespeare has been credited by Harold Bloom with the 'invention of the human', inasmuch as his characters possess a psychological depth that Bloom regards as the defining hallmark of the modern self (Bloom 1999). But a play like *Hamlet* also suggests how Shakespeare finds within that depth an element of the *inhuman*, of unconscious forces that are outside a character's control. In Derrida's analysis of *Romeo and Juliet*, Shakespeare decentres the self by tethering it to an inhuman element—the proper name—that is both separate from and intrinsic to it; Deleuze, Serres, and Latour likewise theorize the networks in Shakespeare's drama that conjoin human and inhuman elements. Shakespeare's decentring of the self by the unconscious, however, was first theorized by Sigmund Freud (1856–1939), the Viennese founder of psychoanalysis.

Freud's understanding of the unconscious is interarticulated with his influential model of the psyche, which distinguishes between the ego (the conscious mind, derived from the Latin for 'I'), the id (unconscious psychic processes, derived from the Latin for 'it'), and the superego (the internalized law that regulates, through repression, the traffic of psychic energy from the unconscious to the conscious). These are not simply three separate provinces of the psyche; they are in dynamic relation with each other. We might see the ego as an elite nightclub into which only very few guests are admitted; the superego is the burly bouncer that protects the club by barring entrance to an unending stream of guests from the id, which are for the most part socially unacceptable thoughts, impulses, and fears. But these unwanted guests still find ways of creeping surreptitiously into the club. Gatecrashers from the id infiltrate the ego in four ways. First, parapraxes—more commonly known as 'Freudian slips' of the tongue—reveal unconscious thoughts. Second, puns and jokes lend expression to unconscious sexual and aggressive impulses. Third, neurotic and even psychotic symptoms reveal unconscious compulsions: for instance, the obsessive urge to repeat behaviour, which Freud associates with the death drive—an unconscious desire to return to an original state of stasis. Most importantly, dreams communicate unconscious desires via processes of condensation (the metaphorical splicing together of two different ideas into one figure) and displacement (the metonymic transfer of qualities from one thought to another). To give one example: a friend of mine, who had recently broken her elbow, had a dream in which she hid her injury by tucking her forearm inside her coat. Even as the gesture acknowledged her infirmity, it also replicated the famous pose of Napoleon—a condensation that yoked her disability with an image that may have reflected an unconscious wish for power. This condensation auguably performed a displacement too. 'Bonaparte' is, after all, a pun on 'bone apart'. So my friend's dream enacted a metonymic movement, at the level of sound, from a phrase that evoked her fracture to the name of an all-conquering general. For all the ingenuity of this interpretation, however, my tentative terms ('may', 'arguably') betray how hard it is to identify with absolute certainty the contents of the unconscious.

Freud did not just theorize the relation of the unconscious to our everyday behaviour and dreams. He also offered an influential account of psychic and sexual development. The infant child, before he is socialized (and many of Freud's theories presume a universal 'he'), harbours a strong erotic desire for his mother. This turns him into his father's competitor, whom he wishes to kill but from whom he fears castration as punishment for his desire. That fear presumes the infant's internalization of a prohibition or law that leads to the formation of the superego: his now illicit desire is repressed to his unconscious, from which it re-emerges only in dreams and neurotic symptoms. Freud famously called this infantile nexus of sexual longing, aggression, and repression the 'Oedipus complex'. The name derives from Sophocles' tragedy *Oedipus Rex*, in which Oedipus, deserted at birth by his royal parents and brought up by shepherds, kills a man whom he doesn't know but who turns out to be his biological father, and has sexual relations with a woman who is, also unbeknownst to him, his biological mother. Finding out what he has done, Oedipus blinds himself, a punishment that Freud reads as a displaced form of castration.

Symbolic castration plays a significant part also in Freud's influential theory of sexual fetishism. In Freud's clinical experience, the fetishist's realization that his mother does not have a penis is a deeply traumatic event, disturbing his narcissistic investment in his own bodily wholeness. Fearing that his mother has been castrated and lost her penis, the fetishist fastens on a substitute object—often something physically close to where her penis should be, such as shoes, underwear, or hair—that not only restores wholeness to the mother in the realm of his fantasy, but also helps him repudiate the threat of his own castration. Because of its seemingly magical power to safeguard against loss, the fetishist invests the substitute object with an erotic charge. Freud's theory of the fetish object is in some ways reminiscent of deconstruction's critique of logocentrism and signification. As a substitute for something that never existed in the first place—the mother's penis—the fetish object is a deconstructive signifier that both generates and punctures the illusion of an original wholeness.

Although Freud elaborated many of the principles of psychoanalysis in clinical case studies, he often illustrated his theories—as the very name of the Oedipus complex suggests—with recourse to literature. Indeed, he saw the creative imagination of writers as performing the operations characteristic of dreams; as a result, literature is able to tap into an author's and her readers' unconscious longings and fears, often with therapeutic value. Freud sees this happening particularly in literary treatments of the uncanny, a phenomenon grounded in partial recognition of an archaic desire that has long been repressed and hence is experienced simultaneously as alien and as strangely familiar. For example, Freud's brilliant close reading of E. T. A. Hoffman's eerie story, 'The Sand-Man', stresses how its uncanny moments engage Hoffman's and our own repressed fears of castration.

It was left to Freud's followers, however, to turn psychoanalysis into a bona fide mode of literary criticism. His English acolyte, Ernest Jones, developed Freud's intuition that *Hamlet* reveals the workings of a repressed Oedipus complex. Jones helped initiate what was to become itself something of an Oedipal rite of passage for psychoanalytic critics—reading the play anew to pay homage to, but also wrest interpretive authority from, their Freudian forefathers. Psychoanalytic literary criticism also owes much to Melanie Klein (who, like Freud, emigrated from Vienna to England to escape Nazi persecution). Klein was one of the principal architects of what has come to be known as object relations theory: that is, the notion that our behaviour bears the archaic trace of our relations to primal objects, including the body parts of our parents. Psychoanalytic critics have used object relations theory to consider not just how literature depicts such relations but also becomes itself an object implicated within them. Shakespeare offers particularly fertile ground for such speculation. As the central figure in the English literary canon, Shakespeare is at the receiving end of many of our most compulsive projections, including Freud's own. For example, Freud late in life joined the ranks of those who disputed Shakespeare's authorship of the plays—an arguably Oedipal act of symbolic parricide, and one that he never fully explained.

Psychoanalysis has often been faulted for being blind to its own historical situatedness. By positing the unconscious as a transhistorical phenomenon, psychoanalysis potentially overlooks how Freud's theories treat as universal phenomena that are in fact specific to modern Western urban culture, such as the nuclear family and a privatized interiority. There is no doubt that some of Freud's thought is symptomatic of an alienated Western modernity. Still, it is remarkable how much confirmation he finds of supposedly modern problems in pre-modern literature. Indeed, Shakespeare looms extraordinarily large in psychoanalytic theory; his plays have been both subject to psychoanalysis and a constitutive presence within it ever since Freud formulated his theory of the Oedipus complex, which he derived as much from his reading of *Hamlet* as from Sophocles' play. But *Hamlet* is by no means the only Shakespearian drama that speaks in the accents of psychoanalysis.

Deciphering Death in *The Merchant of Venice* and *King Lear*: Sigmund Freud

Aside from *Hamlet*, Freud wrote about (amongst other plays) *Richard III*, which he saw as exemplary of the psychopathology of the 'exception' (Freud 1966, xiv:313–15); *Macbeth*, whose criminal anti-hero and -heroine he saw as 'two disunited parts of a single psychical individuality' (Freud 1966, xiv:307–8); and *Henry IV* and *Love's Labour's Lost*, whose jests provided him with illustrations of his theory of jokes and their relation to the unconscious (Freud 1966, viii:144–5). Freud's most extended reflection on Shakespeare's writing, though, is his essay on 'The Theme of the Three Caskets' (1912). Here he seeks to explain the presence of a common fairy-tale motif in the Belmont scenes of *The Merchant of Venice*: the lottery in which Bassanio must choose between three caskets to win Portia as his bride. Even though Bassanio chooses the right casket, the justifications he offers for his choice seem unpersuasive and forced. Freud observes that 'if in psycho-analytic practice, we were confronted with such a speech, we should suspect that there were concealed motives behind the unsatisfying reasons produced' (Freud 1997, 109). It is these concealed motives that Freud proceeds to excavate—an archaeological metaphor that suits his understanding of the psyche as containing truths buried deep in the unconscious.

Freud first discounts a popular interpretation of his time, according to which the subplot of the three caskets is a retelling of an archaic astral myth. According to this interpretation, the Prince of Morocco represents the sun, which explains his choice of the golden casket; the Prince of Aragon symbolizes the moon, and so chooses the silver casket; while Bassanio represents the star youth, and chooses the lead casket. Freud is not satisfied with this explanation, which he regards as simply a reframing of Shakespeare's casket scenes in the terms of yet another story—this one mythic rather than dramatic. Freud regards myth as deriving from universal psychic experience, and thus it too requires explanation. To this end, he applies insights derived from the practices of psychoanalysis, especially dream interpretation.

Freud asserts that dreams often entail the symbolic substitution of one thing or sign for another that is barred from consciousness; myth, he argues, operates in a similar way, lending expression to unconscious desires and fears by substituting them with opaque symbols. And this is how he reads the caskets of *The Merchant of Venice*. If 'what we were concerned with were a dream', he argues, then 'it would occur to us at once that caskets are also women, symbols of what is essential in woman, and therefore of a woman herself—like coffers, boxes, cases, baskets, and so on' (Freud 1997, 111). Therefore Freud concludes that Bassanio's choice among the three caskets is really a choice among three women. We might note here a further association not mentioned in Freud's reading of the caskets as symbols for women—the symbolic link between caskets, coffins, and death, a striking omission given the direction that his analysis will subsequently take. But this link raises a question reminiscent of the formalist and structuralist struggles with the spectres of ambiguity and excessive meaning. Given the potentially limitless array of associations any symbol might have, how do we determine which if any is the right one?

Reading the caskets as symbols of women, Freud then turns to another play by Shakespeare that entails a choice among three women: *King Lear*. Lear must choose among his two elder daughters Goneril and Regan, who flatter their father to prove their love and win his kingdom, and Cordelia, his loving youngest daughter, who opts to remain silent. Lear's choice to reject Cordelia leads to his financial ruin, madness, and then death. In this, *King Lear* presents a counter-example to other myths in which a man correctly chooses the best of three women. Freud, however, looks for the common denominator between Shakespeare's two plays and this mythic tradition. What do the women who are the 'correct' choice (even if they are not chosen) have in common besides beauty? The lead casket bearing Portia's image is all 'paleness' (3.2.106); Cordelia is 'silent' (1.1.60). These qualities relate to dumbness, and Freud observes that 'psycho-analysis will tell us that in dreams dumbness is a common representation of death' (Freud 1997, 113). Applied to *The Merchant of Venice* and *King Lear*, then, the choice of the pale or silent woman represents the choice of a dead woman, and more specifically of death itself.

Freud acknowledges the counter-intuitiveness of this interpretation. How can the choice of the correct woman represent a choice of death? We tend not to choose death freely: it imposes itself on us largely as an implacable necessity. To overcome this dilemma, Freud draws on another psychoanalytic insight expounded in his theory of dreams. As he argues, symbolic substitution often takes the path of semantic opposition:

contradictions of a certain kind—replacements by the precise opposite—offer no serious difficulty to the work of analytic interpretation. We shall not appeal here to the fact that contraries are so often represented by one and the same element in the modes of expression used by the unconscious, as for instance in dreams. But we shall remember that there are motive forces in mental life which bring about replacement by the opposite in the form of what is known as reaction-formation; and it is precisely in the revelation of such hidden forces that we look for the reward of this enquiry. (Freud 1997, 118)

In the unconscious, opposites such as death and love often represent one and the same content. For Freud, then, as for structuralists and deconstructionists, opposites are connected and contain the trace of each other. Hence in dreams and myths, any socially unacceptable or terrifying concept can be readily displaced by its more acceptable or pleasurable opposite.

In *The Merchant of Venice* and *King Lear*, Freud argues, the choice between three caskets or women distorts the well-known myth of the three female fates. The first two fates weave and spin the thread of life; the third, Atropos, cuts it. Shakespeare thus replaces Atropos, the Goddess of Death, with her opposite, the Goddess of Love. That is, Bassanio's and Lear's choices compensate for the *necessity* of death by substituting it with the *choice* of love. The latent psychic meaning of their choices is, therefore, the inevitability of death; but each play distorts this meaning by presenting it as its opposite. This substitution is a wish-fulfilment fantasy in which both death and necessity are imaginatively overcome: 'a choice is made where in reality there is obedience to a compulsion; and what is chosen is not a figure of terror, but the fairest and most desirable of women' (Freud 1997, 119). We might note that this imaginative overcoming of death entails a fetishistic logic. As a symbol, the woman figures a frightening loss that is repudiated through an erotic reinvestment in her as a symbol of love. Something of this fetishistic logic can be glimpsed in *The Merchant of Venice*. Not only does Portia save Bassanio from financial ruin and Antonio from losing his pound of flesh (a fate that reeks of symbolic castration); Bassanio also fetishizes her body, despite its association with the deadly paleness of the lead casket, as a bountiful source of gold, possessed even of 'sunny locks' that 'Hang on her temples like a golden fleece' (1.1.169–70).

In *King Lear*, by contrast, this fetishistic translation of death into golden love is not total. As Freud argues, 'it is impossible to explain the overpowering effect of *King Lear*' if we read it as a failure to choose love (Freud 1997, 120). Such a reading cannot explain the play's final scene, in which Lear, carrying the body of Cordelia on stage, chooses death in the figure of the woman who supposedly represents true love. *King Lear* thus recognizes the necessity of death, and its supersession of love, more explicitly than the casket sequence in *The Merchant of Venice*. This prompts Freud to conclude that the theme of the three caskets is ultimately a distortion of the three guises of the mother:

We might argue that what is represented here are the three inevitable relations that a man has with a woman—the woman who bears him, the woman who is his mate and the woman who destroys him; or that they are the three forms taken by the figure of the mother in the course of man's life— the mother herself, the beloved one who is chosen after her pattern, and lastly the Mother Earth who receives him once more. But it is in vain that an old man yearns for the love of woman as he had it first from his mother; the third of the Fates alone, the silent Goddess of Death, will take him into her arms. (Freud 1997, 121)

In the case of *King Lear*, then, the work of psychic repression can be at least partly undone. Although Freud elsewhere observes that literature often works by creatively distorting unconscious desires and fears, *King Lear* suggests how the literary text can function in a manner not dissimilar to psychoanalysis itself—that is, by bringing repressed unconscious material to consciousness. To the extent that this material is made only partially visible in *King Lear*, however, its effect is uncanny, echoing our own submerged desires and fears. Such, for Freud, is the power of tragedy.

Freud's methods of interpretation in this essay suggest several possibilities for literary criticism. First, the methods of psychoanalytic clinical practice resemble the interpretation of literary texts. More specifically, the structure of literature, myth, and fairy tales—in fact, of all narrative forms—imitates the structure of dreams. That is, they emerge from the unconscious and are distorted by the same censorship mechanisms of displacement, condensation, and wish-fulfilment at work in dreams. Such distortion implies, as it does in psychoanalytic clinical practice, a hierarchy of meaning: the surface or blatant meaning of a text derives from, even as it works to obscure, that text's latent or deeper meaning. The psychoanalytic critic must dig, like an archaeologist, to recover that deeper meaning; doing so often necessitates going outside the text to other resources—myth, clinical case studies—that share a structure, theme, or other similarity with the text under examination. But this in turn raises the question: is the true meaning of a text simply discovered by the psychoanalytic critic, or does she contribute to its creation? To what extent do the desires of the reader also produce the meaning attributed to the text? It is notable, for example, that the Jewish Freud writes about Shakespeare's one play with a Jewish character—the usurer Shylock—yet he makes no reference to him or the scenes in which he appears. Is the fear of death that Freud attributes to the casket scenes of *The Merchant of Venice* a displacement of a fear that he himself felt when reading scenes in which the Jewish Shylock is stripped by his Christian antagonists of his daughter, his possessions, and ultimately his religious identity?

Freud no doubt would have recognized how such questions open up to the possibility of what he called counter-transference—that is, the projection of the analyst's desires and fears onto the person of the analysand or patient. In this, psychoanalytic criticism can help us realize how interpretation is never simply a scientific act of decoding but also a fantasy of truth-seeking driven by many of the same psychic impulses as what it seeks to explain. Yet Freud's essay on *The Merchant of Venice* and *King Lear* largely bypasses this possibility, seeking instead to identify the true meaning of the two plays. Freud thus subscribes to a version of logocentrism in his readings of literature as much as dreams: that is, he regards both as mediated expressions of an unconscious whose pure meanings can, by psycho-analytic procedures, be recovered and hence known objectively.

Reading the Oedipus Complex in *Hamlet*: Ernest Jones

This is a recurrent feature of the earliest psychoanalytic literary criticism, including the work of the Welsh psychoanalytic critic Ernest Jones (1879–1958). When considering Freudian themes in Shakespeare, many of us might call to mind Hamlet's supposedly repressed Oedipal desire for his mother Gertrude—a desire made explicit in the 1948 film adaptation by Laurence Olivier, whose Hamlet roughhouses in bed with a Gertrude played by an actress younger than him. This 'Freudian' reading of the play, however, is in no small part the legacy of Jones.

Freud's own references to *Hamlet*, though frequent, are fairly fleeting. In a letter to his colleague Wilhelm Fliess, written on 15 October 1897, Freud first compared Oedipus to Hamlet. Observing that he has come to regard 'falling in love with the mother and jealousy of the father...as a universal event of early childhood', Freud claims that this 'event' explains the enduring power of *Oedipus Rex*: 'Each member of the audience was once, in germ and in phantasy, just such an Oedipus, and each one recoils in horror from the dream-fulfillment here transplanted into reality, with the whole quota of repression which separates his infantile state from his present one'. He then wonders 'whether the same thing may not lie at the bottom of *Hamlet* as well'. How is it, Freud asks, that Hamlet—who has no compunction about killing Rosencrantz and Guildenstern—can hesitate in killing his uncle Claudius to avenge the latter's murder of his father, unless he too has an 'obscure memory that he himself had meditated the same deed against his father from passion for his mother?' (Freud 1966, i:265–6).

This question provides the kernel of the reading that Freud was to develop in his *Intepretation of Dreams* (1900). Here he repeats his conviction that *Hamlet*, like *Oedipus Rex*, bears witness to the unconscious desires of sons to have sexual relations with their mothers and kill their fathers. But he adds two wrinkles to his interpretation, one historical and the other biographical. Freud argues that *Hamlet* differs from *Oedipus Rex* inasmuch as Shakespeare's play shows, two thousand years after the Greeks, 'the secular advance of repression in the emotional life of mankind' (Freud 1966, i:264): whereas *Oedipus Rex* treats the desire to bed one's mother and murder one's father in the way a dream would—by bringing it out into the open—in *Hamlet* the desire remains firmly repressed, and is legible only by inference. Freud suggests additionally that the play's treatment of this desire is complicated by the then recent death, in 1601, of Shakespeare's own father, about whom his childhood feelings must have been freshly revived while writing *Hamlet*.

But it was left to Ernest Jones to flesh out these notes into a full 'Freudian' reading of the play. Freud's remarks about *Hamlet* suggest three points of departure for a psychoanalytic literary criticism: the analysis of a literary *character* as if he were a patient possessed of an unconscious; the analysis of a historically contingent *culture* and its mechanisms of repression; and the analysis of an *author* and his artistic wellsprings. The first and last approaches were pursued by Jones in his book *Hamlet and Oedipus* (1949), a revision of an earlier book he had published in 1922. In the process, Jones made one of the earliest attempts to transform psychoanalysis into a viable literary as well as psychological theory. His 1949 study takes explicit aim at the then fashionable tendency of American New Critics to bracket off a text from its author: 'A work of art is too often regarded as a finished thing-in-itself, something almost independent of the creator's personality, as if little would be learned about the one or the other by connecting the two studies' (Jones 1954, 14). Yet even as Jones attempts to reconnect the study of literary texts to the study of the minds of authors, he does so in a way that departs from any understanding of a writer as supremely in control of his craft. Instead, he insists that 'an artist has an unconscious mind as well as a conscious one, and his imagination springs at least as fully from the former as from the latter' (Jones 1954, 22).

Jones's splitting of the artist is crucial to his splitting of literary character. First, he treats Hamlet as if he were a real person—not a whole or unified personality, but a divided psyche whose unconscious longings are invisible to his conscious mind. These longings, however, are legible to the psychoanalytic literary critic. Jones asserts that Hamlet had, 'as a child, bitterly resented having had to share his mother's affection even with his own father, had regarded him as a rival, and had secretly wished him out of the way' (Jones 1954, 78). Such thoughts have been driven into Hamlet's unconscious by his filial loyalty and the social taboo against incest. But the actualization of his infantile wish in the murder of his father by a jealous rival produces an obscure and depressive memory of his childhood conflict. Hamlet's uncle thus reflects back to him the most buried part of his own personality, so that he cannot kill Claudius without also killing himself: 'killing his mother's husband would be equivalent to committing the original sin himself' (Jones 1954, 103). Jones argues that *Hamlet* conceals its title character's desires from itself through a dream-like process of displacement or 'decomposition', whereby Hamlet deals with his ambivalent feelings about his father—loving obligation coupled with illicit murderous rage—by performing a further splitting:

In *Hamlet* the two contrasting elements of the normal ambivalent attitude towards the father were expressed towards two sets of people: the pious respect and love towards the memory of his father, and the hatred, contempt and rebellion towards the father-substitutes, Claudius and Polonius. In other words, the original father had been transformed into two fathers, one good, the other bad, corresponding with the division in the son's feelings. (Jones 1954, 122)

For Jones, the twin splittings of Hamlet and his father must stem ultimately from a division in Shakespeare's own mind. He thus reads Hamlet's Oedipal conflict as emerging from Shakespeare's conflicted feelings about his own father.

Jones, like Freud, regards the Oedipus complex as the foundational drama of male identity formation. Even though this drama presumes a sexualized bond between male infant and mother, it triangulates that bond with, and subordinates it to, the infant's relation to the father as rival and role model. The Oedipus complex is for Jones, moreover, the original truth that dramatic character, literary work, and author all express, no matter how obliquely. Jones's logocentric model of literary production is thus at root a masculinist if not a patriarchal one: the relation between son and father is, according to him, the wellspring of psychic and creative activity.

Reading Jealousy in *Othello*: Melanie Klein

For Freud and Jones, the relation with the father is instrumental in the development of the ego. By contrast, Melanie Klein (1882–1960) argues that the primal bond with the mother is just as if not more constitutive of subsequent psychic activity. For Klein, envy is a particularly potent factor in our lives. She sees it as a sadistic form of relationality that dates back to the earliest stages in the infant's psychic development. As we have seen, Freud uses the metaphor of archaeological excavation to recover early psychic activity such as the formation of the Oedipus complex; Klein proposes digging deeper still to consider the earlier relations between the infant and the mother. In *Envy and Gratitude* (1957), she develops Freud's theorization of the life and death drives in order to understand the complex of loving and destructive relations that characterize the infant's early emotional life. And she sees both these drives at work in the infant's relation to the mother and, in particular, her body.

According to Klein, the infant distinguishes early on between its good and bad objects. The good object is the mother's breast, which forms the core of the infant's ego and vitally contributes to its growth; the infant internalizes the breast and the milk it gives not just as physical substance, but also as a psychic symbol of nourishment and love. The mother's breast thus becomes the prototype of what Klein calls the 'phantasy' (spelled with a 'ph' to distinguish it from the more common 'fantasy') of maternal love as the font of goodness, generosity, and creativity. This phantasy, grounded in the oral relation of the infant to the mother's body, is potentially disrupted by a destructive impulse that resents the breast for withholding its nourishment for itself. At the root of this destructive impulse, Klein argues, is envy. Preventing the infant from building up her good object and hence her sense of self, envy, like the greed for the mother's good breast, takes an oral form—the urge to bite and destroy the now bad breast.

Klein's conception of envy is thus different from René Girard's, which presumes triangulation among a model, and imitator, and an object. Indeed, Klein distinguishes between envy and jealousy in a way that subtly serves to underline her shift in focus from Freud's and Jones's triangulated model of ego development to her dyadic one:

> Envy is the angry feeling that another person possesses and enjoys something desirable—the envious impulse being to take it away or spoil it. Moreover, envy implies the subject's relation to one person only and goes back to the earliest exclusive relation with the mother. Jealousy is based on envy, but involves a relation to at least two people; it is mainly concerned with love that the subject feels is his due and has been taken away, from him by his rival. In the everyday conception of jealousy, a man or a woman feels deprived of the loved person by someone else. (Klein 1957, 6–7)

In other words, jealousy is derived from and a displacement of primal envy. It attributes to a third party—for example, the father—a power to take away love; but that power has always already resided in the primary love object, the mother's breast. Or, more accurately, the infant has always already projected that power onto the primary love object. This hints at the destructive underside of projective identification: for Klein, the infant's badness—primarily bad excrements and bad parts of the self—is displaced onto the mother and her breast, which acquire in phantasy a power to withhold nourishment and even identity from the infant.

To illustrate the projective powers of envy and the ways in which these shape instances of jealousy, Klein turns to *Othello*. The play's title character destroys the object he loves—Desdemona—and this typifies for Klein the way in which jealousy betrays the workings of an envy that is little more than greed stimulated by fear. She cites Emilia's remarks about how jealousy is never really about the rival:

> But jealous souls will not be answer'd so.
> They are not ever jealous for the cause,
> But jealous for they are jealous. It is a monster
> Begot upon itself, born on itself.

$$(3.4.154-7)$$

As Klein remarks, 'it could be said that the very envious person is insatiable, he can never be satisfied because his envy stems from within and therefore always finds an object to focus on' (Klein 1957, 8). And tying this hint of envy's 'insatiable' orality to her conviction that *Othello* recognizes the true basis of jealousy in primal envy,

Klein cites Iago's characterization of jealousy as 'the green-eyed monster which doth mock | The meat it feeds on' (3.3.170–1). Of this, she says: 'One is reminded of the saying "to bite the hand which feeds one", which is almost synonymous with biting, destroying, and spoiling the breast' (Klein 1957, 9). If *Hamlet* is for Freud and Jones the barely disguised drama of the son's Oedipal relation to the father, then *Othello* is for Klein the barely disguised drama of the infant's oral relation to the maternal breast.

Klein does not move beyond these few speeches on jealousy in *Othello*. But her reading might be profitably developed with respect to the whole play. Othello's violent swings between regarding Desdemona as the chaste source of his identity and its predatory destroyer repeatedly suggest processes of projective identification that veer between idolization and violence. When she is good, she is 'fair', and Othello is secure; when she is no longer good, she is sullied or spoiled, and for Othello 'chaos is come again' (3.3.93). One might even argue that Othello's projective identification with Desdemona performs a substitutive reversal; although he is old enough to be her parent, he acts as a greedy and frightened child demanding maternal sustenance from her. And he is most upset when he cannot receive that sustenance, or when he fears that she has withheld what he greedily craves from her. It is in such moments that his appetite is disavowed or rather displaced onto hers, which he tellingly apprehends as a form of malicious withholding: 'O curse of marriage, | That we can call these delicate creatures ours, | And not their appetites!' (3.3.272–4). That Klein does not pursue this reading says something about her critical practice: rather than reading Othello as if he was a real patient with an unconscious and a psychic history (as Jones would), she is more interested in how the play is a meditation of sorts on the origins of jealousy. That is to say, she does not psychoanalyse the play (or its characters) so much as see the play as itself an effective instance of psychoanalysis, providing keen insight into the workings of the psyche.

Object relations theory, pioneered by Klein and developed by the English psychoanalyst D. W. Winnicott, has had a significant influence on literary criticism, including criticism of Shakespeare. In addition to providing a framework for reading characters' and authors' relations to phantasy, object relations theory has emphasized how the very act of reading is equally implicated in phantasies that engender both pleasure and frustration. Just as importantly, Klein's emphasis on the maternal body has appealed to feminist literary theorists and critics who have sought an alternative to the father-centred Oedipal paradigm of Freud and Jones. To the extent that Klein reads Shakespeare as revealing the buried unconscious truth of envy, she abides by the logocentric reading practice of Freud and Jones. But inasmuch as she paints a portrait of an ego that is inherently unstable and, in its projective identifications, even impossible, Klein—like Freud—anticipates certain aspects of poststructuralist thought. As we will see, her vision of the desire that endeavours unsuccessfully to coalesce into a whole, unified 'I' is a distinguishing feature of poststructuralist adaptations of psychoanalysis, especially the theories of Jacques Lacan.

6

Lacanian Psychoanalysis

Jacques Lacan, Julia Kristeva, Slavoj Žižek

> I am not what I am.
>
> *Twelfth Night*, 3.1.132; *Othello*, 1.1.65

Shakespeare gives this memorable line to both Viola (in *Twelfth Night*) and Iago (in *Othello*). In each instance, the line alerts us that its speaker is putting on an act: Viola cross-dresses as Cesario to gain employment with Orsino; Iago feigns loyalty to, even as he plots to ruin, Othello. The line is, in Viola's case, a gentle parody and, in Iago's case, a demonic travesty of God's 'I am that I am' (Exodus 3:14), the classic assertion of God's pure self-identity as *logos*. Yet Viola's and Iago's 'I am not what I am', crossing lines of both gender and genre, suggests a pervasive problem intrinsic to the assertion of the 'I'. It is less that there is a real self concealed beneath Viola's or Iago's deceptive exterior than that, in each case, the 'I' does not fully coincide with itself. It contains the trace of something else that it is not, yet also is— and all the more so inasmuch as the 'I' is itself generated from an 'it'. Viola's or Iago's 'I' is a self-contained entity, yet it is also a social self derived from an *image* of 'me' (as male, as loyal) seen by another. Because we tend to privilege the first kind of 'I' as more real, we easily dismiss the second as artificial. Yet Shakespeare's 'I am not what I am' syntactically refuses this distinction: even as the line works to identify its speakers with duplicity, it does not allow us to decide which of its two 'I's is reality and which mere image or 'it'. Each slips into the other, quilting 'I' with 'it'.

This slippage between reality and image, 'I' and 'it', is a distinctive feature of the psychoanalytic theory of Jacques Lacan (1901–81). Freud registers it also in his contested remark about the relation between the unconscious and the conscious, 'Wo Es war, soll Ich werden' (Freud 1966, xxii:80): 'where It was, shall I be'. In the post-Freudian school of ego psychology, which flourished in the United States after the Second World War, the remark was understood to mean that the psychoanalyst can minimize the patient's repression and neurosis by bringing the contents of the unconscious into consciousness. By replacing the 'it' or unconscious id with a conscious and self-identical 'I', ego psychology presumes the ego to be a unified self, a repository of enlightened reason that can triumph over the dark shadows of the id. Lacan vigorously disputed this interpretation, thereby inaugurating a psychoanalytic movement that has strong affinities with deconstruction. He argued that the ego is not the salvation of the patient; rather, it is a projection, an illusion of self-identity that the analyst must disassemble. Hence Lacan interpreted Freud's remark differently from the ego psychologists: the patient's 'I' must come to inhabit the fissure that divides the ego from the unconscious 'it', a position that no longer permits the illusion of a unified self. Moreover, the ego must be seen as itself deriving from a second 'it' external to the patient.

Lacan developed this thesis in his influential essay, 'The Mirror Stage as Formative of the Function of the "I" As Revealed in Psychoanalytic Experience'. In his clinical practice, he noted that an infant between 6 and 18 months experiences its body as fragmented; yet it recognizes its image in a mirror. The infant sees its reflection as a whole, which brings it into conflict with its experience of its body. Yet it proceeds to identify with the reflection: this primary identification is what forms the 'I'. In other words, the 'I' is not intrinsic to the infant, but rather a product of what Lacan terms *méconnaissance*, or false recognition, of an external image (Lacan 1977, 5). Because the mirror stage entails misrecognition of a wholeness that is only imagined, Lacan terms 'Imaginary' the register whereby we identify with phenomena external to us. For the infant, the identifications of the Imaginary extend beyond the mirror image: they also vitally include a crucial aspect of the mother, that is, her desire, with which the infant believes itself to coincide.

The infant's Imaginary identification with the mother's desire is challenged, however, by the recognition that the father has a claim over the mother, and that her desire is not of and for the infant alone. This recognition is a linguistic one: for Lacan, our entrance into language is a potentially wrenching movement from the early bond with the mother into the patriarchal realm of signification, distinguished by the Name of the Father—in French, the *nom du père*, which is pronounced the same way as *non du père*, or 'no of the father'. This 'no' denies the infant its Imaginary identification with the mother's desire, forcing a distinction between it and others. Here Lacan owes a considerable debt to Saussure and structuralist linguistics. For the entry into language also forces the child to identify with various signifiers—her name, the gendered pronoun 'he' or 'she', etc.—that, by being differentially related to other signifiers, ground her within a larger structure. Although the identification with external signifying elements necessarily involves an aspect of the Imaginary, the location of the infant within a larger system of differences that precedes her is the hallmark of the register that Lacan calls the 'Symbolic'. Entry into the Symbolic produces difference not only between 'I' and other signifiers but also between ego and unconscious.

The child's entrance into the Symbolic also inaugurates desire, which Lacan again sees as a function of language. By separating signifiers from their signifieds—and, in particular, by barring the signifier 'I' from identification with the mother's desire, an identification relegated to the unconscious—the Symbolic dispatches the child on a fetishistic quest for a lost wholeness that never was, and that never can be attained. The movement of the desiring 'I' toward wholeness, which would perform a metaphoric union of signifier and signified, is thwarted by the metonymic diversion of the signifier 'I' to other signifiers, or 'objects *a*', that promise the illusion of completing it (e.g. a perfect lover, house, or job). Inasmuch as these 'objects *a*' are signifiers fetishistically substituting within fantasy for a lost Imaginary wholeness, they can never grant a full plenitude to the 'I'. Indeed, for Lacan, we are all—male as much as female—symbolically castrated by and in language, bereft of the signified that would restore to us the Phallus, Lacan's term for what the 'I' has lost by entering the Symbolic.

Even though Lacan stresses that the Phallus is not the biological penis but a sign of what we all lack, some have chafed at the male-centredness of the concept. At least one psychoanalyst indebted to Lacan has re-emphasized the importance of the feminine in the subject's psychosexual development. The French-Bulgarian theorist Julia Kristeva, while preserving many aspects of Lacan's account of the Imaginary and the Symbolic, has stressed the complexities of the infant's pre-linguistic relation with the mother in ways that build on the object relations theory of Melanie Klein. In the earliest stage of development, which she terms the 'Semiotic', the infant does not distinguish itself from its mother or the world around it. Rather, it attempts to orally absorb everything that it experiences as pleasurable without any acknowledgement of boundaries. But Kristeva also posits that, between the Semiotic and the mirror stage, there occurs a crucial phase of abjection. During this time, the infant begins to separate between itself and the maternal, thus creating those boundaries between self and other that must be in place before the entry into the Symbolic. As a result the infant experiences as terrifyingly abject certain objects, such as milk, that blur the boundary between itself and its mother; these experiences of abjection pose the risk of falling back into an earlier, undifferentiated state without selfhood.

In his later work, Lacan emphasized a third category called the 'Real', which he saw as separate from the Symbolic register of language and the Imaginary register of fantasy and the mirror stage. The Real, which is not the same as reality, is distinguished by phenomena that shatter the meaning of the Symbolic and the wholeness fantasized by the Imaginary: death in particular, but also the senseless cracks within those fantasies that we so often mistake for meaningful reality. Lacan's conception of the Real has been developed with especial acuity by the Slovenian critic Slavoj Žižek who, coupling psychoanalysis with elements of Marxism, analyses popular cultural fantasies (from expressions of anti-Semitism to the films of Alfred Hitchcock) for the trace of the Real legible within them. It is on this terrain that Shakespeare's work has proved a powerful interlocutor to Lacanian analysis. In particular, the lurking presence in Shakespeare's writing of compulsive desires that never quite find their objects, that split the 'I', and that resist conversion into meaning is one of its hallmarks. 'In night . . . desire sees best of all', says Venus in *Venus and Adonis* (720). That is, desire does its work beyond and behind the light of reason. And nowhere is this more apparent than in *Hamlet*, which Lacan has styled the 'tragedy of desire'.

Desiring the Phallus in *Hamlet*: Jacques Lacan

Lacan's essay 'Desire and the Interpretation of Desire in *Hamlet*' (1959) is extraordinarily difficult: it is full of digressions, obscure puns, and diagrams that do not quite make sense. This difficulty says something not just about Lacan's characteristically allusive writing style, but also about his conceptions of language and desire. Language is for Lacan both the realm of the Symbolic—the system of differences that generate identity and meaning—and the medium of the unconscious, which operates through parapraxis, displacement, and condensation: that is, through slippages at the level of the material signifier. By promising a fullness of meaning, the Symbolic is immersed in an element of Imaginary fantasy that can be all too easily misrecognized. But the desires unleashed in and by the Symbolic can also produce disturbances that foreground signification's endless slippages. Lacan's essay on *Hamlet* does not simply *describe* the workings of desire; it also *enacts* them in the provocations it poses to the reader and the reader's own desire. By doing so, it differs greatly from Ernest Jones's Oedipal interpretation of the play. If Jones seeks to bring the truth of Hamlet's and Shakespeare's unconscious to rational consciousness—to convert 'it' to 'I'—Lacan seeks to confront readers with their own desire for understanding, and the slippages to which that desire is prone.

He does this in several ways. One is with his three graphs of desire, which he reproduces from his earlier seminar on 'The Subversion of the Subject and the Dialectic of Desire in the Freudian Unconscious'. The graphs, which illustrate the workings of desire through the subject's relation in fantasy to signification and the object of his longing, are topographical diagrams that imply a complex mathematical understanding of psychic activity. In other words, they induce in the reader a desire for meaning and scientific mastery—a desire to know what Lacan knows. And indeed, the graphs do make a kind of logical sense. But that sense can blind us to the graphs' material forms. The first of the three graphs, which depicts the relation of desire to language, consists of an inverted U or bulb that is bisected, or cut, by signification; it resembles a circumcised penis, or more specifically, a penis that has been sliced. The second graph, called *che vuoi*—Italian for 'what do you want?'—depicts the relation of desire in fantasy to its object or other; it looks remarkably like a question mark. And in the final diagram or 'complete graph', which offers a complex mapping of the subject's relation to *jouissance* (or senseless pleasure), we might decipher the shape of a tumescent phallus. In their material forms, then, the three graphs arguably allegorize Lacan's conception of desire: as we enter language, and hanker for a fullness of identity and meaning, we unwittingly submit to a castration that asks the question of the other: what do you want for and from me? And in seeking an answer to that question, we desire that strange sign that Lacan calls the Phallus—a plenitude that bulges with seeming significance yet always eludes our grasp. It is this sign that Lacan's reading of *Hamlet* is devoted both to fleshing out and making frustratingly unobtainable.

With its opening sentence, Lacan's essay provokes the reader to desire: 'As a sort of come-on, I announced that I would speak today about that piece of bait called Ophelia, and I'll be as good as my word' (Lacan 1982, 11). We might ask: what desire does the 'bait called Ophelia' provoke? Lacan expects us to snap at this bait. But what do we expect to acquire by doing so? One answer might be a fuller understanding of Ophelia: her inner psychology and, as the essay's title suggests, her role in relation to Hamlet's desire. Yet Lacan's essay—despite his assurance that he will 'be as good as [his] word' in speaking about Ophelia—makes only passing reference to her. Lacan, it might then seem, is not as good as his word. But what does it mean to be as good as one's word? In everyday usage, the phrase means to deliver on a spoken promise—to match word to action and meaning, to connect signifier to signified. But words in *Hamlet* are unreliable: they punningly slip and slide, drawing attention to their material dimensions rather than their meanings. 'What do you read, my lord?' asks Polonius; Hamlet's obtuse reply, 'Words, words, words' (2.2.191–2), typifies the play's deflection of words from meaningful signifieds to opaque signifiers. For Lacan too, signifiers always slide away from meaning to other signifiers. Thus for Lacan, to be as 'good as my word'—if 'my word' is understood as his theory of signification—is to be diverted from the straight path that connects the signifier 'Ophelia' to her true meaning. And such diversion is precisely what is performed by another signifier, *leurre*, that Lacan associates with Ophelia. In the English translation of the essay, *leurre* is rendered as 'bait'. But it also means 'delusion'. As Lacan will go on to argue, Ophelia as an object of desire (whether Hamlet's or the reader's) is also a delusion—a necessary one, perhaps, but a delusion that masks desire's real aim.

Leurre is also a pun on *l'heure*, meaning hour or time, a key concept in the essay. Lacan asserts that Hamlet is always in the time of the other; that is, he has lost the way of his own desire, as he is perpetually in thrall to the desire of the other. He cannot act on his own desire, despite his pledge to avenge his dead father, because something in him always capitulates to the timetables and hence the wills of others, as when he cheerfully submits to Claudius' fatal proposal that he duel with Laertes. But Hamlet is most in thrall to the desire of his mother. Having pleaded with her to abstain from sexual relations with his uncle, he nonetheless 'sends her to Claudius's bed, into the arms of the man who once again will not fail to make her yield' (Lacan 1982, 13). He acts in concert with Gertrude's will rather than plotting his own course. Hamlet's legendary indecision is therefore not the product of an Oedipal desire *for* his mother, as it is in Freud's and Jones's interpretations. Rather, Lacan's Hamlet is frozen by his fixation *within* his mother's desire, from which he cannot separate himself.

To become the subject of one's own desire rather than the captive of the other's, one has to separate less from the other than from a fantasy object, the Phallus. The Phallus is not the biological penis, but a signifier of what the subject gives up—an Imaginary identification with the (m)other and her desire—to enter the network of differences that comprise the Symbolic. The subject's desire is inaugurated by fetishistically replacing the Phallus with another signifier, the object *a*, to which the subject is drawn inasmuch as he invests it with the trace of what he has lost:

With respect to the object *a*, at once image and pathos, the subject feels himself to be in an imaginary situation of otherness. This object satisfies no need and is itself already relative, i.e., placed in relation to the subject. It is obvious from simple phenomenology . . . that the subject is present in the fantasy. And the object is the object of desire only by virtue of being the end-term of the fantasy. The object takes the place, I would say, of what the subject is—symbolically—deprived of. . . . Thus the imaginary object is in a position to condense in itself the virtues or the dimension of being and to become that veritable delusion of being [*leurre de l'être*]. (Lacan 1982, 15)

To become Hamlet's 'object *a*', Ophelia would have had to substitute for the Phallus of which he was deprived upon entering the Symbolic. For Lacan, *Hamlet* hints that this is the function she was meant to play, and he argues (in possibly tongue-in-cheek fashion) that the etymology of her name is 'O Phallos'. As a substitute for the Phallus, however, Ophelia is a *leurre de l'être* or delusion of *being*, inasmuch as Ophelia's existence as a differentiated object is not an intrinsic aspect of reality but is instead dependent on the subject's fantasy. With this phrase, Lacan puns on *leurre de lettre*, or delusion of the *letter*, inasmuch as the subject's fantasy is produced by the agency of signifiers within the Symbolic; and *leurre de l'autre*, or delusion of the *other*, inasmuch as Ophelia's otherness is a fantasy that masks how the subject takes her as his object to replace something he fears he has lost in himself. These delusions, however, are necessary if Hamlet is to become the subject of his own desire. And they presume also a powerful deconstructive paradox: to avoid the time of the other, in which he fails to separate from others' desires, Hamlet must submit to another punning sense of *leurre de l'être—l'heure de l'Autre*. This is the time of the Other with a capital 'O', Lacan's term for language, which insists on the otherness of subject to object.

Yet in the first three acts of the play, Hamlet neurotically rejects Ophelia as his object *a*. Why? Freud theorized that mourning performs a carefully timed withdrawal of desire from a lost object in order that the subject may be freed to desire another object. Lacan, building on Freud's theory, notes that Hamlet does not have enough time to mourn the loss of his father, thanks to his mother's hasty remarriage to Claudius. Hence Hamlet's ability to transfer desire to another object is tragically arrested. Beholden to his mother's desire, he is not able to mourn the loss of the Phallus, and so he cannot perform the substitution in desire that mourning his father's death would permit. In rejecting Ophelia as his other, however, Hamlet paradoxically cannot avoid the time of the other. He finally begins to desire Ophelia after her death in Act 5, but 'only insofar as the object of Hamlet's desire has become an impossible object' (Lacan 1982, 36). And Ophelia becomes this impossible object in a fashion that again involves Hamlet's Imaginary identification with another's desire. Seeing Laertes' powerful display of grief for Ophelia in the cemetery, Hamlet leaps into her grave to prove to Laertes that he can 'rant as well as thou' (5.1.269). As Lacan notes, Hamlet's aggressive response to Laertes betrays the 'paroxysm of absorption in the imaginary register, formally expressed as a mirror relationship, a mirrored reaction. The one you fight is the one you admire most' (Lacan 1982, 31). This Imaginary identification with Laertes and his mourning momentarily unblocks Hamlet's desire and sends it in the direction of the object *a*. Yet it also prevents him from becoming the subject of his desire, inasmuch as he remains in the time of the other, fixated within Laertes's desire. Even in the play's final act, Hamlet submits to Claudius' will. He can only become the subject of his desire and kill Claudius once 'he has made the complete sacrifice—without wanting to, moreover—of all narcissistic attachments, i.e., when he is mortally wounded and knows it' (Lacan 1982, 51). In other words, it is impossible for Hamlet to reconnect with his desire and its lost object, the Phallus, without surrendering his subjectivity and dying.

This essay illustrates how Lacan combines elements of structuralist and deconstructive thought in his reworking of Freudian psychoanalysis. Whereas Freud regards the unconscious as if it were amorphous, subterranean magma seeking vents through which it can irrupt and bring its contents out into the open, Lacan regards the unconscious as ordered—indeed, he claims it to be structured like a language—yet impossible to know in any unmediated form. Lacan reproduces the structuralist emphasis on systems of difference as opposed to positive identities, which is why he analyses the unconscious as a linguistic structure rather than in terms of its contents and treats the Symbolic as a web of differences rather than as individual words describing pre-existing objects. But in foregrounding the slippages of the signifier by means of which the unconscious troubles the orderly differences of the Symbolic, Lacan's thought is more in sympathy with deconstruction.

Excavating the Maternal Bond in *Romeo and Juliet*: Julia Kristeva

The tension between language's orderly differences and the disorderly slippages induced by desire is the hallmark of Lacanian theory in general and Lacanian interpretation of Shakespeare in particular. For

Lacan, this tension is very much grounded in the vexations of the Phallus. For Julia Kriseva (1941–), by contrast, the tension between differentiation and disorder is more a function of the pre-linguistic relation to the mother. Kristeva left her native Bulgaria in the 1960s for France, where she studied first structuralism and then Lacanian psychoanalysis. Supplementing Lacan's association of the Symbolic domain of language with the Name of the Father, her writing initially valorized an archaic pre-linguistic state associated with the mother which, instead of the Imaginary, she termed the Semiotic. In this state, where the infant is undifferentiated from the mother, communication consists of gurgles of meaningless noises that indicate pleasure rather than symbolization. In her influential study *Powers of Horror: An Essay on Abjection*, Kristeva developed her theorization of this pre-Symbolic phase in less idealizing fashion. Following Melanie Klein, she stressed the importance of the mother to the subject's formation. According to Kristeva, the pre-Symbolic infant's *jouissance*—Lacan's term for senseless pleasure—entails a bodily fusion with the mother. But this pleasure is matched and countermanded by a horror of the 'abject', Kristeva's term for the maternal object-that-is-not-quite-an-object (because it is pre-Symbolic, and hence prior to the differences of signification). Like Lacan's Phallus, the abject blurs the fragile boundary between the child's and the mother's identities. Kristeva follows Klein in seeing the infant's relation to the mother as torn between gratitude and envy, love and hate, pleasure and abjection; but these primal ambivalences clear space for the later linguistic processes of differentiation and identification that shape subjectivity and desire in the Symbolic (Kristeva 1982).

This assumption is central to Kristeva's essay, 'Romeo and Juliet: Love-Hatred in the Couple' (1985). She starts her reading by noting how Shakespeare's tragedy reproduces the fantasy of outlaw love, a love that can survive only by being outside the law—that is, outside the space of the Symbolic—and hence, as a capital offence, it courts death. This seems to place love in the space of the feminine; death is a punishment that the patriarchal law metes out to a love that it opposes with hatred. Yet, in a deconstructive twist, Kristeva notes that far from being external to love, hatred is integral to it in *Romeo and Juliet*: 'my only love sprung from my only hate!' says Juliet (1.5.135). In other words, it is no accident that both Romeo and Juliet fall for a member of another family they have been socialized to hate, as love in Kristeva's analysis emerges from the same mainspring as hatred: 'we are dealing with the intrinsic presence of hatred in amatory feeling itself' (Kristeva 1987, 222). Kristeva notes the tension between Romeo's idealizing solar metaphor for love—a sun-like singularity that dazzles everything in its solar system, of which it is the organizing centre—and Juliet's more destructive nocturnal metaphors, which disperse and fragment: 'Come, gentle night…and, when I shall die, | Take him and cut him out in little stars' (3.2.20–2). This is not simply the tension between a male and a female understanding of love; for Kristeva, the lovers' metaphors transcend gender and underline the constitutive power of idealization and destruction in subject formation.

In a biographical detour, Kristeva proposes that Shakespeare wrote *Romeo and Juliet* in the year that his son Hamnet died (1596). Succumbing *both* to nostalgia for the adolescent love that had produced Hamnet *and* to hatred for his abandoned wife, Shakespeare idealized his youthful love in Romeo and Juliet and transferred his hatred to the play's feuding parents. Yet, Kristeva notes, this strategy—reminiscent of Ernest Jones's account of Hamlet's decondensation of his Oedipal ambivalence—performs a mystification of how love works. Hatred is not something that comes *after* love, but is always already integral to it. Shakespeare's nostalgia for adolescent love, Kristeva argues, derives from a deeper nostalgia for his mother that is itself shaded with hatred. She sees this duality as integral also to Romeo and Juliet's love.

The fact that the lovers are teenagers is important for Kristeva. In her experience as an analyst, the onset of sexuality produces destabilizations that are combated by fantasies of marriage and lasting love. These fantasies are driven by nostalgia for the pleasure of the primary maternal bond. In their choice of partner, then, both men and women—whether hetero- or homosexual—look to recreate their bond with their mother. Yet that bond also necessitates the object-relation of hatred. Kristeva argues that *Romeo and Juliet* recognizes the ground of this ambivalence in Friar Lawrence's conflation of womb and tomb: 'The earth that's nature's mother is her tomb; what is her burying grave, that is her womb' (2.2.9–10). Lurking in this remark, Kristeva argues, is a partial recognition of the fatal danger posed to the subject by the bond with the mother:

The jubilatory vanishing of identity at the heart of a nostalgic love for a maternal embrace is nevertheless felt by the adult as a loss, even as a mortal danger. The defense mechanisms then react, kneaded by drives and by egotic and superegotic hatred, in order to give back shape, identity, and existence to the *same* swallowed up in the *other*. The alternating love/hatred braids passions tangle, and its eternal return never produces a 'better' couple than the sadomasochistic one. (Kristeva 1987, 223–4)

For Kristeva, in other words, hatred is a protection against the death of the self threatened by fusion with the mother. For a love relation to prosper and ward off the threat of undifferentiation, it needs to incorporate hatred.

Kristeva imagines what would have happened if Romeo and Juliet had escaped their persecutors and survived: either time would have transformed their outlaw passion into 'the banal, humdrum, lacklus-ter lassitude of a tired and cynical collusion'; or they would have continued to be a passionate couple, 'but covering the entire gamut of sadomasochism that the two partners already heralded in the yet relatively quiet version of the Shakespearean text' (Kristeva 1987, 217). For Kristeva, Romeo's idealizations of love cannot disguise a violent compulsion—and a compulsion to violence—integral to his and Juliet's love, even if that compulsion is disavowed by the lovers and their playwright as the hatefulness of others.

Reading the Real in *Richard II*: Slavoj Žižek

In this disavowal, Kristeva anticipates Slavoj Žižek's account of the relations between fantasy and the Real. Žižek (1949–) is one of the best exegetes of Lacan, whose work he has popularized in a series of brilliant and often witty studies of popular culture, including *Looking Awry: An Introduction to Jacques Lacan through Popular Culture* (1991), *Everything You Always Wanted To Know about Lacan But Were Afraid To Ask Hitchcock* (1992), and *How to Read Lacan* (2007). But Žižek also transforms Lacan, for his writing stages a dialogue between psychoanalysis and Marxism about the relation of ideology to fantasy, as outlined in his first English-language book, *The Sublime Object of*

Ideology (1989). Žižek maintains that in Marxism, ideology shares the contours of fantasy as theorized by Lacan; both wholly structure the subject's sense of reality. Like Lacan, Žižek sees the Real as antithetical to that reality, which the subject experiences as a meaningfully ordered totality. For Žižek, the Real instead names aberrations within reality that puncture its meaningfulness to the subject and potentially generate sites of active political resistance.

Looking Awry (1991) may illustrate Lacanian theory with instances of modern popular culture; but throughout, Shakespeare serves as titular shorthand for the irruption of the Real within reality. One chapter is called 'All's Well That Ends Well', another 'Much Ado about a Thing'; even the book's title is a quote from *Richard II*. In the first chapter, 'From Reality to the Real', Žižek offers a reading of *Richard II* to illustrate Lacan's thesis concerning the object *a* of desire. We may think we know what the object of our desire is: but what constitutes the desire is not the object itself, so much as the pleasure of movement towards it. Here Žižek draws on Lacan's distinction between the *goal* and the *aim* of desire: the goal is the end object, which makes desire intelligible in terms of the object and makes the object intelligible in terms of desire. By contrast, the aim is the direction of desire, which traces a senseless movement independent of the object. If the goal of desire characterizes the fantasy that structures a meaningful reality, the aim of desire hints at the Real that both drives and is hidden by the fantasy. Popular culture—science fiction stories, murder mysteries, but also Shakespeare—often discloses this tension between goal and aim, the 'something' and the 'nothing' of desire.

Richard II provides Žižek with an exemplary illustration of how the Real can puncture the reality of desire and reveal the latter's meaningfulness to be a 'something produced from nothing'. The play, Žižek quips, 'proves beyond any doubt that Shakespeare had read Lacan' (Žižek 1991, 9). Indeed, *Richard II* illustrates particularly well Lacan's understanding of the void that haunts the fantasy of identity: 'the basic problem of the drama is that of the *hystericization of a king*, a process whereby the king loses the second, sublime body that makes him a king, is confronted with the void of his subjectivity outside the symbolic mandate-title "king," and is thus forced into a series of theatrical, hysterical outbursts, from self-pity to sarcastic and clownish madness' (Žižek 1991, 9). Žižek is particularly interested in one dialogue that demonstrates the disjunction between the subject's object of desire and that object as seen by others. King Richard has left on a war expedition; the Queen, succumbing to a presentiment of evil, is consumed with a sadness she cannot explain. Bushy tries to console her, claiming that her grief is baseless:

> Each substance of a grief hath twenty shadows
> Which shows like grief itself, but is not so.
> For sorrow's eye, glazed with blinding tears,
> Divides one thing entire to many objects—
> Like perspectives, which rightly gazed upon,
> Show nothing but confusion; eyed awry
> Distinguish form. So your sweet majesty,
> Looking awry upon your lord's departure,
> Find shapes of grief more than himself to wail,
> Which, looked on as it is, is naught but shadows
> Of what it is not.

> (2.2.14–24)

As Žižek points out in his updated discussion of *Richard II* in *How To Read Lacan*, Bushy describes here the object *a*: 'an entity that has no substantial consistency, which is in itself "nothing but confusion", and which acquires a definite shape only when viewed from a standpoint distorted by the subject's desires and fears—as such, a mere "shadow of what it is not". *Objet a* is the strange object which is nothing but the inscription of the subject itself in the field of objects, in the guise of a blotch that takes shape only when part of this field is anamorphically distorted by the subject's desire' (Žižek 2007, 69). Žižek reminds us that the most famous anamorphic painting, Holbein's *The Ambassadors*, concerns death: when we look from the proper standpoint at the anamorphically prolonged 'stain' in the lower part of the painting, it reveals itself as the death skull, which blurs the ambassadors' meaningful identities into nothingness. This aspect of anamorphism is underlined by Richard's later monologue, in which he characterizes Death, placed in the void in the middle of his 'hollow crown' (3.2.156), as an antic jester who lets him play the part of a king only to puncture his inflated substance with a pin and reduce him to nothing.

Žižek rejects the idea that, in this speech, Richard fails to accept his true identity as a mere human divested of his royal title. Instead, he argues that the lesson of the play is that *any* identity is groundless. Although Richard perceives that his identity as king is an effect of anamorphosis, getting rid of this unsubstantial apparition does not leave him with the reality of what he 'really' is. For all reality is an effect of anamorphosis, a 'shadow of nothing', and what we see if we look at it directly is a formless void. What remains after we are deprived of Symbolic identification is, precisely, nothing: 'The "Death" figure in the middle of the crown is not simply death, but the subject himself reduced to the void' (Žižek 2007, 70). This is Richard's position also when confronted with Henry's demand to resign the crown:

> Ay, no; no, ay; for I must nothing be;
> Therefore no, no, for I resign to thee.
> Now mark me, how I will undo myself.
> I give this heavy weight from off my head
> And this unwieldy sceptre from my hand...
>
> (4.1.191–5)

As Žižek argues, Richard's reply to Henry's request entails a complex set of puns on 'Ay, no; no, ay'. Those four words can be read simply as a repeated refusal, accompanied with the exclamatory 'ay'. If we understand 'ay' as 'I', however, they can be read again as a refusal, but this of the very existence of the 'I': 'I (say) no (because there is) no I (to do it)'. And we can also hear the words as 'I know no I' (Žižek 2007, 71). Identity may be the goal of Richard's desire, but it is annulled by the hint of the Real—the irruption of his nothingness—that exposes his desire's objectless aim.

Žižek's critical practice might be understood as a psychoanalytically inflected, more politicized descendant of Russian formalism: he shows how Shakespeare's drama defamiliarizes the world as we think we know it. *Richard II* performs this function, however, not because of Shakespeare's skilful experiments with literary form, but because it reveals instabilities in reality that, by looking awry, we have been trained not to see. Žižek practises a hermeneutics of suspicion shared by many of the literary theories to be considered in the following chapters, which likewise think with Shakespeare to critique the apparently seamless ideological fantasies of patriarchy, heteronormativity, bourgeois capitalism, and European imperialism. The process of looking awry to sustain fantasy is something that Shakespeare's theatre repeatedly exposes. With its women played by boys, and kings played by commoners, Shakespearian theatre is itself an anamorphic form that keeps drawing attention to the material conditions of its illusions and, therefore, to what Žižek calls 'the crack' within the Symbolic (Žižek 1997, 214).

7

Feminism

Virginia Woolf, Hélène Cixous, Elaine Showalter

> I see a woman may be made a fool
> If she had not a spirit to resist.
>
> *The Taming of the Shrew*, 3.3.91–2

Shakespeare's infamous 'shrew', Katherina, voices an irresistible imperative: women should resist. But resist what, exactly? The authority of individual men—her father Baptista, her husband Petruccio—who believe women should obey men? Patriarchal institutions—marriage, the family, education—that prescribe and circumscribe what women can and cannot do? Or even demeaning conventions of representing women—including that of the 'shrew' of the play in which she appears—which have been a persistent feature of literature, art, and theatre? And how should she resist? By violent opposition or separatism? By seeking a place within the institutions from which women have been excluded? By changing the terms of representation itself? These questions anticipate the challenges posed by feminism, one of the most powerful movements in both political activism and literary criticism over the last century. Feminism, like Katherina, is broadly concerned with the possibility of female resistance. But what, exactly, does feminism resist? And how does it resist?

As a political movement, feminism has come in many waves: the women's rights and suffragette campaigns of the nineteenth and early twentieth centuries, the Women's Liberation movement of the 1960s and 1970s, the internationalist and Third World coalitions of recent years. With each wave, feminism has (despite the assumptions of its detractors) resisted not men so much as patriarchy, the system of relations that presumes the superiority of men. In political, social, and economic spheres, resistance to patriarchy has meant enfranchising women to vote, granting them reproductive rights, and lobbying for equal pay. Because feminism has always been concerned with the representation—artistic as much as political—of women, it has long been committed also to the task of literary criticism. Yet the proper task of a feminist literary criticism has been intensely debated. Should it seek to shed light on, and transform, the material conditions that shape literary production and reception? Deconstruct the patriarchal logics that undergird the very conception of 'woman' itself? Or simply advocate for more responsible representations of women by writers and by literary critics (including the expansion of the canon to include women writers)? These questions, which have been posed in different ways by various feminist literary critics, are to a certain extent symptomatic of distinct geographical critical traditions: British, French, and American.

Many first-wave feminists, including Virginia Woolf, were interested in the conditions of female authorship. Woolf asked whether, in a patriarchal society, an intelligent woman can match the accomplishment of a male writer like Shakespeare, and whether the absence of a female Shakespeare is due to differences of social conditioning or of biology. Here we can see a tension between a constructivist and an essentialist view of women, one that recurs in later feminist criticism. Woolf's answer is that, for the most part, material circumstances are paramount in fostering creativity—a position that has shaped much British feminism, which often in alliance with Marxism, has insisted on the need to transform the conditions within which women live and work.

French feminist theory has, by contrast, devoted more attention to how the very category of 'woman' is a patriarchal construct that needs to be rewritten. In its insistence that action precedes essence, the philosophical movement known as existentialism influenced feminist thinkers such as Simone de Beauvoir, who claimed that one is not born a woman; one becomes a woman. Lacanian psychoanalysis has also provided a fertile spur to French feminism, both as foil and as ally. On the one hand, Lacan's insistence that the unified subject is a mirage, and that men as much as women are castrated, has enraged those French feminists who ridicule the supposed phallocentrism of psychoanalysis; on the other hand, it has helped other feminists articulate a radical critique of unitary selfhood as a fiction of patriarchy. Finally, deconstruction has provided French feminists with a new set of tools for thinking through and against the binary oppositions of patriarchy, as well as modelling a new language for non-patriarchal writing, or *écriture féminine*, as theorized by Hélène Cixous and Luce Irigaray. Yet in Cixous's case, this writing is not just something women alone are capable of: Shakespeare's *Antony and Cleopatra* provides her with the exemplary instance of a liberatory *écriture féminine* that critiques fixed identities and meanings.

French feminism has been received ambivalently in the United States, where feminists have found the 'spirit to resist' many of its assumptions. Apart from a suspicion of French feminists' deliberately elliptical prose style, American feminists have often been reluctant to embrace French critical methods—not just *écriture féminine*, but also deconstruction and Lacanian psychoanalysis—that challenge conceptions of identity, which they view as the ground of political activism. Yet if Shakespeare's drama has offered French feminists a means for critiquing the phantasm of singular identity, Shakespeare's female characters have also prompted American feminists to reassert the category of 'woman' as the rallying point for resistance to patriarchy. Exemplary on this score is Elaine Showalter's essay on Ophelia, madness, and the responsibilities of feminist criticism. But even as it questions the gambits of *écriture féminine* and Lacanian theory, it shows how both raise questions that remain ongoing concerns.

Shakespeare and the Question of Female Authorship: Virginia Woolf

In the late 1920s, Virginia Woolf was invited to speak at Cambridge on the subject of women and fiction. While mulling over how to tackle such an impossibly large topic, she walked across a grass plot on the university grounds. She was immediately intercepted by a man who furiously gesticulated at her with an expression of horror: 'he was a Beadle; I was a woman. This was the turf; there was the path' (Woolf 1929, 1). Woolf's encounter led her to speculate about the psychology of the patriarch and the attribution of inferiority to half the population, and the ways in which women are structurally positioned as looking glasses in which men see themselves reflected back as twice their natural size. But her grand musings were interrupted by the mundane necessity of paying the bill for her lunch at the Cambridge dining hall, which she could afford thanks to a bequest from an aunt of £500 per year. This anecdote—of a hallowed institution quick to defend its patriarchal 'turf' and the material supports necessary both to reproducing the institution and buying her a foothold within it—frames Woolf's discussion of female creativity in her essay 'Shakespeare's Sister' (1929).

Woolf concerns herself with a puzzle posed by another hallowed institution, the English Renaissance: why did this time of unrivalled literary flowering produce no female equivalent to Shakespeare? To answer this question, she turns not to women as such, but to the conditions of literary production. And here she challenges what was to become, with the ascendancy of formalism and structuralism, the notion of the literary work as a self-contained artefact detached from its author or the society in which it was produced:

fiction, imaginative work that is, is not dropped like a pebble upon the ground . . . fiction is like a spider's web, attached so lightly perhaps, but still attached to life at all four corners. Often the attachment is scarcely perceptible; Shakespeare's plays, for instance, seem to hang there complete by themselves. But when the web is pulled askew, hooked up at the edge, torn in the middle, one remembers that these webs are not spun in midair by incorporeal creatures, but are the work of suffering human beings, and are attached to grossly material things, like health and money and the houses we live in. (Woolf 1929, 3–4)

Shakespeare's plays might give the illusion of being free-standing works of genius; but they emerge from material conditions that divide people along lines not just of class but also of gender. Because women were married early, made to perform menial domestic labour, and deprived of access to education and a 'room of their own', even a sister of Shakespeare would have experienced very different material circumstances from him. And for this reason alone, Woolf surmises that no woman could achieve what Shakespeare did.

Woolf then conducts a thought experiment: 'Let me imagine . . . what would have happened had Shakespeare had a wonderfully gifted sister, called Judith, let us say' (Woolf 1929, 5). Woolf's Judith

Shakespeare is every bit as imaginative and intellectually curious as her brother. But she is not sent to school and, while still in her teens, is betrothed to the son of a neighbouring wool-stapler at the insistence of her father, who beats her when she refuses the marriage. Looking to find an outlet for her literary gifts, she escapes to London. Like her brother, she adores theatre; she hopes to act as well as write, but she is allowed to do neither. An actor-manager takes pity on her and gets her pregnant; mortally ashamed, she kills herself on a winter's night, and her remains now lie anonymously buried at a crossroads outside the Elephant and Castle. Woolf repeatedly stresses that the sole difference between William and Judith Shakespeare is the access each has to institutions and vocations in which their talent can flower—although there is a hint of biological essentialism too in Woolf's account of Judith's decision to kill herself: 'who shall measure the heat and violence of the poet's heart when caught and tangled in a woman's body?' (Woolf 1929, 6). Yet even this suggestion of an innate female physiology is tempered by Woolf's conviction that the latter is ultimately the product of the social environment: 'any woman born with a great gift in the sixteenth century would have certainly gone crazed, shot herself, or ended her days in some lonely cottage outside the village, half witch, half wizard, feared and mocked at . . . To have lived a free life in London in the sixteenth century would have meant for a woman who was a poet and playwright a nervous stress and dilemma which might well have killed her. Had she survived, whatever she had written would have been twisted and deformed, issuing from a strained and morbid imagination' (Woolf 1929, 6).

Woolf's argument here is philosophically materialist—the assumption that one's being does not precede one's material conditions, but is rather determined by them. This is the philosophical tradition from which Karl Marx also derived his thought (see Chapter 9). Materialist explanations are at odds with fantasies of transcendent genius, and Woolf accordingly anticipates that her readers will 'object that in all this I have made too much of the importance of material things'. But she goes on to assert that 'five hundred a year stands for the power to contemplate, that a lock on the door means the power to think for oneself . . . Intellectual freedom depends upon material things. Poetry depends upon intellectual freedom. And women have always been poor' (Woolf 1929, 7). Yet this 'always' is historical, not universal:

'My belief is that if we live another century or so...and have five hundred a year each of us and rooms of our own...then the opportunity will come and the dead poet who was Shakespeare's sister will put on the body which she has so often laid down. Drawing her life from the lives of the unknown who were her fore-runners, as her brother did before her, she will be born' (Woolf 1929, 7–8).

As this shows, Woolf's feminist vision of Shakespeare's sister is inflected not just by materialism but also by a secular form of Christian progressivism—the conviction that a better future will eventually come to redeem the imperfect present. (The echo of Christianity is most apparent in her prophecy of a she-messiah's birth that will mark the advent of a new epoch.) Indeed, Woolf's mixture of materialism and progressivism has been very much a feature of feminism in its British guises, which have insisted on both the material conditions that constrain women and the possibility of radical change. But Woolf has also allowed us to see Shakespeare differently—not simply as the proper name for free-standing works of remarkable ambiguity or structural complexity, nor as the brilliant divided psyche that produced characters of unparalleled psychological depth, but also as a socially situated author working within specific conditions more conducive to his gender than to his sister's.

Antony and Cleopatra and the Question of *Écriture Féminine*: Hélène Cixous

For Woolf, women's material lot—including their bodies—militates against their creativity. By contrast, the French-Algerian feminist Hélène Cixous (1937–) insists that feminine creativity is grounded in the body: 'Woman must write her body', she commands (Cixous 1986, 84). In her essay 'The Laugh of the Medusa' (1974), Cixous invokes the snake-haired gorgon of classical myth to begin writing that body: 'we're stormy, and that which is ours breaks loose from us without our fearing any debilitation. Our glances, our smiles, are spent; laughs exude from all our mouths; our blood flows and we extend ourselves without ever reaching an end' (Cixous 1976, 877). The laughter of Cixous's boundless female body recalls the laughter of Mikhail Bakhtin's grotesque body. And that laughter serves a similarly anti-authoritarian function for each—in Cixous's case, destabilizing the tyranny of the patriarchal body. Not surprisingly, Cixous's injunction to 'write the body' has been interpreted as partaking of a biological essentialism, according to which men's bodies are naturally oppressive, and women's bodies are naturally liberatory. But this critique misunderstands the very phrase 'writing the body'. For Cixous, the body—whether male or female—does not precede the act of writing it; rather, it is materialized in and by writing, an argument she makes most forcefully in her essay 'Sorties: Out and Out: Attacks/Ways Out/Forays' (1975).

Cixous critiques the traditional patriarchal writing of male and female bodies. This writing participates in a larger system of differences that she terms, adapting Derrida, 'phallogocentric': it privileges the phallus and *logos* as guarantors of presence opposed to the feminized spectres of castration and unintelligibility. At the start of her essay, she enumerates a sequence of gendered binary oppositions in which the masculine term is associated with self-identical presence and the feminine term with lack:

Where is she?
Activity/passivity
Sun/Moon
Culture/Nature
Day/Night

Father/Mother
Head/Heart
Intelligible/Palpable
Logos/Pathos
Form, convex, step, advance, semen, progress.
Matter, concave, ground—where steps are taken, holding- and
    dumping-ground
Man
———
Woman (Cixous 1986, 63)

The hierarchal logic of these binary oppositions is exemplified by the excerpt's last two lines, which graphically locate 'Man' over 'Woman' and divide them with a bar. 'Sorties', French for attacks and ways out, describes Cixous's feminist practice: she seeks not just to attack phallogocentrism, but also to find a way out of its hierarchies. And she does so with a theory of *écriture féminine*. The phrase, which means feminine writing, not only suggests a deliberately allusive alternative to phallogocentric writing, but also draws on Derrida's sense of writing as *différance*. In short, *écriture féminine* is a deconstructive rewriting of the Western patriarchal text of the body—although its fluid metaphors may recall Deleuze and Serres more than Derrida.

As the above list of binary pairs suggests, phallogocentrism marks women and their bodies under the sign of lack or absence. But by having no singular centre (whether phallus or *logos*), the woman of the patriarchal text stands in a different relation to otherness. Whereas the patriarchal man must defend his corporeal and linguistic integrity by violently opposing the otherness of femininity, apprehended as castration and/or madness, the woman's body and speech—like Bakhtin's conceptions of the grotesque and the dialogic—are open to, and reveal the trace of, otherness. As written in and by phallogocentrism, then, the female body is more than just lacking; it is plural, resisting the singular logic of the 'Self-Same'. If the woman represents another body to that of the phallogocentric male, this other body is defined precisely by its love of the other within the body, whether it takes the form of pregnancy, other genders, or other sexual possibilities. Cixous sees this embrace of otherness also as the defining hallmark of literature: 'Other-Love is writing's first name' (Cixous 1986, 99). And it is in literature that Cixous finds the other body and the other in the body. This explains her title, 'The Laugh of the Medusa', as well as her many digressions in 'Sorties' through the works of Homer, Kleist, and Shakespeare. For Cixous, each writer resists phallogocentrism by revealing alternatives, male as much as female, to the singular body that refuses otherness. It is not that women's bodies are intrinsically plural while men's bodies are intrinsically singular. Rather, the plurality of the woman's body as written in and by the phallogocentric text has the deconstructive power to reveal the plurality also of the man's body, which need no longer 'gravitate around the penis' (Cixous 1986, 87).

For Cixous, the 'writing of the body' that undoes the phallogocentric text has already been performed by 'that being-of-a-thousand beings called Shakespeare'; his plays are scenes of endless becoming, where 'man turns back into woman, woman into man' (Cixous 1986, 98). Although she admires the gender fluidity of *Romeo and Juliet*, whose lovers she sees as dissenting from patriarchal identities, it is *Antony and Cleopatra* that for her best exemplifies *écriture féminine*, inasmuch as that play writes the body by writing the other into the body. The Egyptian Cleopatra, in her legendary 'infinite variety' (2.2.241), is for Cixous the apotheosis of transformative multiplicity: 'The feisty queen, to whom everything is becoming—scolding, laughing, crying—at every instant another face, at each breath a passion, flesh struggling with a desire for more love, more life, more pleasure, at every moment, the queen with ten tongues; she spoke them all' (Cixous 1986, 123). Because of her protean theatricality, Cleopatra is often derided for her lack of a singular identity. She seems to confirm that criticism when, in the play's final scene, she aspires at last to be 'marble-constant' (5.2.236), a phrase that suggests not just the fixity of Roman monuments but also the phallic solidity of patriarchal masculinity. Yet this is less a denial of Cleopatra's multiplicity than a confirmation of it, another bravura performance that demonstrates her embrace of infinite variety—a variety that embodies masculine as much as feminine characteristics.

Cixous does not perform any simple identification between herself and Cleopatra (North African queens both, celebrating fecundity and multiplicity). She equally valorizes Antony, at least the Antony who loves Cleopatra and loves the feminine within himself: 'Antony is not left behind. Although he may have a hard time keeping up with Cleopatra in the realm of invention, he wins in another generosity—the one that for a man consists of daring to strip himself of power and glory and to love and admire a woman enough to take pride happily in rivaling with her in passion' (Cixous 1986, 124). As Caesar notes with horror, Antony 'is not more manlike | Than Cleopatra, nor [she] | More womanly than he' (1.4.5–7); and Antony willingly submits to Cleopatra's sexual games, in which she dresses him up in her 'tires and mantles', while wearing his 'sword Philippan' (2.5.22–3). But perhaps Antony's keenest experience of *écriture féminine*'s decentred, 'endlessly becoming' body is just prior to his suicide, when he discusses his state with his servant Eros:

> ANTONY   Sometime we see a cloud that's dragonish,
>   A vapour sometime like a bear or lion,
>   A towered citadel, a pendent rock,
>   A forked mountain, or blue promontory

> With trees upon't that nod unto the world
> And mock our eyes with air. Thou hast seen these signs;
> They are black vesper's pageants.
> EROS   Ay, my lord.
> ANTONY   That which is now a horse, even with a thought
> The rack distains, and makes it indistinct
> As water is in water.
> EROS   It does, my lord.
> ANTONY   My good knave Eros, now thy captain is
> Even such a body. Here I am Antony,
> Yet cannot hold this visible shape, my knave.
>
> > (4.15.2–14)

Antony realizes how the masculine ideals of fixity and phallic singularity ('A towered citadel, a pendent rock') are literally phantasms that disavow the metamorphic plurality of a world whose natural element is fluid. Of course, Antony's epiphany is simultaneously a lament for his lost Roman 'shape', a loss he experiences as a symbolic castration: as he says to Cleopatra's eunuch Mardian a few lines after this speech, 'thy vile lady | ... has robbed me of my sword' (4.15.23–4). Yet Cixous insists that *Antony and Cleopatra* ultimately vindicates the decentred world of *écriture féminine* shared by its title characters, 'far from kingdoms, from caesars, from brawls, from the cravings of penis and sword' (Cixous 1986, 130).

If Antony (dressed in Cleopatra's clothes) and Cleopatra (wearing his sword Phillippan) embody how 'man turns back into woman, woman into man', that reversal exemplifies also Cixous's *écriture féminine*, where seeming opposites cross over and find unexpected common ground. This strategy equally characterizes her own relation with Shakespeare, who bears the traces of Cixous even as her text bears the traces of Shakespeare. In the English version of 'Sorties', Shakespeare is never quoted as such; his words have either been translated back into English from Cixous's French translation, or are paraphrased in her poetic reworkings of the play. Similarly, Shakespeare haunts Cixous's own words in her many intertextual allusions to plays like *Hamlet*. For example, on the perennial question of psychoanalysis—what do women want?—she answers, 'To sleep, perchance to dream' (Cixous 1986, 67). 'Feminine writing' for Cixous thus amounts to a dialogic quilting of her words with Shakespeare's and Shakespeare's with Cixous's: she not only finds *écriture féminine* in Shakespeare, but also performs it in her dialogue with him.

As Cixous's alliances with Antony and Shakespeare show, *écriture féminine* is not a writing confined to women and their bodies. But women are perhaps better placed to recognize *écriture féminine*'s value, inasmuch as they are structurally placed outside the patriarchal fantasy of singularity and selfsameness. Cixous thus resists the phallogocentrism of Western metaphysics in ways that ultimately problematize the very notion of gender identity, even as *écriture féminine* becomes a gendered synonym for the bodies and speech acts that undo the logic of patriarchy.

Hamlet and the Question of Feminist Ethics: Elaine Showalter

Elaine Showalter (1941–), one of the most influential feminist literary critics in the United States, is a proponent of what she calls 'gynocritics', a female framework for the study of women's literature and women's experiences. But perhaps her most widely read and studied essay is 'Representing Ophelia: Women, Madness, and the Responsibilities of Feminist Criticism' (1985). Showalter's essay begins with a sharp critique of Jacques Lacan. Although Lacan starts his seminar on *Hamlet* by promising to speak of Ophelia, assuring his readers that he will be 'as good as my word', Showalter laments that he is '*not* as good as his word'. This is because he 'goes on for some forty-one pages to speak about Hamlet, and when he does mention Ophelia, she is merely what Lacan calls "the object Ophelia"—that is, the object of Hamlet's male desire' (Showalter 1994, 220). Showalter, by contrast, insists that feminists should be as good as their word and speak of Ophelia 'herself'. She thus signals her hostility to both the 'bait-and-switch' tactics of psychoanalysis (which she sees as patriarchal in its tendency to analyse women only as 'objects' in relation to male subjects) and the deferrals of deconstruction (which she regards as politically questionable, depriving women of a voice with which to resist patriarchy).

Showalter does indeed speak of Ophelia, but as we will see, it is not the Ophelia we might expect. As Showalter concedes, Ophelia speaks very little in *Hamlet*. She appears in only five of the play's twenty scenes; her tragedy is not shared with the audience in soliloquies as Hamlet's is; what we know about her is largely due to what male characters tell us in a handful of unclear flashbacks. Despite Ophelia's relative marginality in *Hamlet*, she has commanded a disproportionate attention in popular culture, from John Everett Millais's painting of drowned Ophelia (1852) to the Indigo Girls' folk-rock album 'Swamp Ophelia' (1994). Ophelia, in other words, is a blank screen in the play: just like the 'nothing' between her legs on which Hamlet lewdly focuses (3.2.106–7), Ophelia is the nothing within *Hamlet* onto which critics, actors, writers, and artists repeatedly project their fantasies. And these fantasies keep looping back, in ways that hint at an ongoing cultural obsession, to the relations between femininity, female sexuality, and insanity. Confronting the tension between the paucity of information in *Hamlet* concerning Ophelia and the cultural fascination with her sexuality and madness, Showalter asks: what is feminism's responsibility toward her 'as character and as woman'?

American feminist literary critics have often attempted to advocate for female characters as if the latter were real people. Showalter recognizes that such a practice will not quite do for Ophelia, given how little the text reveals about her. But Showalter also questions the value of French feminism, for whom 'Ophelia might confirm the impossibility of representing the feminine in patriarchal discourses as other than madness, incoherence, fluidity, or silence' (Showalter 1994, 222). It is tempting to imagine how Cixous would respond to Ophelia's mad language—about which the Gentleman says, 'Her speech is nothing' (4.5.7). Cixous might regard this 'nothing' as a disruption of phallogocentrism and a model for *écriture féminine*. But for Showalter, recuperating Ophelia's 'nothing' is not an attractive option: 'to dissolve her into a female symbolism of absence is to endorse our own marginality' (Showalter 1994, 223). So Showalter by and large rejects *écriture féminine*, for all its deconstructive potential, as incapable of representing women politically as much as linguistically.

Instead, Showalter argues that 'Ophelia *does* have a story of her own that feminist criticism can tell; it is neither her life story, nor her love story, nor Lacan's story, but rather the *history* of her representation' (Showalter 1994, 223). Her essay thus turns away from

Shakespeare's play-text to trace the iconography of Ophelia in nine-
teenth- and twentieth-century painting, photography, psychiatry, and
theatrical production. Showalter sees this iconography as largely the
product of patriarchal fantasies about femininity, female sexuality, and
madness—fantasies that she attributes in particular to the rise of
psychiatry and psychoanalysis. But she also argues that women have
begun to challenge such fantasies, particularly on stage, where female
bodies and voices have generated new feminist interpretations of
Ophelia.

For Showalter, Ophelia's nineteenth- and twentieth-century iconography is partly licensed by the text of *Hamlet* itself. Whereas
Hamlet's madness is presented as metaphysical, Ophelia's is seen as
entirely feminine. Her behaviour and appearance (including her dish-
evelled hair and torn clothes) are characteristic of the female affliction
that Elizabethans called variously love melancholy and the green
sickness, or erotomania. Her turn to song in her last appearance
communicates not just her madness but also her specifically female
experience of sexuality:

> Tomorrow is Saint Valentine's day,
>   All in the morning betime,
> And I a maid at your window,
>   To be your Valentine.
> Then up he rose, and donned his clothes,
>   And dupped the chamber door,
> Let in the maid, that out a maid
>   Never departed more....
>
> .   .   .   .
>
> Young men will do't if they come to't,
>   By Cock, they are to blame.

$$(4.5.47\text{-}54, 59\text{-}60)$$

Some modern readers have interpreted Ophelia's salacious Saint
Valentine's song about the deflowering of a maid as proof she has
been similarly treated by Hamlet. But Ophelia's obsession with sex
was probably interpreted by Elizabethans as proof of the opposite.
Many of Shakespeare's contemporaries believed that a young woman's
womb was a semi-autonomous creature that needed to be sexually
fed; if it did not receive sustenance, it would detach itself and roam

through the body looking for food, ultimately ascending through the neck to feast on the brain, causing hysteria (derived from *husteros*, Greek for womb).

Showalter notes how Ophelia's association with hysteria persisted well into the nineteenth century, coinciding with the birth of psychiatry. In visual culture, including Millais's painting and Delacroix's lithographs of Ophelia, she was repeatedly depicted in the erotic trance of the hysteric, affirming the early clinical studies of hysteria by Jean-Martin Charcot and, later, his student Sigmund Freud. Psychiatrists wrote about Ophelia as a case study in madness; asylum superintendents also photographed mad women decorated with theatrical accessories reminiscent of Ophelia, including flowers in their hair. Yet actresses in the early twentieth century began to challenge the conventional interpretation of Ophelia's madness, arguing that it was caused by her mistreatment rather than her biology. Her madness has also been recuperated by feminist theatre practitioners as a protest and rebellion: in Melissa Murray's 1979 agitprop play *Ophelia*, Ophelia becomes a lesbian and escapes with a woman servant to join a guerilla commune. Yet Showalter questions whether such ideological defiance is what feminism should aspire to. In her estimation, feminist literary criticism 'must aim for a maximum interdisciplinary contextualism, in which the complexity of attitudes to the feminine can be analyzed in their fullest cultural and historical frame' (Showalter 1994, 237). She argues that such complexity is disregarded by any attempt to make sense of Ophelia's madness, whether as a hysterical virgin with a wandering womb or as a lesbian separatist rejecting patriarchal logic. All these interpretations are motivated by a desire to fix and explain Ophelia—a desire, in the process, to speak for her. And this is exactly the gambit of patriarchy.

So what is the solution? How do we allow Ophelia to speak for 'herself', especially when there is no self that speaks? Showalter argues that feminists must start by recognizing that

there is no 'true' Ophelia for whom feminist criticism must unambiguously speak, but perhaps only a Cubist Ophelia of multiple perspectives, more than the sum of all her parts. . . . in exposing the ideology of representation, feminist critics have also the responsibility to acknowledge and to examine the boundaries of our own ideological positions as products of our gender and our time. A degree of humility in an age of critical hubris can be our greatest strength, for it is by occupying this position of historical self-consciousness in both feminism and critics that we maintain our credibility in representing Ophelia, and that, unlike Lacan, when we promise to speak about her, we make good our word. (Showalter 1997, 238)

Showalter here asks that feminism recognize the contingency of history, a fuller realization of Simone de Beauvoir's insistence that one is not born a woman but becomes one—albeit within different cultural frameworks. Although Showalter confines her analysis to English, European, and American constructions of Ophelia, she suggests here the direction that a more internationalist feminist criticism of Shakespeare has subsequently taken. Chantal Zabus's *Tempests after Shakespeare* (2003), for example, devotes much of its analysis to feminist and post-patriarchal rewritings of *The Tempest*, in which Miranda and Sycorax are diversely appropriated and transformed by women writers from not just the United Kingdom, the United States, and largely white settler societies like Canada and Australia, but also Third World nations in Africa, Asia, and the Caribbean. Such studies underline Woolf's contention that a text is not free-standing, but tethered to the world—and not just the world in which its author produced it, but also the changing worlds in which it is reproduced or rewritten. In these changing worlds, the meaning of 'woman' also keeps changing; it is impossible to regard the word 'woman' as a signifier with a transparent, fixed signified. Rather, like the signature or aphorism as described by Derrida, it is continually detached from its contexts and countersigned.

Showalter's Cubist Ophelia might allow her to claim that 'unlike Lacan, when we promise to speak about her, we make good our word'. Still, Showalter's forceful resistance to Lacanian theory as well as to French feminism disavows the affinities of her argument with both. Although she scoffs at Lacan's tongue-in-cheek etymology of Ophelia as 'O Phallos', she too treats Ophelia as a primal lack, substituted by an endless chain of signifiers or re-presentations. That is, like Lacan, she ultimately tells us less about Ophelia than about those who make her their desired object. And, like Lacan and Cixous, Showalter embraces this endless process of substitution and multiplication as mystified by an essentialist investment (whether phallogocentric or not) in the singular and the selfsame. In other words, there is an anti-identitarian subtext to Showalter's essay, one potentially at odds with her assertion of feminism's responsibility to re-present Ophelia 'as character and as woman'. Yet we might view this tension between the irreducibility of the singular 'woman' and the impossibility of identity—that is, between difference and *différance*— not as a shortcoming but as an enabling disturbance. As we will see in the next chapter, queer theory regards it as such, making the tension between sexual identity and its impossibility the engine of its critical practice.

8

Queer Theory

Eve Kosofsky Sedgwick, Jonathan Dollimore,
Lee Edelman

> Know thou first,
> I loved the maid I married; never man
> Sighed truer breath. But that I see thee here,
> Thou noble thing, more dances my rapt heart
> Than when I first my wedded mistress saw
> Bestride my threshold. Why, thou Mars...
>
> *Coriolanus*, 4.5.112–17

With this speech, the Volscian warrior Tullus Aufidius voices a desire that is hard to pin down. He admits that he 'loved the maid I married'; but the spectacle of his Roman adversary Coriolanus, he says, sets his heart dancing more than the sight of his wife did on their wedding night. The comparison suggests, even as it doesn't quite own up to, a homoerotic desire. What, then, is Aufidius' sexual identity? Hetero-? Homo-? Both? Neither? The question of his sexuality is complicated further by the fact that his profession of love for Coriolanus is the sanctioned desire of a patriarchal world in which relations between men take precedence over relations between men and women. In such a world, a beloved wife remains a nameless 'maid' or 'mistress' while a beloved male competitor is elevated to the status of a 'Mars'. Aufidius' desire, then, has no singular object: we apprehend it, rather, in its oscillating movement between 'maid' and 'Mars'. This desire that leads away from any fixed identity or object, and that potentially 'mars' even as it is 'made' from the structures of the social, is the theme of queer theory.

Queer theory derives in large part from gay and lesbian criticism, which was itself an offshoot of second-wave feminism. Just as Elaine Showalter's gynocriticism focused on female writers and characters from a female perspective, so did critics like Adrienne Rich advocate in the 1970s for their gay and lesbian literary counterparts. But queer theory is in one respect crucially different from gay and lesbian criticism. While the latter presumes the stability of the homosexual and the heterosexual, the 'queer' of queer theory describes something less identifiable. The word originally meant 'strange'; applied as a negative epithet to those who supposedly deviate from sexual normalcy, 'queer' has designated less an essential identity than a perversion or lack of any such identity. It is in this sense that the term has been appropriated by queer theory in order to shake up certainties of sexuality and gender. As queer theorist Lee Edelman writes, 'queerness can never define an identity; it can only ever disturb one' (Edelman 2004, 17).

The transformation of queer disturbance into an entire theoretical movement has drawn on two key traditions in the study of sexuality, each of which problematizes the fixity of sexual identities: psycho-analysis and sexual historiography. Yet these traditions are often in tension with each other. Freud theorized the 'polymorphously per-verse' sexuality (Freud 2000, 57) of the infant; in his analysis, the child has to learn to be a heterosexual, passing through a necessary homo-erotic identification (for the son, with the father; for the daughter, with the mother) before moving to object choices of the opposite sex. In psychoanalysis, then, perverse sexuality precedes the social, which channels desire into normative object relations that repress homo-sexuality. By contrast, the French philosopher of history Michel Foucault (see also Chapter 11) insisted sexuality does not precede but rather is entirely generated by the social. In his influential *The History of Sexuality*, he critiqued what he termed Freud's repressive hypothesis; for Foucault, all sexual identities are constructed within regimes of knowledge or 'discourse', whereby power organizes people into categories of normality and deviance. Hence in his analysis, homo- and heterosexuality were invented in the nineteenth century within the discourse of clinical psychiatry. This discourse represented a break with a previous religious discourse of sexual deviance. Whereas in medieval Europe 'sodomy' had described a sinful act or 'temporary aberration', in the nineteenth century the 'homosexual' became a pathological identity or 'species' (Foucault 1978, 43).

In America and Britain, queer theory has traced somewhat different paths, even as both have drawn from psychoanalysis and Foucault. In America, it has tended to be driven by structuralist and deconstructive critiques of identity. Judith Butler, for example, has argued that any gender or sexual identity is not a function of biology, but is rather performative, a repetition of stylized acts that have no clear origin; we are all, effectively, in drag. And in a particularly influential argument, Eve Kosofsky Sedgwick has explored how the 'homosocial' continuum of same-sex relations has not always differentiated homoerotic from straight male bonding. In Britain, queer theory has acquired a slightly different accent. Just as British feminism has been more materialist than its American counterpart, so has British queer theory tended to place more emphasis on the dynamics of social change. The radical politics of sexual perversion are examined by British theorists such as Jonathan Dollimore, who regards nonnormative sexuality as a mode of dissidence. Yet for Dollimore, sexual perversity does not stand outside but emerges from contradictions within dominant formations; queerness can thus resist the sexually normative by inhabiting and exposing its internal contradictions.

On this score, Dollimore's thought has affinities with what has been dubbed the 'anti-social hypothesis' of a more recent American strain of queer theory. In a riposte to the heteronormative embrace of the child as the future of society, Lee Edelman notes how this embrace is perversely dependent on the queer—or what he calls, punning on Lacan's and Žižek's accounts of the *sinthome* as the subject's relation to the senseless compulsion that sustains fantasy, the 'sinthomosexual'. The sinthomosexual is so named not just because her non-reproductive sexuality is symptomatic of a death drive that threatens futurity, but also because the homophobic violence repeatedly committed against her in defence of the future is itself symptomatic of a disavowed, senseless compulsion at the heart of heteronormative sociality.

As Edelman's argument suggests, queerness has been increasingly uncoupled from sexual acts and linked to other phenomena such as aberrations within signification and temporality. This more capacious understanding of queerness is demonstrated by Edelman's recent work on queer education, which finds a counterpart in Shakespeare's own version of sexual pedagogy. In Act 4 of *As You Like It*, Rosalind, disguised as the male Ganymede, teaches her love Orlando how to woo the woman he loves (Rosalind). But Ganymede's lesson involves 'him' pretending to be a woman for Orlando to practise on, thereby forcing the latter to woo a boy masquerading as a girl who is in fact really a girl—even though in the play's first performances Rosalind was played, of course, by a boy. As Rosalind's pedagogy suggests, Shakespeare's drama repeatedly explores desire's undecidable origins and destinations.

Homosociality and the Sonnets: Eve Kosofsky Sedgwick

So too do his Sonnets, as Eve Kosofsky Sedgwick (1950–2009) argues. Sedgwick's earliest work emerges from a significant tension within feminism. Whereas French feminism emphasizes the structural difference between men and women within the phallogocentric text, materialist feminism stresses changing configurations of gender in relation to changing material conditions. If French feminism can teach its materialist counterpart something about the differential structures of gender and sexuality, materialism can equally address French theory's neglect of history. To this end, Sedgwick attempts a synthesis between the two. As the title of her book *Between Men: English Literature and Male Homosocial Desire* (1985) suggests, Sedgwick theorizes the structural problem of male–male (or what she calls 'homosocial') bonds and women's position within them. But she also acknowledges historical transformations of homosociality, inasmuch as our rigid division between male homosexuality and (say) locker-room male bonding departs from earlier homosocial continuums, such as that of ancient Greece.

Sedgwick derives her analysis of male homosocial relations from René Girard's theory of mimetic desire. Girard takes as transhistorically axiomatic the structure of the erotic triangle, which features two rivals and a shared love object. For him, it is not the object but rather emulation between the rivals that produces desire for the object. Yet the bond between the rivals can be just as intense, even more so, than that with the beloved. Girard in effect universalizes the Oedipal triangle, in which the father–son bond is more intense than that with the mother; but for him, the gender of the subjects in the triangle does not matter. Yet as Gayle Rubin notes in her influential feminist critique of Lévi-Strauss, the male–male relation within which the woman is triangulated is the structural basis of patriarchal power. Marriage is traditionally a relation between two men (a husband and a father-in-law), within which the wife/daughter is exchangeable property. Sedgwick likewise insists on the gender asymmetries of Girard's erotic triangle, arguing that the gender configuration of the triangle makes a difference. Two men exchanging a woman materialize very different power relations from those instantiated by a triangle in which (say) two women compete for a man, or a man and a woman compete for a man. In addition to teasing out the power relations at play in the gender imbalances of any erotic triangle—an explicitly feminist concern—Sedgwick is also interested in the configurations of sexuality such triangles produce, particularly with regard to male–male relations. To what extent does the homosocial bond between two men in relation to a woman conduce to homoeroticism or homophobia? And how may different historical articulations of the homosocial bond complicate our modern opposition of 'hetero-' and 'homo-'? To answer these questions, Sedgwick reads a variety of literary texts from the seventeenth to the nineteenth centuries, starting with Shakespeare's Sonnets.

In her chapter 'Swan in Love', Sedgwick examines the Sonnets in order to tease out some themes that will recur in her subsequent analyses of writers such as Wycherley, Sterne, Thackeray, Eliot, Tennyson, and Whitman. Sedgwick acknowledges that hers is a historically deracinated reading, inasmuch as she proceeds from the belated nineteenth-century interpretation of the Sonnets as a novel-istic narrative featuring three principal characters: the speaker, Will; the Fair Youth; and the Dark Lady. In this interpretation, the speaker sometimes competes with the Fair Youth for the Dark Lady, and at other times with the Dark Lady for the Fair Youth; hence the Sonnets seem to assert a symmetry between the two love objects. When the Dark Lady and the Fair Youth hook up in Sonnet 42, for example, the speaker insists that 'Both find each other, and I lose both twain, | And both for my sake lay me on this cross' (42.11–12). The symmetry is asserted again in Sonnet 144; but this time gender tilts the balance:

> Two loves I have of comfort and despair,
> Which like two spirits do suggest me still.

The better angel is a man right fair,
The worser spirit a woman coloured ill.
To win me soon to hell my female evil
Tempteth my better angel from my side,
And would corrupt my saint to be a devil,
Wooing his purity with her foul pride;
And whether that my angel be turned fiend
Suspect I may, yet not directly tell;
But being both from me, both to each friend,
I guess one angel in another's hell.
       Yet this shall I ne'er know, but live in doubt
       Till my bad angel fire my good one out.

(144.1–14)

As Sedgwick notes, Sonnet 144's dominant syntactic structure is symmetrical; but 'semantic differences eddy about and finally wash over the sonnet's syntactic formality' (Sedgwick 1985, 31). That is, she does not emulate Roman Jakobson's teasing out of endless symmetries from the Sonnets, but focuses instead on the destabilizing force of gender. Apart from coding the Dark Lady—the 'bad angel'—as 'ill' and 'foul' in opposition to the youth's fairness and purity, Sonnet 144 also divides them syntactically: the youth has only one, passive verb ('be turn'd'), while the Dark Lady has three active verbs ('Tempteth', 'would corrupt', 'fire'). The female desires and acts, while the youth is acted upon. This asymmetry is underscored by the sonnet's repetition of the word 'hell', a synonym for the Dark Lady's immorality and her vagina. There is no corresponding 'heaven' that the youth can incarnate; instead, he is dispatched to her inferno.

Sonnet 144 may depart from the conventional patriarchal association, noted by Hélène Cixous in 'Sorties', of men with activity and women with passivity. But Sedgwick is interested in how this specific asymmetry and the misogyny that informs it are structurally crucial to the sexual dimension of male–male bonds conceptualized by the Sonnets as a whole. In addition to the gender asymmetry of the Fair Youth and the Dark Lady, there is an additional asymmetry between the heterosexuality of the Fair Youth sequence and the heterosexuality of the Dark Lady sequence. Non-reproductive heterosexuality in the Dark Lady sequence is presented as a dangerous corruption that sends men to hell. By contrast, reproductive heterosexuality in the Fair

Youth sequence guarantees an eternal life on earth, if not in heaven. Here, women are notable for their virtual absence; they are merely the passive means by which men breed male heirs for the gratification of other men. In other words, heterosexuality is here conceived as the support for a male homosocial universe, in which bonds between men—even erotic ones—are paramount. The infamously slippery Sonnet 20 describes the youth as the 'master-mistress of my passion', intended for the speaker until nature gave him 'one thing to my purpose nothing' (20.2, 12). Yet the youth's sexual dalliances with women provokes in the speaker not jealousy, but a breezy confidence that male bonds will still take precedence: 'Mine be thy love, and thy love's use their treasure' (20.14). Noting the intense homoeroticism of this line, which seems to distinguish between merely reproductive sex between men and women and true love between men, Sedgwick says,

My persistence in referring to the fair youth sonnets as heterosexual may require more explanation. If all this is heterosexual, the commonsensical reader may ask, then what on earth does it take to be homosexual? One thing that it takes is a cultural context that defines the homosexual as against the heterosexual. My point is obviously not to deny or de-emphasize the love between men in the Sonnets, the intense and often genitally oriented language that describes that love, or even the possibility that the love described may have been genitally acted out. . . . However, I am saying that within the world sketched in these sonnets, there is not an equal opposition or a choice posited between two such institutions as homosexuality (under whatever name) and heterosexuality. (Sedgwick 1985, 35)

Sedgwick's argument here owes a demonstrable debt to Foucault. Homosexuality is not a transhistorical essence; it is, rather, a historically constructed difference from heterosexuality, a difference that does not yet exist in Shakespeare's time.

Yet, as we have seen, Sedgwick's pre-modern heterosexuality also differs from itself. When the speaker's love object is the Fair Youth, the youth's heterosexual relations pose no real obstacle to the speaker's bond with him. But when the speaker's love object is the Dark Lady, heterosexuality becomes a dangerous disturbance. As is suggested by Sonnet 144's vision of an 'angel' possessed of a vaginal 'hell', the Dark Lady exemplifies a rapacious self-division: 'dark' yet 'fair', she is what Sedgwick calls 'an oxymoronic militant' (Sedgwick 1985, 44). The speaker feels himself contagiously altered by her, moreover, experiencing this alteration as an unlooked-for, traumatic loss of his own self. In the Fair Youth sonnets, by contrast, the speaker's psychic strategy is to voluntarily absorb the shock of any self-division in the youth. Indeed, the speaker repudiates the youth's self-division; Sedgwick notes that 'if anything, the fair youth, "woman's face" and all, is presented as exaggeratedly phallic—unitary, straightforward, unreflective, pink, and dense' (Sedgwick 1985, 44). For Sedgwick, then, the Sonnet's male–male and male–female bonds evince a powerful asymmetry with respect to identity: 'the tensions implicit in the male–male bond are spatially conceived (you are this way, I am that way) and hence imagined as stable; while the tensions of the male–female bond are temporally conceived (as you are, so shall I be) and hence obviously volatile' (Sedgwick 1985, 45). The stability of the former and the volatility of the latter underline how, even when the speaker experiences a loss of self in relation to the youth, he still participates within a sum of male power. The speaker experiences the loss of self in relation to the lady, however, as a total degeneration of substance that divides him both from himself and from male homosociality.

Sedgwick's reading of the Sonnets has helped delimit queer theory as a field distinct from, even as it is indebted to, gay and lesbian studies. With her adaptation of structuralist analysis, Sedgwick undermines any reading strategy that would seek to ground the Sonnets in particular, and sexuality in general, within fixed identities of hetero- and homosexuality. Such identities are merely self-contradictory effects of historically contingent, unstable webs of relationality. As Sedgwick insists in her essay's last sentence, 'the strength and shape of the bond by which "the sexual" is connected to the genital changes as extragenital bonds and forms of power change, and in turn the nature of that bond affects their distribution' (Sedgwick 1985, 48). Sedgwick's essay does not consider how such change might happen, however, or how one might even dissent from 'forms of power'.

The Perverse Dynamic and *Othello*: Jonathan Dollimore

It is the possibility of such dissidence that Jonathan Dollimore (1948–) theorizes. Unlike some other theorists who turned to Shakespeare only after writing theory, Dollimore theorized perversion after writing on Shakespeare. His earliest publications were written from the perspective of cultural materialism, an outgrowth of Marxism that we will consider in Chapter 11: in works such as *Radical Tragedy*, he critiques the notion of a pure human nature that precedes culture and shows how Renaissance tragic drama, including Shakespeare's *King Lear*, *Coriolanus*, and *Antony and Cleopatra*, exposes the notion of a pre-social self as a fantasy riven by the contradictions of the social. In *Sexual Dissidence: Augustine to Wilde, Freud to Foucault* (1991), he adapts his analysis to consider homosexuality and what he calls the perverse dynamic. This is the dynamic by which dominant formations, such as heterosexuality, are haunted by their supposed opposites: 'the perverse dynamic denotes certain instabilities and contradictions within dominant structures which exist by virtue of exactly what those structures simultaneously contain and exclude ... [it] signifies that fearful interconnectedness whereby the antithetical inheres within, and is partly produced by, what it opposes' (Dollimore 1991, 33). In this, Dollimore leans heavily on Derrida's theorization of *différance*, though he reworks it within a framework of sexual dissidence. But what is perhaps most surprising and original about Dollimore's argument is how he traces the perverse dynamic back to medieval theological discourse, especially St Augustine's writing, to show how perversity negotiates between understandings of evil as a mode of being and evil as pure lack or non-being.

At times Augustine insists on the necessity of representing 'evil as absolutely other', as a City of Sin *separate* from the City of God (Dollimore 1991, 138). Yet elsewhere, he argues that evil is a perversion that involves a deviation emanating from *within* 'nature' as created by God, a regression towards a state of privation or non-being. Augustine thus oscillates between viewing perversion as substantial and as lack, as other and as immanent. This theological tension is replayed in modern debates about transgression, such as the one with which Dollimore starts his book: the opposed understandings of homosexual dissidence occasioned by the meeting between Oscar Wilde and André Gide in Algiers in 1895. Gide's sexual experiences in Algiers, incited by Wilde, prompted him to understand his homosexuality as his authentic, essential self—a mode of being that he had previously repressed. By contrast, Wilde saw his homosexuality as revealing the artifice of any human 'nature'. Dollimore does not so much arbitrate between the two positions—though he favours Wilde's—as read them as symptomatic of the perverse dynamic and its dialectical structure. That is, the perverse is simultaneously articulated as a free-standing entity and as a lack of being that emerges from within, and shatters, human nature. This paradox—as Dollimore calls it, citing Cleanth Brooks (Dollimore 1991, 105)—is enabled by displacements that a) lend ontological substance to outsiders who incarnate a disavowed lack within the 'natural' social order and b) project an external danger back onto elements within the latter. It is the paths of these displacements, and their relations to sexual perversity, that Dollimore traces in his reading of *Othello*.

As Dollimore notes, *Othello* obsessively imagines desire in terms of errant nature: Brabanzio says it is against 'all rules of nature' (1.3.101) that Desdemona should desire Othello, and that 'For nature so preposterously to err' (1.3.62)—'preposterous' being the term for a sexual inversion that confuses the behind ('post'-) for the front ('pre'-)—Desdemona must have been seduced by witchcraft. Here Brabanzio imagines her sexual transgression as caused by an agency outside her. Yet Iago and Othello worry at another possibility, that her transgression is intrinsic to rather than external to her nature:

> OTHELLO   And yet, how nature erring from itself—
> IAGO   Ay, there's the point; as, to be bold with you,
>   Not to affect many proposèd matches
>   Of her own clime, complexion, and degree,
>   Whereto we see in all things nature tends.
>   Foh, one may smell in such a will most rank,
>   Foul disproportions, thoughts unnatural!
>   (3.3.232–8)

Iago argues that Desdemona's choice of foreign Othello over her countrymen makes her a sexual pervert. He thus extends the 'erring' movement of Othello's line, which imagines Desdemona as possessed of a supposedly pure 'nature' from which she temporarily deviates. For Iago, however, she fully embodies the 'unnatural' as a separate category of (non)being. Schematizing this speech in relation to the perverse dynamic, Dollimore says: 'In its splitting the natural produces the perverse as a disavowal of itself and a displacement of an opposite (the unnatural) which, because of the binary interdependence of the two (the natural and the unnatural), is also an inextricable part of itself' (Dollimore 1991, 154). Nature, therefore, partakes of what it would exclude; but Iago controls the destabilizing force of that contradiction by externalizing and substantializing the (non)identity of the unnatural.

Yet even as the perverse dynamic generates displacements in the direction of an 'unnatural' exteriority, it simultaneously recasts external threats as internal deviations. *Othello* begins with a perceived military threat to Venice and its colony, Cyprus, from the Ottoman Turks. That threat is quickly eliminated by the storm that miraculously sinks the invading Turkish fleet. But the Turkish threat re-emerges in the Venetian characters as a figure for their perversions: 'The perverse subject—the desiring woman—becomes, through imagined sexual transgression, a surrogate alien, a surrogate Turk' (Dollimore 1991, 156). It is not just Desdemona who is refigured as a Turk. When Cassio drunkenly brawls with Roderigo, Othello asks: 'Are we turned Turks, and to ourselves do that | Which heaven hath forbid the Ottomites?' (2.3.153–4); and at play's end, before killing himself, Othello declares that it is he who has turned Turk, re-enacting upon his own body his earlier murder in Aleppo of a 'a malignant and a turbaned Turk' (5.2.362) who had slandered Venice. Dollimore, noting that the play makes explicit the processes of displacement whereby the unnatural is rewritten as the alien and the alien is projected into the interior, argues that it is left to the reader to endorse or repudiate those processes. Criticism of the play has done both, which is why, he argues, *Othello* can be made both to confirm and to discount the charge that it is racist.

But one might ask what Dollimore's queer reading of the perverse dynamic in *Othello*, centred on Desdemona and Iago, reveals about homosexuality in the play. A popular interpretation of Iago's malignity, parlayed in Oliver Parker's 1995 film version of *Othello*, is that he is really a repressed homosexual motivated by sexual jealousy over Othello; Iago's 'true' sexuality surfaces in his fraudulent tale about the sleeping Cassio, who supposedly misidentifies him as his lover and kisses him on his lips. Dollimore is quick to discount this interpretation. Referencing Sedgwick, he argues that the perverse dynamic whereby Desdemona is rewritten as an 'unnatural' alien works to cement, at her expense, the homosocial bonds between Iago and

Othello. But he adds that 'we would be mistaken to conclude that "repressed homosexuality" is the "real" motivation of the homosocial bond since such a conclusion would obscure much and reveal little' (Dollimore 1991, 158). A queer reading of a text does not necessarily aim to identify homosexuals. Instead, as in Dollimore's interpretation, it seeks to reveal the larger processes of displacement that produce and trouble categories of sexual normality and perversion.

If a conservative world view is structured through binary oppositions between order and disorder, the natural and the unnatural, sanctioned love and sexual deviation, that structure, Dollimore argues, is inherently unstable. It is 'given the lie by the perverse dynamic, which indicates that political and sexual ordering is always internally disordered by the deviations it produces and displaces and defines itself against' (Dollimore 1991, 160). And that disordering opens up space for future dissidence from sexual and social normality. Although Dollimore never uses the word 'queer' in his discussion of *Othello*, his theorization of perversity anticipates how queer theory has increasingly come to understand its object not as a sexual identity so much as a disturbance, a complex of disavowals and displacements that accompanies the fantasmatic production of a 'something' (i.e. the supposed identity of both the sexually 'normal' subject and the pervert) out of 'nothing'. As such, this project has potential affinities with aspects of Lacanian psychoanalysis, especially Žižek's theorization of the Real and the impossibility of identity.

Queer Education and *Hamlet*: Lee Edelman

These affinities are made explicit in the work of Lee Edelman (1953–). Just as Dollimore's account of the perverse dynamic insists on the displacements that enable normativity to project as other what it seeks to exclude from itself, so too does Edelman's account of queer theory and the death drive, outlined in his book *No Future* (2004), explain homophobia as a displacement or projection of a tendency that reproductive heterosexuality disavows in itself. Whereas Dollimore sees the perverse dynamic as generating dissident possibilities for the future, however, Edelman critiques the very notion of futurity. The future, as promised by the figure of the child, is often fantasized as a meaningful time under threat from a homosexuality associated with a meaningless death drive: that is, homophobia makes homosexuality synonymous with a senseless, repetitive compulsion as well as the death sentence of AIDS, both of which refuse the future-oriented goal of sexual reproduction. But even as the ideology of reproductive futurism attributes the deadly spectre of senseless compulsion to the queer, Edelman argues—by way of Lacan and Žižek—that the future promised by the child is itself a fantasy driven by senseless compulsion. Such compulsion is nowhere more evident than in the excessive homophobic violence repeatedly directed at the queer 'enemies' of futurity. Rather than seek a place in the future or in the social institutions that work to bring it about, Edelman argues, queers might instead actively embody the negativity of the death drive and its refusal of a meaningful future.

Even Edelman's admirers sometimes find this foreclosure on futurity unsettling. In his endorsement of *No Future*, printed on the book's jacket, the queer theorist Leo Bersani writes: 'Edelman's extraordinary text is so powerful that we could perhaps reproach him only for not spelling out the mode in which we might survive our necessary assent to its argument'. Edelman's subsequent project, titled *Bad Education*, takes up this question of survival in relation to what he calls the 'queer event': the irruption, within fantasies of how 'we might survive', of a void that disturbs identity and futurity. Although this queer event derives its name and critical force from queer sexualities, Edelman makes the term 'queer' refuse any straight equation with homosexuality. In particular, he considers how the queer event attends education, the means by which our reserves of knowledge can supposedly survive us by being transmitted to the next generation. Edelman illustrates this more expansive usage of 'queer' and its relation to education in his essay 'Hamlet's Wounded Name' (2010).

The title of Edelman's essay is taken from a line at play's end, in which the dying Hamlet tells Horatio that his is 'a wounded name' (5.2.286). Hamlet may refer here not just to his own name but also to his father's. Their shared 'wounded name' suggests a world in which wrongs have been committed by evil uncles and treacherous mothers against the Hamlet line; but it also suggests for Edelman, following Lacan and Žižek, how the play presents the Symbolic as a structure of signification that *both* projects its survival into the future through patrilineal transmission *and* bears a wound that rends asunder the identities it supposedly secures. The Symbolic order, Edelman argues, is grounded in the very logic of *or*der, as indicated by the play's six most famous words: 'To be, *or* not to be' (3.1.58). That 'or' asserts an absolute distinction between two entities, life and death. But *Hamlet* deconstructs this distinction, and not just in its title character's infamous assertion of his posthumousness: 'I am dead, Horatio . . . Horatio, I am dead' (5.2.275, 280). For Edelman, the play most profoundly disturbs the distinction between life and death with the survivals it projects, through processes of education, of the Symbolic *or*der.

In an interview just before his own death, Jacques Derrida cited the German philosopher Walter Benjamin's distinction between '*überleben*, on the one hand, to survive death as a book can survive the death of its author or a child the death of its parents, and, on the other hand, *fortleben*, *living on*, to continue to live' (Derrida 2005, 26; Edelman 2010, 3). For Edelman, this distinction is in a crucial way undone by the child. The child is expected *both* to survive its parents *and* to represent the survival of the parents as genetic code. Yet, as he notes, 'because such genetic "living on" can offer, by itself, no assurance of survival in and as cultural memory, the child as biological survivor (*fortleben*) requires an educational supplement to make its survival equivalent to a book (*überleben*)' (Edelman 2010, 3–4). This educational supplement, which renders the child's memory a book in which the living words of previous generations are inscribed, is uncannily realized in Hamlet's response to the ghost's command, 'Remember me':

> Remember thee?
> Yea, from the table of my memory
> I'll wipe away all trivial fond records,
> All saws of books, all forms, all pressures past,
> That youth and observation copied there,
> And thy commandment all alone shall live
> Within the book and volume of my brain
> Unmixed with baser matter.
>
> (1.5.97–104)

In a manner that recalls de Man's account of prosopopeia, Hamlet lends life to his father even as he transforms himself into a mere object, a book on which his father's command is inscribed. He keeps that command 'alive' by becoming the agent of his father's will, the instrument of a vitality to which he must subordinate his own. As an exemplary instance of reproductive futurism's figural child, Hamlet signifies survival; but as such, he can never survive as himself, doomed as he is to disappear by a process of education that compels him to voice another's script.

In *Archive Fever*, Derrida considers one of the key institutions of the Symbolic order—the archive—by means of which past knowledge is remembered and transmitted to the future (Derrida 1998). For Derrida, the pledge of the archive to remember in and for the future is everywhere informed by repetition: the repetition of the meaningful past as the meaningful future, the repetition of the assent to remember as the grounds of a meaningful self projected into the future, and a more profound repetition compulsion premised on the forgetting of its own meaninglessness—that is, the urge, beyond all meaning, to embrace the fantasy of saving meaning for the future. In other words, Derrida sees the archive as the guarantor of futurity and the survival of the Symbolic; but he also concedes it to be haunted by the spectre of a death drive that troubles even as it enables the archive's promise of education for the future. For Edelman, this is the dilemma that disturbs *Hamlet*—and Hamlet. The prince turns his brain into an archive that memorializes his father's law, assenting to purge a Denmark where 'the time is out of joint' (1.5.189) so that he may restraighten time and point it to a meaningful future. But his assent unleashes a compulsion that tears him apart, ensuring that time—and being itself—is forever out of joint.

Hamlet's father enjoins on him a fierce rejection of perverse sexuality: 'Let not the royal bed of Denmark be | A couch for luxury and damnèd incest' (1.5.82–3). The son likewise seeks to distinguish 'Hyperion' from a 'satyr' (1.2.140), his godly father from bestial Claudius. As Hamlet's invocation of the sexually incorrigible satyr suggests, this distinction works to place sexual perversity, like death, in a nameable category of non-being—a monstrous human/inhuman hybrid—from which singular being must be distinguished. Yet the task of obeying the Father's law, of separating being from a monstrous sexuality that would split it, spawns in Hamlet an equally monstrous compulsion that fractures him to the point of madness. As Edelman argues,

Hamlet is 'torn between the enforcement of sexual norms to repair what is out of joint and the extravagance of his passion for enforcing those norms, which exceeds all normative bounds. By being too much his father's child, he would have no children be fathered; defending too well the institution of marriage, he would have no marriage at all' (Edelman 2010, 10). Like the archive, then, Hamlet evinces a death drive that remembers not the past in order to (re)produce a meaningful future but rather a queer event that cannot be named, an event that is both the condition of entry into the Symbolic *or*der and the instrument of its demise.

While Lacan grounds his reading of *Hamlet* as the tragedy of desire in a teasing etymology of Ophelia's name as 'O Phallos', Edelman tethers his reading of the play's queer event to a similarly tongue-in-cheek etymology of Hamlet's name. Summoned to follow his father's ghost, but restrained by Marcellus and Horatio, Hamlet cries out: 'By heaven, I'll make a ghost of him that lets me!' (1.4.62). Edelman observes that

Playing on the double sense of 'let'—to permit or allow, on the one hand, and to hinder or prevent, on the other—these words free Hamlet to follow his father, the 'ghost of him that lets me': the ghost of him who gave life and preempts it; the ghost who confirms, in more ways than one, that time is out of joint; the ghost whose example dooms Hamlet at once to be *and* not to be—that is, to be and not to be 'Hamlet', the name by which he's prevented from being what it gives him leave to be. But that, of course, is what Hamlet means, even literally: '[I] am let'. It's also what normativity means in the world we inherit from Hamlet: to be let, constrained, or prevented by the power that gives us permission to be, even while it incites, perversely, our passion to constrain what appears as perverse. (Edelman 2010, 11)

The ghost's injunction that Hamlet 'remember!' so that he may be educated (or 'let') into a normative identity and a better future has been repeated in the play's reception. Harold Bloom's claim that *Hamlet* invents the 'human' demands that the play be memorialized as the foundational archive of what it is to be truly ourselves, an archive that offers invaluable lessons to us and future generations. Yet the compulsion to remember the play this way, like Hamlet's compulsion to remember his father, forgets the queer event of its own meaningless aim even as it strives to obtain the meaningful goal of its fantasy. Edelman's essay thus prompts the question: what might be the object of an explicitly queer education, especially one that calls into question the very fantasy of a future meaningful object? Here it is worth noting, perhaps, that 'educate' derives from the Latin for 'lead away'. This etymology suggests an intransitive motion rather than a meaningful destination, a goalless leading away that traces the queer anatomy of compulsion.

Part III

Culture and Society

9

Marxism

Karl Marx, Georg Lukács, Bertolt Brecht

> We cannot miss him. He does make our fire,
> Fetch in our wood, and serves in offices
> That profit us.—What ho! Slave, Caliban!
>
> *The Tempest*, 1.2.314–16

Prospero refers here to just one character, his slave Caliban. But in his remarks, a whole complex of social and economic relations is outlined. What Prospero describes is more than simply a relationship of bondage between master and slave; it is also a relationship from which he and his daughter Miranda 'profit', inasmuch as Caliban does the backbreaking work that enables their life. This is a relationship based on tension and conflict, one that eventually provokes Caliban to rebellion. The idea that social relations are grounded in economic relations of production, and that these relations profit some classes in ways that lead others to revolt, is the basis of Marxism. If the theoretical movements of this book's first four chapters focus on language and structure, and those of the next four on desire and identity, Marxism and its offshoots make culture and society the ground zero of their critical practice.

A middle-class German exiled to Britain in 1848, Karl Marx (1818–83) devoted his life to analysing and strategizing against the effects of industrial capitalism. Together with his fellow expatriate Friedrich Engels, Marx denounced the misery produced by the capitalist exploitation of deskilled or alienated workers, whom he called the proletariat. The latter are alienated psychologically inasmuch as they have become automatons who perform mind-numbingly repetitive factory work. But they are alienated economically as well, having sold their labour to capitalists who also own their places of work, tools, and products. Marx's solution to this state of affairs was communism—a classless society based on common ownership of the economic means of production. No matter how untenable it might seem in light of the Soviet communist experiment of the twentieth century, Marx's solution was based on a rigorous theorization and analysis of history. Many nineteenth-century Europeans understood history as the march of progress: some tended to see this march in terms of the rise of national identity and sovereignty, while the German idealist philosopher G. W. F. Hegel saw history as a progression of the Spirit. Marx, however, understood history to be driven by the struggle between different social classes, irrespective of national identity, for economic and political advantage—a competition most nakedly evident in the age of capitalism. In contrast to nationalist historians, then, Marx conceived of history with an internationalist inflection (evident in his famous battlecry, 'Workers of the world, unite!'). And in contrast to Hegel and his notion of progress grounded in the perfection of Spirit, Marx insisted on the economic basis of human history. But even as Marx reacted against Hegel's idealism, he borrowed from him the concept of the dialectic, or the notion that struggle between two opposed forces produces change. Indeed, change is crucial to all of Marx's thought. In his early writings, he famously asserted that while philosophers have tried simply to understand the world, the point is to change it. But whereas Hegel saw the dialectic operating solely in the realm of Spirit, Marx insisted that change was largely a product of contradictions within the material realms of social organization and economic production. Hence Marx's claim that his was a philosophy of dialectical materialism.

The dialectical cast of Marx's thought is most visible in his analyses of different modes of production in European history. He devoted considerable attention to feudalism, the hierarchical system of medieval polity in which peasants worked the estates of a hereditary lord to whom they owed tribute (usually in the form of a percentage of the fruits of their labour). During the Renaissance, Marx argued, the feudal system collapsed under the weight of its internal contradictions, and in doing so paved the way for the rise of capitalism.

Marx predicted that capitalism will likewise crumble as a result of its own foundational contradiction—the bourgeoisie's need for an alienated working class, who will eventually rebel against their oppressors. Such analyses might seem to view social change simply as the inevitable consequence of structural problems within an economic system. Marx nevertheless stressed the active role people play in bringing about change. Men and women, he insisted, make their own history, even if it is not under conditions of their own choosing.

Throughout Marx's analyses of historical change persists a model of social formation founded on a division between the economic base (the material means of production, distribution, and exchange) and the cultural superstructure (religion, law, philosophy, language, literature, art). For Marx, the latter is not free-standing, but determined (or shaped) by the base. This model provided the rudiments for what was to become Marxist literary criticism: that is, the notion that literature reflects the economic and social organization of the time and place in which it is written. What precisely this reflection entails for Marx, however, is unclear. In fact, his understanding of literature's relation to its historical contexts remained imprecise throughout his writing. If he sometimes advanced a deterministic understanding of literature, he on occasion implied that art has a degree of autonomy from prevailing economic circumstances. The tension between a deterministic and a relatively autonomous view of literature was to be a recurring issue in Marxist literary criticism in the twentieth century.

Although Marx laid the foundations for a materialist literary criticism, the latter did not become a fully fledged practice until the rise of communism after the Russian Revolution. Lenin, the first leader of the Soviet Union, had argued that literature should become an instrument of the Communist Party. Under his successor Stalin, this goal was translated into a state-mandated 'socialist realism' in which literature was expected to reflect the truth of the communist base—a policy that spawned a dreary brood of homogeneous novels, poems, and plays populated by upstanding proletarian heroes. But even far less programmatic Marxist critics of the time, such as the Hungarian Georg Lukács, championed realism for the light it could cast on the true material conditions of society. In all these Marxist embraces of literary reflectionism, we can see an unresolved tension between literature as mirror and as prescription. Literature is understood to be determined by its material conditions of production; yet it is imagined to play a shaping and sometimes revolutionary role in relation to the latter.

Many Marxists outside the Soviet Union rejected the realist aesthetic in order to theorize literature's revolutionary potential. A good case in point is the German playwright Bertolt Brecht, who proposed a theory of anti-illusionist theatre. Unlike naturalist drama, which presents its characters' behaviour as the product of a universal, unchanging human nature, Brecht's theatre sought to impress on its audiences how all behaviour is shaped by contradictory material conditions that can be challenged and transformed. To this end, Brecht employed a device that he called the 'alienation-effect', which interrupts a play to show how seemingly natural human feelings, actions, and identities are the products of social forces and contradictions. Brecht found particular support for his theory in Shakespeare's drama, which repeatedly draws attention to the various social and theatrical conventions that shape its characters' behaviour. We might think, for example, of the Induction scenes in *The Taming of the Shrew*. These dramatize a trick played on a drunken tinker, who is made to believe he is a Lord. As part of the hoax, the tinker is dressed up in rich apparel and presented with an aristocratic 'wife', played by a pageboy. The Induction scenes thus employ alienation effects that disclose how both nobility and femininity are not natural identities, but socially scripted roles. Brecht's theorization of epic theatre, however, is only one in a long line of Marxist engagements with Shakespeare that begins with Marx himself.

Timon of Athens and the Power of Money: Karl Marx

Karl Marx was an ardent reader of Shakespeare, and his love of Shakespeare's drama complicated the model of economic determinism informing his conception of the cultural superstructure. This model, which suggests that certain systems of social and economic organization will produce certain types of literature, guides Marx's pioneering sketches of materialist literary criticism compiled in the *Grundrisse* (1857–8). Here he promises to consider classical Greek literature and Shakespeare's drama in relation to their societies' different means of material production. Homer's and Shakespeare's genius suggest a cultural flowering 'out of all proportion to the general development of society, hence also to the material foundation, the skeletal structure as it were, of its organization' (Marx 1975, 245). Homer's *Iliad* and Shakespeare's *Hamlet*, in other words, might strike us as timeless works of art that transcend their historical moments. But Marx insists that such a view is a mystification. In the case of the Greeks, their literature derives from a mythology very much shaped by the material conditions of their lived relation with nature: 'Is the view of nature and of social relations on which the Greek imagination and hence Greek [mythology] is based possible with self-acting mule spindles and railways and locomotives and electrical telegraphs? What chance has Vulcan against Roberts & Co., Jupiter against the lightning-rod and Hermes against the Credit Mobilier?' (Marx 1975, 245–6). Greek mythology presumes a world in which nature can be mastered only in the imagination, and in such a world, nature is a force far greater than the nature subsequently tamed by the technologies of industrial capitalism. Marx never follows through with his promise to discuss Shakespeare in the *Grundrisse*. In the context of his larger argument, however, he might have similarly asserted that Shakespeare's plays are 'bound up with certain forms of social development' even as 'they still afford us artistic pleasure' (Marx 1975, 246). That is, they reflect the material conditions of their production even as they seem to rise above them; they are, to adapt Ben Jonson, more of an age than for all time.

Yet Marx's one extended essay on Shakespeare, 'The Power of Money in Bourgeois Society' (1844), reads *Timon of Athens* as less of an age and more for all time. In this early piece, Marx does not situate the play within the specific material conditions of Shakespeare's England. Instead, he lends it a more general applicability: for him, the play 'excellently depicts the real nature of money' (Marx 1975, 103). Marx's point of departure is the scene in which the once wealthy Timon, having lost his fortune, has exchanged his luxurious life in Athens for solitude in the wilderness, fancy food for filthy roots, and his philanthropic disposition for a bitter misanthropy. He discovers a treasure trove of gold buried in the ground, which prompts him to inveigh at length against the evils of money:

Gold? Yellow, glittering, precious gold?
No, gods, I am no idle votarist:
Roots, you clear heavens. Thus much of this will make
Black white, foul fair, wrong right,
Base noble, old young, coward valiant.
Ha, you gods! Why this, what, this, you gods? Why, this
Will lug your priests and servants from your sides,
Pluck stout men's pillows from below their heads.

.   .   .   .

Come, damnèd earth,
Thou common whore of mankind, that puts odds
Among the rout of nations...

(4.3.26–33, 42–4)

For Marx, Timon's speech shows a transhistorical awareness of how money enables people to become their opposites based on their ability to buy what they do not have. It is thus the 'alienated *ability of mankind*', the '*truly creative power*' that allows anyone who has it to convert mere thought into action (Marx 1975, 104). Marx sees this alienation as a perversion of the natural order of humans and objects. When I consume an object—'as in eating, drinking, working up of the object' (Marx 1975, 102)—I rightfully exert my agency over it as a human subject; but when I use gold to buy what I don't have, I cede my agency to a mere metal and give it a 'creative power' that should belong to me alone, a power suggested in Timon's speech by the active verbs he assigns to gold: it 'will make', 'will lug', 'will knit and break', and so on (4.3.35). Timon represents money's perversion of the subject/object relation by means of two metaphors. On the one hand, money is a 'common whore' (4.3.43): it forces a confusion of the 'false' for the 'true', the merely bought for the genuinely reciprocal, the pathetic customer for the powerful lover. But later in the scene, Timon refers to money as a 'visible god' (4.3.379): it performs a miraculous inversion of the natural properties of spirit and matter, subject and object. Whether as common whore or visible god, money alienates the human subject from him/herself—which, of course, presumes that there was a whole, unitary subject to begin with.

Marx's essay is less a reading of *Timon of Athens* than an appropriation of its language and its tone. Indeed, Shakespeare's misanthropic satire is close to Marx's own. *Timon*'s topsy-turvy world, in which

money has the power to make 'Black white, foul fair, wrong right, |
Base noble, old young, coward valiant' (4.3.29–30), is matched by
Marx's caustic insistence that money transforms 'fidelity into infide-
lity, love into hate, hate into love, virtue into vice, vice into virtue,
servant into master, master into servant, idiocy into intelligence and
intelligence into idiocy' (Marx 1975, 105). As this suggests, Marx is
particularly drawn to *Timon of Athens*'s trope of inversion, or what he
calls 'the world upside-down' (Marx 1975, 105). For him, this trope
does not possess a rejuvenating carnivalesque power as it does
for Mikhail Bakhtin; instead it signals an apocalyptic perversion of
nature, as in René Girard's reading of Ulysses' speech on 'degree' in
Troilus and Cressida. Marx uses the trope again in *The German
Ideology*, where he argues that, in Hegel's philosophy, 'men and their
circumstances appear upside-down as in a *camera obscura*' (Marx 1975,
154); and in *The Communist Manifesto*, where he asserts that, under
capitalism, 'all that is solid melts into air, all that is holy is profaned'
(Marx and Engels 1975, 476).

With its attention to the inversions engendered by the false god of
money, moreover, Marx's reading of *Timon of Athens* also anticipates
his theory of commodity fetishism (which differs from, even as
it parallels, Freud's theory of sexual fetishism). In capitalism, commodities are invested with a magical aura—their exchange value—
which derives from human labour, but is mistakenly believed to be an
autonomous abstraction residing in the object itself. As a result,
relationships between people—that is, between producers of value—
are transformed into relationships between exchangeable inanimate
objects. Commodities, like money in Timon's speech, usurp the
sovereign agency of humans. This attribution of human qualities to
material objects is what Marxists call reification; it not only inverts
the subject/object relation, alienating humans from their creative
abilities, but also fantasizes seemingly autonomous entities out
of what are really effects of social relations. By suggesting to Marx
the trope of unnatural inversion, therefore, *Timon of Athens* was
instrumental in shaping the distinctive language of his theoretical
apparatus.

But it is not the only play that influenced his vocabulary. Marx
also resorted extensively to the characters and language of *Hamlet*.
That play's uncanny ghost and undertakers lurk in *The Communist*

Manifesto's images of a 'specter haunting Europe' and the bourgeoisie producing its own 'grave-diggers' (Marx and Engels 1975, 473, 483). And in *The Eighteenth Brumaire of Louis Bonaparte*, Marx misquotes Hamlet's 'well grubbed old mole' (cf. 'Well said, old mole', 1.5.164) to figure the subterranean processes of social transformation that will eventually lead to capitalism's demise (Marx 1975, 606). These apparitions of the Elizabethan *Hamlet* in the Victorian Marx's writing suggest how he understands the communist future to be enabled by the untimely irruption of the past. He thus does not see history as a linear progression: for Marx, as for Shakespeare, 'the time is out of joint' (1.5.189). Shakespeare everywhere enables Marx's language. Yet although Marx's theory may be in this sense Shakespearian, he did not elaborate a sustained literary theory of Shakespeare. That was the accomplishment of later generations of Marxists.

Shakespeare's Histories and the Decline of Feudalism: Georg Lukács

The Hungarian critic Georg Lukács (1885–1971) arguably did more than anyone else in the first half of the twentieth century to produce a comprehensive Marxist literary theory and critical practice. Like Mikhail Bakhtin and many of the Russian formalists, he was attracted to the radical potential of the novel. But he was suspicious of the formal experiments of the modernists, and favoured instead the more traditional aesthetic of realism, which he thought better confronted reality as an objective totality of social relations. Lukács adapted Marx's theories to explain how a literary work is expressive not just of its author's class consciousness but also of the economic base. Modernism, like capitalism, fragments subjective experience in a way that detaches it from its social context and views it as isolated or autonomous; Lukács sees this as a form of reification. (Hence many Marxists believe that psychoanalytic accounts of subjectivity, inasmuch as they seem to divorce the individual from the political sphere, exemplify capitalist reification.) By contrast, realism understands subjective experience as shaped by the larger web of social relations in a given historical moment. For this reason, Lukács saw the historical novels of Sir Walter Scott as more radical than the modernist fiction of Franz Kafka, inasmuch as Scott's aristocratic nostalgia afforded him a critical distance from the capitalist system—albeit in a reactionary guise—that allowed him to represent its social relations with more accuracy.

Lukács advanced his reading of Scott in his 1937 study *The Historical Novel*. The nineteenth-century historical novel exemplifed by Scott's oeuvre, he argued, should be understood not only in terms of the genre's unique formal elements, but also in relation to the contradictions of capitalism. His analysis of the latter, however, leads him out of the nineteenth century. In his second section, 'Historical Novel and Historical Drama', Lukács treats Shakespeare's tragedies and histories as precursors of Scott's novels. In Shakespeare's hands, the two genres converge not just in their subject matter but also in their ability to capture social totality during the decline of feudalism. Lukács repeatedly borrows Hegel's term 'collision' to represent the interpersonal and intergenerational human conflicts in Shakespeare's tragedies that, in his analysis, spring from larger social contradictions between old feudal relations and newer capitalist ones. He views the tragedy of *King Lear*, for example, as a cross-generational 'collision' between codes of hierarchy and individualism that highlights the 'break-up of the feudal family' (Lukács 1983, 93–4). Likewise, the individualization of the lovers in *Romeo and Juliet* 'cannot weaken, but only strengthen the universally social character of the collision . . . it is precisely individual love here which breaks through the bounds of feudal family enmities' (Lukács 1983, 112). He sees such a collision also in *Hamlet*, which makes clear 'how much a personal destiny can evoke the impression of a great historical change . . . all the qualities of a character, from the ruling passions down to the smallest "intimate", yet dramatic, subtlety, are coloured by the age' (Lukács 1983, 118). Shakespearian tragedy, in other words, does not treat its heroes as isolated individuals but as part of a totality of social relations, even if that totality is riven with conflict and contradiction.

In his subsection on 'The Development of Historicism in Drama and Dramaturgy', Lukács offers a detailed analysis of Shakespeare's histories. Like the tragedies, the histories grasp the 'inner contradictions of feudalism, pointing inevitably to its dissolution' (Lukács 1983, 153). What most interests Shakespeare, according to Lukács, are the human conflicts generated by feudalism's demise. Shakespeare sees the triumphant humanist character of the rising new world, but also sees it causing the breakdown of a patriarchal society humanly and morally better in many respects and more closely bound to the interests of the people. Shakespeare sees the triumph of humanism, but also foresees the rule of money in this advancing new world, the oppression and exploitation of masses, a world of rampant egoism and ruthless greed. In particular, the types representing the social-moral, human-moral decay of feudalism are portrayed in his historical plays with incomparable power and realism and sharply opposed to the old, inwardly still unproblematic and uncorrupted, nobility. (Shakespeare feels a keen, personal sympathy for this latter type, at times idealizes him, but as a great, clear-sighted poet regards his doom as inevitable.) (Lukács 1983, 153)

Shakespeare's ambivalence is evident in *Henry IV Part 1*: the personal conflict between Hal and Hotspur is dramatized as the standoff between a charismatic spokesperson for a potentially ruthless bourgeois individualism and an equally charismatic spokesperson for a patently doomed feudal honour. Likewise, Lukács reads Richard III's predatory wooing of Lady Anne as not just a battle of 'two human wills' but also a 'historical witness to the magnificent energy and thoroughly amoral cynicism' (Lukács 1983, 155) of feudal dissolution. And when *Henry VI Part 3* brings onto the battlefield a son who has killed a father and a father who has killed a son, we are privy to more than just a familial tragedy:

> From London by the king was I pressed forth;
> My father, being the Earl of Warwick's man,
> Came on the part of York, pressed by his master;
> And I, who at his hands received my life,
> Have by my hands of life bereavèd him.
>
> (2.5.64–8)

In Lukács's analysis, the son's speech presents a personal tragedy but also exposes the larger social forces that have shaped it. As such, the speech underlines how 'Shakespeare always looks for these magnificent human confrontations in history and finds them in the real historical struggle of the War of the Roses... the human features absorb the most essential elements of this great historical crisis' (Lukács 1983, 154). However, Shakespeare does not present this 'great historical crisis' as a collision between social classes. As Lukács's contemporary (and frequent critic) Theodor Adorno notes, dissenting from the popular Marxist wisdom that history is the history of class struggles, 'in Shakespeare the social antagonisms are visible everywhere, but they manifest themselves primarily in individuals' (Adorno 1984, 361).

Lukács assumes that realism's sheer breadth of representation is in and of itself progressive: for him, simply seeing the historical forces at play in a realist text will make us repudiate capitalism's logic of reification. By contrast, he sees modernism, with its aesthetic of fragmentation, as only encouraging this logic by fostering the illusion that there is no prior organic whole from which capitalism has alienated us. Indeed, the impossibility of wholeness theorized diversely by deconstruction, Lacanian psychoanalysis, and queer theory would have registered for Lukács as symptomatic of capitalist reification.

Coriolanus and the Staging of Contradiction: Bertolt Brecht

In his antipathy to modernism, Lukács was opposed by the German playwright Bertolt Brecht (1898–1956), who rejected the idea that progress comes simply from recognizing an objectively accurate representation of social totality. Instead, he promoted a Marxist aesthetic of formal experimentation and fragmentation. Like Lukács, however, he enlisted Shakespeare for his theory of radical drama. Brecht had a somewhat ambivalent attitude to Shakespeare. On the one hand, he derided productions of Shakespeare on the modern stage for licensing a cult of bourgeois individualism: in the theatre of his day, the lives of Shakespeare's heroes were usually presented as shaped by fate or personal tragic flaws rather than by social factors. On the other hand, he admired many aspects of Shakespearian drama. Like Lukács, he insisted on the power of Shakespeare's plays to expose contradictions. But for Brecht this power did not stem from the realistic representation of social totality. Influenced by the Russian formalists, Brecht argued that theatre can defamiliarize our sense of what is real or natural, particularly through the use of formal devices or 'alienation-effects' that puncture the seamless illusions of realism and reveal the aesthetic and social contradictions these might conceal. For Brecht, many of the techniques of Shakespeare's theatre—empty

stages, clowning, plays-within-plays, boy-actors playing women—
have precisely this anti-illusionist potential.

Throughout his career as a playwright and director, Brecht repeatedly returned to Shakespeare. In the 1930s, he rewrote *Measure for
Measure* (which he regarded as Shakespeare's most progressive play)
as *Roundheads and Peakheads*, a parable of the hold Adolf Hitler held
over Germans; Shakespeare's Angelo becomes Angelo Iberin, a tyrant
who replaces the absent Regent and incites a race war to maintain his
grip on power. Brecht again borrowed from Shakespeare in his other,
more famous allegory of Hitler, *The Resistible Rise of Arturo Ui*, which
depicts the career of a Chicago mobster who is compared repeatedly
to Richard III and learns public speaking by reciting Mark Antony's
famous speech from *Julius Caesar*. As these examples suggest, Brecht's
interest in Shakespeare differed from Lukács's. Whereas Lukács
sought to recover the totality of social relations in Shakespeare's
historical moment, Brecht underscored how problems posed by
Shakespeare's drama could resonate for audiences in the present.
That isn't to say Brecht had no interest in staging the historical
contradictions of Shakespeare's time. He praised the alienation
effect achieved by a set designer who, reading the Macbeths
as neurotically ambitious petty nobles, made their castle 'a semi-
dilapidated grey keep of striking poverty' (Brecht 1992, 231); this
choice exposed the conflict between medieval feudalism and a
new code of individualistic upward mobility. Brecht also wrote a
rehearsal scene for *Hamlet*, in which Hamlet learns from a Danish
fisherman about the widespread rejection of feudal codes of violence,
which explains his subsequent inability to avenge his father's death.
Elsewhere, however, Brecht insists that *Hamlet*'s applicability to the
present moment engenders potential alienation effects for the modern
stage. 'The theatre has to speak up decisively for the interests of its
own time', he argues; he thus proceeds to read the play (and Hamlet)
as demonstrating the failure of Wittenberg's humanist Reason in
addressing the breakdown of the old order, a problem that resonates
with that of 'the dark and bloody period in which I am writing—the
criminal classes, the widespread doubt in the power of reason, constantly being misused' (Brecht 1992, 201). Here Brecht upholds his
friend Walter Benjamin's claim that, unlike the historicist, who seeks

to recreate the past as it really was, the materialist 'seizes on a memory as it flashes up in a moment of danger' (Benjamin 1969, 255).

Brecht devoted special attention on stage and in his writing to a specific Shakespearian tragedy: *Coriolanus*. He wrote but never quite finished an adaptation of the play, and one of his most powerful theoretical essays is a dialogue, 'Study of the First Scene of Shakespeare's "Coriolanus" ' (1953). As we have seen in chapter 4, the scene is one of the most action-packed openings to any of Shakespeare's plays: the insurrection of the Roman plebeians, hungry because of food shortages and irate that the upper-class patricians hoard the city's grain for themselves; the patrician Menenius Agrippa's attempt to quell the mutiny by telling the fable of the belly and the foolhardy rebellion of the body's lower members; the plebeians' uncertain response to the fable; the entrance of the plebeian-hating patrician warrior Martius; the creation of the offices of two Tribunes to represent the plebeians; the outbreak of war with the Volscians. Brecht and his interlocutors note how, in the bourgeois theatre, *Coriolanus'* kaleidoscopic first scene is presented largely from the single perspective of Martius. The plebeians' revolt is seen as proof of their untrustworthiness, with Martius' heroic nature serving as the play's yardstick of value. For Brecht, by contrast, the scene presents multiple contradictions that should cause readerly and audience discomfort. *Coriolanus* offers less an overview of social totality, as Lukács might insist, than a proliferating array of local conflicts plastered over by tendentious assertions of unity. These conflicts and their effacement also pose interesting problems of staging.

Textually, the scene's contradictions are evident from the moment of the plebeians' entrance. Rather than regarding them as a homogeneous group united in their opposition to the patricians, Brecht teases out the fissures in their supposed alliance (as suggested by the Second Citizen's questioning of their motives for rebellion): 'neither we nor the audience must be allowed to overlook the contradictions that are bridged over, suppressed, ruled out, now that sheer hunger makes a conflict with the patricians unavoidable' (Brecht 1992, 253). This contradiction is accompanied by numerous others: 'the unrest of the starving plebeians plus the war against their neighbours, the Volscians; the plebeians' hatred for Marcius, the people's enemy—plus his patriotism; the creation of the People's Tribune—plus

Marcius's appointment to a leading role in the war' (Brecht 1992, 255). Lest we regard these contradictions, à la Lukács, simply as elements of an explanatory social totality, Brecht is equally interested in moments of textual mystery that do not quite add up, that resist explanation and provoke discomfort. The plebeians' uncertain response to Menenius Agrippa's fable, his accusation that the plebeians are 'passing cowardly' (1.1.192), and the stage direction '*Citizens steal away*' (1.1.241)—which Brecht insists was added later to Shakespeare's text—are three such instances. How does one stage the scene's irresolvable tensions, as well as its sundry textual mysteries, without suppressing the larger problems they pose?

Brecht deals first with the question of the plebeians: are they as weak as Martius and the bourgeois theatre's interpretation of them insist? Brecht proposes that they enter with weapons that they have had to improvise, which suggests their relative weakness; yet inasmuch as they also make the Roman army's weapons, they are skilful in improvising their own, and so their inventiveness—Brecht suggests 'butcher's knives on broomsticks, converted fireirons' (Brecht 1992, 257)—might be a source of strength. This staging choice encourages a dialectical reading of the plebeians as structurally disadvantaged yet also possessed of a genuine power. To tackle the problem of Menenius Agrippa's fable and the plebeians' uncertain response to it, Brecht proposes a staging choice that amounts to an alienation effect, one that drives a wedge between the moral of unity proposed by the fable and the social contradictions it plasters over:

We've got to show Agrippa's (vain) attempt to use ideology, in a purely demagogic way, in order to bring about that union between plebeians and patricians which in reality is effected a little—not very much—later by the outbreak of war. . . . I've been considering one possibility: I'd suggest having Marcius and his armed men enter rather earlier than is indicated by Agrippa's 'Hail, noble Marcius!' and the stage direction which was probably inserted because of this remark. The plebeians would then see the armed men looming up behind the speaker, and it would be perfectly reasonable for them to show signs of indecision. . . . in these few moments, we observe that Agrippa's ideology is based on force, on armed force, wielded by Romans. (Brecht 1992, 258)

Finally, Brecht considers the abrupt show of unity between plebeians and patricians in response to the Volscian war. Citing Mao Zedong's essay 'On Contradiction', which asserts that significant social conflicts are often absorbed and concealed within nationalist struggles, Brecht insists that the conflict between plebeians and patricians—the class struggle not fully effaced by Menenius Agrippa's myth of the united social body—'has been put into cold storage by the emergence of the new contradiction, the national war against the Volscians' (Brecht 1992, 262). But that first contradiction has by no means disappeared, and it can be made visible in performance. Brecht proposes staging the layering of national conflict over class struggle by having Cominius, the consul of the patricians, grin as he takes the plebeians' 'home-made weapons designed for civil war and then give[s] them back to their owners for use in the patriotic one' (Brecht 1992, 263).

As this might suggest, Brecht and Lukács model very different attitudes to social contradiction. Lukács understands contradiction as a Hegelian collision between old and new forces—in Shakespeare's case, feudalism and capitalism—with the new always prevailing as a necessary if sometimes traumatic step in the long historical march towards freedom. This is ultimately a comforting narrative of progress. By contrast, Brecht views contradiction not as a necessary step en route to a better future, but as an intractable problem with no immediate or clear solution. As he and his interlocutor 'R' note at the end of the dialogue, 'the position of the oppressed classes can be strengthened by the threat of war and weakened by its outbreak... lack of a solution can unite the oppressed class and arriving at a solution can divide it' (Brecht 1992, 264). There is no Lukácsian comfort provided here by either contradiction or solution; indeed, the staging of each must cause discomfort to an audience. But that discomfort is, for Brecht, a necessary stimulus to analysis and revolutionary action. With his embrace of the multivalent properties of contradiction and solution, Brecht not only reworks elements of Russian formalism but also anticipates certain themes in poststructuralist thought. This hint of affinity was to blossom, in subsequent decades, into a full-fledged dialogue between Marxism and poststructuralism, particularly deconstruction and Lacanian psychoanalysis.

10

Poststructuralist Marxisms

Terry Eagleton, Jacques Derrida, Fredric Jameson

> Ware pencils, ho! Let me not die your debtor,
> My red dominical, my golden letter.
> O, that your face were not so full of O's!
>
> *Love's Labour's Lost*, 5.2.43–5

With these words, Rosaline provides a seemingly perfect illustration of Jacques Derrida's dictum that 'il n'y a pas de hors-texte', there is nothing outside the text. She dismisses Berowne's love letter to her as meaningless: it consists merely of material signifiers—a 'red dominical' (the letter used to mark Sundays on calendars), a 'golden letter', a brace of 'O's'. Yet Rosaline also resorts to a striking prosopopeia, allowing Berowne's meaningless letters to usurp his attributes: his written 'O's' are features on a 'face', as if that textual face was not only frozen in an expression of amorous passion but also scarred by the circular pocks of venereal disease. Once dead letters come to life like this, there is nothing outside them. Importantly, however, Rosaline's speech also traces a web of economic relations. She risks becoming 'debtor' to 'dominical' and 'letter'—that is, deriving her identity from words—in a way that presumes a credit economy of loan and repayment. The economic implications of her speech do not stop there. Her attribution of bodies to letters and dramatic character to alphabetic character rehearses the capitalist logic of commodity fetishism described by Marx: inert matter acquires a life of its own, independent from and even at the expense of human life. For Rosaline, then, language has an extraordinary shaping power. It is not, as the cultural superstructure in traditional Marxism is, simply determined by the economic base. But neither is it independent of the economic. Instead it both shapes and is shaped by the economic, suggesting a potential for dialogue between poststructuralist and Marxist literary theory.

This potential has been realized in a variety of ways from the 1960s to the present. In that time, Marxism has faced two significant challenges as a political movement: the repressiveness of totalitarian Soviet-style communism after the rule of Stalin, and the supposed victory of Western market capitalism after the fall of the Berlin Wall in late 1989. Yet both challenges have reinvigorated Marxist philosophy and literary theory. Stalinism's rigidly deterministic version of the base/superstructure model has been critiqued by Marxists in conversation with poststructuralist theories of language and causality. And poststructuralist theories of historiography and temporality have provided a rejoinder to the conviction of conservative philosophers that, with the fall of the Berlin Wall, the world has acquired a capitalist perfection that forever consigns Marxism to the dustbin of history.

In its most deterministic formulation, the base/superstructure model presumes a logocentric conception of literature—the presumption that a text must reflect the prior truth of the economic base. The French Marxist Louis Althusser (1918–90) argued that such a view is informed by theories of 'transitive' and 'expressive' causality. Transitive causality posits an origin external to the effects it produces: striking a billiard ball with a cue, for instance, causes the ball to move and hit other balls. Expressive causality presumes a totality in which one essential part organizes the rest: in Ernest Jones's Freudian reading of *Hamlet*, for example, the essence of the play is the Oedipus complex, and everything in the play is to a lesser or greater degree an expression of it. The base/superstructure model can be easily seen in terms of either paradigm. The economic base is either an external cause that determines literature as a cue determines the movement of a billiard ball or it is the essence of the social totality of which literature is but one expression. Yet Althusser argued that Marx also hints at another, more nuanced theory of 'structural' causality in his economic treatise, *Capital*. In this text, Marx explores how a social formation devoted to producing commodities will be distinguished throughout by variations on the commodity form, whereby phenomena that are parts of the totality of social relations (such as Berowne's letters) are reified as autonomous entities. This theory does not presume an external cause or essential part of a system but rather—as in Saussure—a mode of structuration that articulates the system as a differentiated totality. Literature, therefore, is not rigidly determined by a prior economic base. But neither can it be completely independent of the economic. Rather than seeing the economic as an autonomous domain different from and prior to art, Althusser argues, we must read this difference as itself symptomatic of the commodity form that is integral to—yet also conceals—relations within the social totality. We thus need to interpret any cultural phenomenon not in isolation but in relation to the absences or exclusions that constitute it. Here we might recognize Althusser's debt not just to Saussure but also to Lacan. This debt is particularly apparent in his theory of interpellation. For Althusser, ideology interpellates us as subjects: just as the Lacanian infant internalizes the external image it sees in the mirror, ideological state apparatuses (or ISAs) such as church, school, and the media 'hail' us with identities to which we willingly accede, thereby locking us into supposedly autonomous subject positions within the totality.

Althusser's work has provided the template for Marxism's dialogue, since the 1960s, with numerous structuralist and poststructuralist theoretical positions. His influence is apparent, for example, in *The Political Unconscious*, by the American Marxist Fredric Jameson. Although Jameson's book popularized the injunction to 'always historicize!' (Jameson 1981, 9)—the *cri de guerre* not just of a generation of Marxist literary critics but also, as we will see in Chapter 11, of new historicists and cultural materialists—it argues that to historicize means doing far more than simply reading a work of literature in relation to the economic and social conditions of its moment of production. Indeed, Jameson understands history through the prisms of Althusser's structural causality and Lacan's Real—that is, as an unrepresentable absence that nonetheless puts pressure on representation. We see a similar theorization of history in the writing of the British Marxist Terry Eagleton. One of the best-known exegetes of poststructuralist literary theory, Eagleton has drawn on Althusser to theorize how history enters literature as an ideological absence whose effects can be witnessed in disturbances of signification not unlike those theorized by Derrida, Lacan, and Cixous.

If Marxists have dialogued with poststructuralist thought, then the traffic has not been all one-way. *Specters of Marx*, one of Derrida's later works, represents a comprehensive if somewhat unorthodox attempt to tease out a Marxist lineage for deconstruction. In particular, Derrida finds in Marx's writing a deconstructive understanding of being and time that opens up to the hope of universal justice in an unknowable future. As the diverse instances of Jameson, Eagleton, and Derrida show, the two-way dialogue between Marxism and poststructuralism has led to new modes of interpretation that cannot be univocally subsumed under either heading. I thus use the plural form, poststructuralist Marxisms, deliberately here: out of the dialogue has emerged no one singular theoretical synthesis, but rather an array of new Marxisms and new poststructuralisms. Their emergence underscores the increasingly syncretic modes of interpretation currently favoured by literary theorists, who tend to couple formal textual analysis with questions of politics and history.

It is precisely this syncretism that has made Shakespeare's texts fertile ground for poststructuralist Marxisms. If his plays are characterized by slippages of language and identity (as diversely theorized by deconstruction, psychoanalysis, French feminism, and queer theory), they also bear witness to and even long for profound social transformations (as theorized by Marxism). We needn't see these features as separate, or as necessitating separate theoretical accounts or vocabularies. In a world where social relations are in flux, language can be equally volatile. As in French feminism, this volatility sometimes models utopian alternatives to the present social order: *différance* can thus acquire a revolutionary potential. Yet as Rosaline's remark about Berowne's human-like love letters makes clear, the autonomous power of language in Shakespeare can also be symptomatic of the logic of reification. Either way, Shakespeare's use of language might tell us something about capitalism and its alternatives not just in his time, but also in our own—and, indeed, in a possible time to come. To highlight the tension in Shakespeare's drama between language as an enabling medium of social transformation and as a disturbingly reified entity is less a Marxist poststructuralist projection back onto the plays than a recognition of one of their abiding concerns.

Language and Reification in *Macbeth* and *Twelfth Night*: Terry Eagleton

In *William Shakespeare* (1986), Eagleton (1943–) exemplifies the syncretism of his Marxism: promiscuous in his critical engagements, he offers spectacular amalgamations of formalist, structuralist, deconstructive, Freudian, Lacanian, and feminist theory. Yet Eagleton repeatedly insists that the affinity each has with Shakespeare is ultimately circumscribed by problems specific to the commodity form. In this, his aim is not simply to shed light on Shakespeare's plays but also to articulate a capitalist problematic of language in relation to the body of speakers and the material world at large:

As signs come to surpass the body they also threaten to escape its sensuous control, dissevering themselves from the material world and dominating that which they are meant to serve. The clearest example of this process is perhaps what Marx in *Capital* termed the 'fetishism of commodities', in which human products under capitalism, once alienated from the control of their producers, begin to set up relations between themselves which powerfully determine the social relations between men and women. Think of the stock exchange, in which interactions between stocks and shares, the signs of the accumulated labour of individuals, may result in mass unemployment. (Eagleton 1986, 97–8)

Here Eagleton draws on Marx to offer an Althusserian reading of signs and their reification, cut off from both the people who use them and the world they supposedly represent. He regards the problem of reification not just as a theme explicitly broached by Shakespeare, but also as a factor behind the emergence in literary theory of multiple methods—including Marxism—that are fascinated with the slippages of signification. Yet for Eagleton, Marxism is not just one theory amongst others. It is the metatheory that can begin to reintegrate these different perspectives, as he argues in his readings of *Macbeth* and *Twelfth Night*.

Eagleton's discussion of *Macbeth* builds on what he perceives to be Shakespeare's contradictory attitude to language. On the one hand, Shakespeare values 'settled meanings, shared definitions and regularities of grammar' which help to constitute 'a well-ordered state'; on the other, his love of order is called into question by his 'flamboyant punning, troping and riddling' (Eagleton 1986, 1). The transgressive power of language is modelled by *Macbeth*'s witches. Eagleton sees their slippery speech (which, Macbeth says, 'palter[s] with us in a double sense' [5.10.20]) as generating local effects that, at first glance, lend themselves particularly well to virtually every one of the theoretical methods we have considered so far:

- *Formalism.* Eagleton begins by invoking Empson's and Brooks's belief in the objective reader, albeit to a counter-intuitive end: 'To any unprejudiced reader... it is surely clear that positive value in *Macbeth* lies with the three witches' (Eagleton 1986, 1–2). In the manner of Brooks, he praises the witches' 'three-in-one' ambiguity (Eagleton 1986, 2). And he alludes to Bakhtin when he characterizes *Macbeth* as 'a dark carnival in which all formal values are satirized and deranged' (Eagleton 1986, 5).

- *Structuralism.* Eagleton notes how the more conservative side of Shakespeare invests, like Saussure, in a 'stability of signs—each word securely in place, each signifier (mark or sound) corresponding to its signified (or meaning)' (Eagleton 1986, 1). He also insists that *Macbeth* deploys binary oppositions that show how 'official society can only ever imagine its radical "other" as chaos rather than creativity, and is thus bound to define the sisters as evil' (Eagleton 1986, 3).

- *Deconstruction.* Eagleton sees the witches' riddling speech as ambiguous, but less in formalist than in Derridean fashion: when they say 'fair is foul and foul is fair' (1.1.12), they do not so much invert one of the play's key oppositions 'as deconstruct it' (Eagleton 1986, 3).

- *Freudian Psychoanalysis.* For Eagleton, the witches illustrate Freud's theory of the id and repression: they 'figure as the "unconscious" of the drama, that which must be exiled and repressed as dangerous but which is always likely to return with a vengeance' (Eagleton 1986, 2).

- *Lacanian Psychoanalysis.* Yet in its slipperiness and unknowability, the unconscious embodied by the witches is less that of Freud than of Lacan: it 'is a discourse in which meaning falters and slides'. This discourse of the unconscious, with its 'teasing word-play', infiltrates Macbeth and reveals in him 'a lack which hollows his being into desire' (Eagleton 1986, 2). His desire sets him on an unending quest for 'an identity which continually eludes him; he becomes a floating signifier in ceaseless, doomed pursuit of an anchoring signified' (Eagleton 1986, 3).

- *Feminism.* Most insistently, Eagleton sees the witches as embodying elements of Cixous's *écriture féminine.* By incorporating both female and male elements, they refuse the singularity of phallogocentrism; their 'words and bodies mock rigorous boundaries and make sport of fixed positions', and they are 'radical separatists who scorn male power' (Eagleton 1986, 3).

As this suggests, Eagleton finds much in *Macbeth* that resonates with contemporary theoretical movements. Yet Eagleton is not convinced that any of these can offer by themselves a convincing analysis of *Macbeth*'s witches and their slippery language. Instead, he harnesses the power of each theory within a larger Marxist rubric: that is, he sees each as explaining, even as it is susceptible to, the logic of reification.

The pivot in his discussion is Lady Macbeth. To many readers, she might seem to be the play's fourth witch. Like the Weird Sisters, she is an androgynous equivocator—she demands to be 'unsexed' (1.5.39) and uses slippery double-talk to tap into Macbeth's unconscious and makes him challenge the established order. Yet for Eagleton, her transgression differs from theirs: she seeks not to overturn the system but to achieve a better place within it for herself and her husband. She is thus a 'bourgeois individualist' (Eagleton 1986, 4), appropriating the creative dissolution of the witches in order simply to reproduce the same old oppressive laws of hierarchy and gender. Quoting the *Communist Manifesto*'s remark that, for the bourgeoisie, 'All that is solid melts into air, all that is holy is profaned', Eagleton notes the ambivalence of transgression under capitalism. On the one hand, it is anti-authoritarian like the witches. On the other, it reproduces the very violence that defines capitalism. The Macbeths' code of bourgeois individualism works to sever their language from reality, forcing them into double-speak to conceal their murderous desires: 'When language is cut loose from reality, signifiers split from signifieds, the result is a radical fissure between consciousness and material life ... The Macbeths are finally torn apart in the contradiction between body and language, between the frozen bonds of traditional allegiance and the unassuageable dynamic of desire' (Eagleton 1986, 7). The witches are seemingly exempt from this contradiction, for their bodies are as mutable and protean as their language. But *Macbeth* fears their feminine fluidity as an anarchic disruption, and not just because the play ultimately upholds patriarchal order. As Eagleton argues, *Macbeth* is understandably worried that the slipperiness of their language is close 'to a certain destructive tendency in bourgeois thought which levels all differences to the same dead level, in the anarchy and arbitrariness of the market-place' (Eagleton 1986, 8). For all its transgressive power, then, the witches' riddling language—in which the fair is convertible into and hence indistinguishable from the foul—rehearses the logic of reification.

Eagleton explores linguistic reification again in his reading of *Twelfth Night*. Like *Macbeth*, the play is obsessed with how words become dissociated from their material contexts and acquire a self-reproducing life independent of reality. In their reification, moreover, *Twelfth Night*'s words resemble money. After Viola has given him a coin, Feste asks for a second:

FESTE   Would not a pair of these have bred, sir?
VIOLA   Yes, being kept together and put to use.
FESTE   I would play Lord Pandarus of Phrygia, sir, to bring a
    Cressida to this Troilus.

(3.1.43–6)

Viola reminds Feste of the coins' 'use' value; but he reifies them as the classical lovers Troilus and Cressida, thereby allowing money, 'the supposed servant of humanity' (Eagleton 1986, 29), to 'breed' independently. This mirrors what happens with words in *Twelfth Night*. Rather than designating clear referents, the play's language is riddled with puns and tropes that again suggest a sexually promiscuous breeding: as Viola says, 'they that dally nicely with words may quickly make them wanton' (3.1.13–14). Such 'wanton words' lose their transparent connection to signifieds and convert language 'into one sealed circuit of abstract exchange, just as the commodity form does with material goods' (Eagleton 1986, 27). In such a world, language is no longer controlled by humans but instead possesses sovereignty over them. Hence Malvolio is manipulated into courting Olivia by

meaningless dead letters—'M. O. A. I. doth sway my life' (2.5.97)—
and he follows the script of Maria's forged love letter to a T (as it
were). Even though Malvolio's fecklessness is singled out for particular derision, he is not alone in submitting to the sovereignty of words.
Olivia and Orsino act out their lovesick states as if they were scripted;
indeed, Olivia chastises Viola for speaking 'out of [her] text' (1.5.204).
And Viola and Sir Andrew Aguecheek's duel is the consequence of
their submission to letters written about them. Everywhere in *Twelfth
Night*, words control human behaviour rather than vice versa.

For Eagleton, then, *Twelfth Night*—like *Macbeth*—exposes how
what Derrida celebrates as *différance* is in fact a symptom of the
commodity form: 'language devours and incorporates reality until it
stands in danger of collapsing under its own excess. The signifier,
whether of speech, money or desire, creates and dominates the signified' (Eagleton 1986, 34). Deconstruction, like Lacanian psychoanalysis and French feminism, remains useful for Eagleton as a
model of how language functions under capitalism. But he suspects
that, by celebrating the free play of signifiers independent of the
humans who utter them and the referents they point to, deconstruction pays homage to rather than demystifies the logic of reification.

Hauntology and the Future-to-Come in *Hamlet*: Jacques Derrida

If Eagleton first affirms then ultimately distances himself from *Macbeth*'s witches in order to make a Marxist critique of their complicity
with capitalist reification, the Derrida who wrote *Specters of Marx*
might ultimately have taken their side, and in the name of Marxism.
Like the witches, Derrida's Marx prophesies the future—yet like
them, he conjures a future that is spectral, unknowable, and marked
by *différance*. In Derrida's reading, this prophetic Marx, like the
witches, is also a necromancer, communing with the dead spirit(s)
of Shakespeare. Yet the Shakespearian spirit that looms largest for
Derrida's Marx is conjured not from the witches' cauldron in *Macbeth*,
but from the purgatory of *Hamlet*.

Derrida wrote *Specters of Marx* shortly after the fall of the
Berlin Wall. This momentous event prompted the triumphalist
claim by the conservative political theorist Francis Fukuyama that
History, understood by Hegel as the march of Spirit toward a final

state of perfection, had now indeed reached its promised end: capitalism had prevailed as the apotheosis of human freedom, and Marxism was now dead and buried. Derrida's book is in no small part a critique of not just Fukuyama's but also Hegel's teleological conception of History. 'Teleology', deriving from the Greek *telos* (end or purpose) and *logos*, holds that there is an inherent purpose or final cause for all that exists; time moves inexorably forward towards a final fullness and self-identity of meaning. Thus in Hegel's teleological conception of History, there can be no trace or remainder of a past that might divide this final, perfected *logos* from itself. Instead the past is dead. Derrida counters that, like Freud's theory of the return of the repressed, the 'dead' past often returns to haunt the present. And this haunting, far from representing the apparition of a ghost that must be exorcized and laid to rest, divides the present from itself in a way that opens up to the possibility of radical otherness, an otherness that takes the hopeful form of unknowable possibilities for future justice. The ghost addresses us from that position of otherness, and we are forced to respond to its call. In this, Derrida endorses a quasi-religious view of time, what he calls a 'messianic eschatology' (Derrida 1994, 72) that differs from Hegelian teleology inasmuch as it welcomes *différance* and endless impurity rather than oneness and final purity. Even after the fall of communism, Derrida argues, Marxism haunts the supposed end of History insofar as it maintains a call for and from otherness, asking us to seek a justice beyond the 'free' market. But Marx is not simply a ghost from the past who enjoins us to a radically different future from that promised by the proponents of Hegelian History and capitalism. In Derrida's reading, Marx is a philosopher who is himself obsessed with ghosts and haunting.

Derrida argues that, in works such as *Capital*, Marx invokes ghosts as figures of impurity or impropriety in order to exorcize them. The commodity form is, for Marx, an object that behaves improperly like a subject; in German, he calls it a *Spuk*, or ghost, and he attempts to banish its spectre by replacing it with use value, in which the object stands once more in proper relation to the subject. Yet elsewhere, Marx welcomes ghosts. 'A specter is haunting Europe': these are the famous words that begin the *Communist Manifesto*, and in this case, Marx (together with Engels) welcomes rather than banishes the ghostly apparition. The spectre is communism, conjured less from a dead past than from an untimely alternative to the present. Hence when it comes to the representation of ghosts—what Derrida calls 'spectropoetics'—Marx's philosophy is divided from itself. It is poised between 'ontology', the study of being, and 'hauntology', Derrida's coinage for the study of phenomena that bear the spectral traces of what are supposedly dead and gone. Derrida acknowledges that there are many versions of Marx's spirit that haunt our current moment. He professes himself repelled by the purist Marxisms that have led to totalitarianism and the gulag; but he embraces the spirit of the impure Marx who, rather than giving up the ghost, welcomes it.

The spectre that dominates Derrida's reading of Marx, though, is Shakespearian:

> Oh, Marx's love for Shakespeare! It is well known.... Even though Marx more often quotes *Timon of Athens*, the *Manifesto* seems to evoke or convoke, right from the start, the first coming of the silent ghost, the apparition of the spirit that does not answer, on those ramparts of Elsinore which is then the old Europe. For if this first theatrical apparition already marked a repetition, it implicated political power in the folds of this iteration ('In the same figure, like the King that's dead', says Barnardo as soon as he thinks he recognizes the 'Thing,' in his irrepressible desire for identification). From what could be called the other time, from the other scene, from the eve of the play, the witnesses of history fear and hope for a return, then, 'again' and 'again', a coming and going. (*Marcellus*: 'What, ha's this thing appear'd againe tonight?' Then: *Enter the Ghost, Exit the Ghost, Enter the Ghost, as before*). A question of repetition: a specter is always a *revenant*. One cannot control its comings and goings because it *begins by coming back*. (Derrida 1994, 10–11)

The ghost of Hamlet's father, like any spectre, is thus a figure of *différance*—and not just because he represents a dead past that lives in the present, but also because his very being consists from the outset of a return that divides being from itself. In the ghost, and because of the ghost, 'the time is' (as Hamlet says) 'out of joint' (1.5.189)—a line that so captivates Derrida that he cites it as the epigraph to *Specters of Marx* and repeats it on fifteen occasions throughout the text. The ghost's untimeliness might recall Derrida's discussion of contretemps and the proper name in *Romeo and Juliet*. But the untimely ghost in *Hamlet* differs subtly from the untimely proper names of Shakespeare's earlier tragedy. For Derrida, the ghost embodies an unknowable otherness: 'Even though in his ghost the King looks like himself ("As thou art to thy selfe", says Horatio), that does not prevent him from looking without being seen: his apparition makes him appear still invisible beneath his armor ("Such was the very Armour he had on . . .")' (Derrida 1994, 6). Yet in his unknowability, the ghost voices an injunction to justice, one that demands an ability to converse with his spectral otherness. 'Thou art a scholar; speak to it, Horatio', says Marcellus (1.1.40). But Horatio cannot speak to or even for the ghost; instead, Derrida argues, it is another scholar, several centuries later—Marx—who would be 'finally capable . . . of thinking the possibility of the specter, the specter as possibility' (Derrida 1994, 13). Marx, like Hamlet before him, recognizes the ghost to recognize how his own out-of-joint time might promise the hope of future justice.

If Marx plays the role of Hamlet in relation to the ghost of Shakespeare's texts, Derrida in turn plays Hamlet in relation to the spectre of Marx, speaking to his spirit in order to heed its injunction. Beyond the call for justice, however, Marx's injunction remains hard for Derrida to fathom, as it does not plot a clear programme for revolutionary action. This shows how closely Derrida's reading of Marx replays a complex network of positions staked out within *Hamlet*. The Prince hears the ghost's command, recognizes the justice of it, but remains uncertain about how to act. And that, Derrida notes, is partly because of his uncertainty about the ghost: 'It may always be a case of still someone else. Another can always lie, he can disguise himself as a ghost, another ghost may also be passing himself off as this one' (Derrida 1994, 7). Even when it speaks as Hamlet's father, the ghost is both a figure of justice and the author of unspecified crimes. In a speech extensively analysed by Derrida, the ghost tells Hamlet:

> I am thy father's spirit,
> Doomed for a certain term to walk the night;
> And for the day confined to fast in fires,
> Till the foul crimes done in my days of nature
> Are burned and purged away.
>
> (1.5.9–13)

Hamlet is confronted with a dilemma: the spirit that asks him to set the world right is itself guilty of mortal sins, 'foul crimes' that must be 'purged' in purgatory. Hamlet himself will undertake the purifying purge of his father, albeit on earth rather than in purgatory: confronted with the spectacle of a spectre that may be 'a spirit of health or a goblin damned' (1.4.21), he opts for the former, purifying his impure father to make him a 'Hyperion' (1.2.140). Derrida does something similar. The spirit of Marx is a bundle of contradictions, his name having been invoked in support of repressive totalitarianism as well as principles of justice. Like Hamlet, Derrida settles on what he considers the best version of the spirit. But here he differs from Hamlet: whereas Hamlet seeks to purge sin from a father to make him pure, Derrida seeks to purge purity from a Marx who, by embracing spectrality, opens up to the justice of unknowable otherness in a future-to-come.

What distinguishes Derrida's Shakespeare as much as Derrida's Marx is the centrality to both of this deconstructive understanding of the future-to-come. Such a future diverges from the heteronormative conception of the future critiqued by Lee Edelman and queer theory. The heteronormative future reproduces the patriarchal Symbolic order that insists on singular identities. By contrast, Derrida's future-to-come takes the form of a heterogeneity that values *différance* over identity. This heterogeneity is glimpsed in the ghost, whose spectral apparition leaves us uncertain as to whether 'it prepares the coming of the future-to-come or if it recalls the repetition of the same, of the same thing as ghost ("What, ha's this thing appear'd againe tonight?")' (Derrida 1994, 44–5). For Derrida, this state of uncertainty is an 'opening', one that 'must preserve ... heterogeneity as the only chance of an affirmed or rather reaffirmed future. It is the future itself, it comes from there. The future is its memory' (Derrida 1994, 45). Still, one might share Edelman's suspicion that, however much it presents itself as infinitely open to something unknown yet to come, Derrida's future still performs a compulsory return to (or 'memory' of) the patriarchal law of the ghostly father.

Utopian Horizons in Shakespeare and Criticism: Fredric Jameson

For some, Derrida's purgation of Marx doesn't leave much that is Marxist. Terry Eagleton has asked: how Marxist can Derrida's

Marxism be if it not only rejects dialectical reason and the category of class but also sees the critique of commodity fetishism as exemplifying the 'pure' Marx who refuses hauntology (Eagleton 1999)? Indeed, Derrida's 'impure' Marx might come across simply as a deconstructionist *avant la lettre*. Yet even as Eagleton has faulted Derrida for not being Marxist enough, the American Marxist Fredric Jameson (1934–) has applauded certain aspects of Derrida's Marxist hauntology. Jameson is particularly attracted to Derrida's conception of the future-to-come, which bears some similarity to his own theorization of the utopian dimension of Marxism (Jameson 1999). This is a dimension that Jameson likewise illustrates in relation to Shakespeare.

In *The Political Unconscious*, Jameson issues to literary critics an injunction that has proved as confounding as the ghost's in *Hamlet*: 'Always historicize!' (Jameson 1981, 9). For Jameson, the task of historicizing is not quite the same as what Lukács means by 'historicism'—that is, reading literary texts in relation to contemporaneous collisions between old and new modes of production. For Lukács, literature offers a more or less transparent window onto history. By contrast, Jameson understands history, like the Lacanian Real, to be unrepresentable, even as it is the 'ultimate horizon' of literary production. Yet history's traces can be recognized in the interplay between the formal dimensions of a text and its interpretation. Jameson analyses this interplay in his chapter on 'Magical Narratives', where he considers the genre of romance. The latter can be understood in two different ways: synchronically—that is, as a genre distinguished at any time by certain formal features (conflict averted by a utopian happy ending); and diachronically—that is, as a genre diversely appropriated and transformed by writers over time. Jameson attempts a synthesis of the two approaches. On the one hand, he insists that a Marxist literary criticism must attend to diachronic changes. On the other, he recognizes that, in its master historical narrative of conflict averted by a utopian happy ending, Marxism itself exemplifies romance in its synchronic aspect.

Jameson sees the genre as typified by Shakespeare's romances. Indeed, Leontes' speech about his supposedly dead wife Hermione's now living statue at the conclusion of *The Winter's Tale* provides Jameson with his chapter's epigraph:

O, she's warm!
If this be magic, let it be an art
Lawful as eating.

(5.3.109–11)

On the one hand, Jameson like Lukács interprets Shakespearian romance as historically situated within a larger diachronic process: a late play like *The Winter's Tale* or *Pericles*, or even an early quasi-romance like *The Comedy of Errors* or *The Merchant of Venice*, recalls with nostalgia an old world even as it opposes 'the phantasmagoria of "imagination" to the bustling commercial activity at work all around it' (Jameson 1981, 148). Yet Leontes' remark also speaks to the utopian longing for a better world that is a defining feature not only of the genre as a whole but also of Marxism's vision of history. Far from discrediting this vision, Jameson suggests, the element of romantic utopianism helps explain Marxism's persistence and vitality. And he argues that utopian desire like Leontes', which takes as its object a 'magic' alternative to the seemingly iron-clad necessities of the current 'lawful' order, is crucial to both a progressive politics and a progressive critical practice.

In his short piece 'Radicalizing Radical Shakespeare', the afterword to a collection of essays called *Materialist Shakespeare* (1996), Jameson makes the case again for a utopian interpretive practice. Just as Marxism can tell us something about romance and romance can tell us about Marxism, 'we find ourselves asking not merely what [radical] critical theory has to tell us about Shakespeare . . . but also what Shakespeare has to tell us about radical criticism' (Jameson 1995, 320). Jameson, like Eagleton, notes how Shakespeare's wordplay anticipates poststructuralist theories of language; and although he echoes Eagleton in his insistence that Marxism provides the most comprehensive and sophisticated analytic paradigm available, he adds that certain deconstructive effects in Shakespeare's plays—such as the challenges they pose to conceptions of the unified subject and of the singular author—can provide a stimulus to a newer, less restrictive Marxism. As a consequence, Marxists might use Shakespeare as a resource for a 'transcendent Utopian vision or horizon of interpretation' (Jameson 1995, 322).

Jameson suggests three ways in which a utopian horizon of inter-pretation might be applied to and by Shakespeare. The first is a traditional mode of Marxist criticism reminiscent of Lukács: 'Shakespeare would thus be the name for the space and locus of transition as such—the immense historical dislocations and sufferings of an incomprehensible and seismic shift from the feudal to the commercial and later on the capitalist' (Jameson 1995, 325). *King Lear*, he suggests, is one play that might sustain more analysis of this kind. The second is a more topical approach that would read Shakespeare in relation to current events of his day and the ideo-logical disturbances that accompany them. This approach, like the first, would unearth utopian possibilities that suggest alternative futures not just to Shakespeare's time but also to our own. But Jameson most vigorously champions a third line of utopian criticism, which entails a comprehensive engagement of issues raised by post-structuralist theory in order to question some of the pieties of trad-itional Marxist criticism. In particular, Shakespeare's drama presents ways of thinking about social class and ideological affiliation that resonate with poststructuralist critiques of identity:

If what is suggested here is the old notion of a unified subject that 'adheres' to this or that class determination, then the questions and problems raised are not complicated enough, particularly for this theatrical moment of a still pre-bourgeois mode of language and expression. One would prefer to suggest that, whatever the multiple subjectivities of a 'Shakespeare himself' (clearly an ideological construct in its own right), the play form imposes a model in which the subject does not so much 'have' this or that ideology as it constitutes an opening into multiple objective ideologies at play... (Jameson 1995, 326)

The advantage of such an approach is not just that it exposes, in the manner of Brecht, powerful contradictions effaced by our perception of what is natural. These contradictions also suggest a utopian alter-native to conceptions of unified subjectivity. 'Utopia', after all, is not only a pun on the Greek *eutopos* (a good place) but also *utopos* (no place). As Theseus reminds us in *A Midsummer Night's Dream*, behind 'a local habitation and a name' is 'airy nothing' (5.1.17, 16). That 'nothing' may mark a frightening irruption of the Lacanian Real within the fantasy of identity, but it is also a literally utopian alternative to the constraints of Althusserian interpellation. With his insistence on how the plural and contradictory subject of Shakespearian drama is simultaneously a political matter, Jameson not only asks that Marxism converse with poststructuralism. He also hints at the terrain occupied by new historicism and cultural materialism.

11

New Historicism and Cultural Materialism

Michel Foucault, Stephen Greenblatt, Alan Sinfield

Lord Angelo dukes it well in his absence; he puts transgression to't.

Measure for Measure, 3.1.341–2

In these lines, Lucio complains about Angelo, the stern puritan-minded substitute for Vienna's absent Duke Vincentio. Since assuming office, Angelo has cracked down hard on sexual immorality. Indeed, he has prosecuted fornicators with so much vigour that Lucio deems him to have put 'transgression to't'. Of course, Angelo is guilty of sexual transgression himself: he lusts for Isabella and attempts to coerce her into sex. But the transgression to which Lucio refers is not just Angelo's. It is also the Duke's, inasmuch as he has deliberately set up Angelo in the expectation that he will profit politically from his substitute's behaviour. In any reading of Lucio's line, then, transgression is not something that straightforwardly opposes authority but is rather intrinsically part of it. This paradox is at the heart of the theoretical challenge posed by new historicism and its close cousin, cultural materialism.

The term 'new historicism' was coined by the American Shakespearian Stephen Greenblatt in the 1980s to differentiate his and others' scholarship from the historicisms of the early twentieth century. Critiqued by formalists such as Cleanth Brooks, these older historicisms interpreted any literary text as a reflection of its historical moment. E. M. W. Tillyard, for example, argued that all Elizabethans believed in a hierarchically organized universe, and that good literature from the period simply reflects that belief. Even the Marxist historicism modelled by Lukács saw a literary work as reflecting the social 'collisions' of its time. The historicism of Greenblatt and his peers is different from Tillyard's or Lukács's. Influenced by poststructuralism, they reject the reflectionism of the older historicisms. And even as they embrace a materialist lineage, new historicists are not particularly interested in economic matters. Instead, in a largely untheorized variation on Althusser's theory of structural causality, new historicists seek to clarify the formal homologies between literature and other aspects of the cultural superstructure. In the process, Greenblatt replaces traditional Marxist conceptions of history and power with ideas inflected by the work of Michel Foucault in particular.

In *Power/Knowledge*, Foucault critiques the 'economic functionality' of Marxist conceptions of power (Foucault 1979, 88). These have tended to regard power as a commodity—the means of production—which in capitalism is the property of the bourgeoisie. By contrast, Foucault understands power not as a singular *thing* to be owned by a dominant class but rather as a pervasive *force* that circulates impersonally through discourse. By the latter, he means any system of knowledge created within the institutions and disciplines of the 'human sciences', such as medicine, psychology, and anthropology. Producing the human as an object of knowledge that can be defined in opposition to forms of deviance (madness, sexual perversity, criminality, etc.), discourse—like Althusser's ideological state apparatus—interpellates the individual within a grid of power: 'the individual', Foucault observes, 'is not the vis-à-vis of power; it is, I believe, one of its prime effects' (Foucault 1979, 98). As the notion of a 'grid' suggests, Foucault imagines power more on the model of electricity, which *produces* specific effects rather than *repressing* individual victims. Yet power's grid is not unchanging. Various discourses combine together within a configuration of knowledge and power, or an *episteme*, distinctive to an epoch; but that configuration can change, forcing an epistemic shift. For example, power in the pre-modern *episteme* is grounded in visibility: the monarch's power derives from the display of his body in pageants and ceremonies, and capital punishment entails the spectacular maiming and killing of criminals. By contrast, power in the modern *episteme* functions more invisibly: authority is often unseen, and criminals are locked up, studied, and disciplined (or privately executed) rather than publicly punished.

New historicists draw on Foucault's notion of discourse, insisting that power in any culture operates through systems of knowledge and representation. Indeed, Foucault's insistence that power is not a commodity but an energy field that circulates through the various discourses that comprise an *episteme* resonates with one of new historicism's most characteristic gambits: parallel readings of literary and non-literary texts. A new historicist essay will typically read a work by Shakespeare in conjunction with (say) a contemporaneous account of New World exploration, or a medical text, or a treatise on witchcraft. In doing so, it endeavours to show how similar configurations of knowledge and power circulate through each. For formalists, this parallelism is scandalous, a lamentable decentring of the literary; the uniqueness of literature is parenthesized in order to foreground the homologies between (say) the discourse of theatrical imposture in *King Lear* and anti-Catholic treatises on exorcism. Some might contend, however, that new historicism expands the empire of the literary, applying skills of close reading to a host of archival documents previously considered beyond the purview of literary criticism.

Echoing Foucault's conception of the individual as an effect of power rather than as its potential victim, new historicists have been preoccupied with how seemingly subversive identities (such as atheists, witches, or sexual deviants) are contained by and even sustain the very power grid they seem to contest. As this might suggest, new historicists' analyses of power—like Foucault's—have a functionalist bias: unlike Marxists, they tend to examine how contradictions function to maintain a social formation rather than destabilize it. Here new historicists owe a debt also to the cultural anthropologist Clifford Geertz, who sees any culture as a complex yet ultimately integrated system of symbolic forms and narrative strategies. Hence, to adapt a distinction from structuralist linguistics, if Marxism tends to encourage diachronic analysis, i.e. examination of how contradictions lead to change over time, new historicism tends to engage in synchronic analysis, i.e. attention to the organization of knowledge and power within a single moment.

While the new historicism has been an almost exclusively American movement, its close counterpart, cultural materialism, is British.

Like the new historicism, cultural materialism has vigorously distinguished itself from Tillyard's historicism; it has attended to the
relations between literature and culture; and it has theorized patterns
of subversion and containment. Also like the new historicism, cultural
materialism has elaborated many of its principal assumptions in
studies of Shakespeare, as we have already seen with Jonathan Dollimore's analysis of the perverse dynamic and *Othello*. But there are
also significant differences. Whereas Foucault has provided new historicists with their primary theoretical influence, the British theorist
Raymond Williams has filled a similar role for cultural materialists.
Roughly contemporaneous with Foucault, Williams was similarly
interested in how power operates through language and culture. But
his analysis of power was more dialectical and less functionalist than
Foucault's. Williams theorized culture as a site of struggle, subdivided
into dominant, residual, and emergent formations or structures of
feeling. This has led cultural materialists to adopt a somewhat different attitude to subversion and containment. Whereas new historicists
have tended to produce functionalist narratives of how subversion
props up rather than challenges power, cultural materialists such as
Alan Sinfield have sought to expose within dominant ideological
formations 'fault lines' that generate dissident positions and the
possibility of change. Both camps, in other words, are likely to
agree with Lucio's observation in *Measure for Measure* that there is a
symbiotic relation between authority and transgression. But they tend
to interpret that relation rather differently. Whereas new historicists
might regard Angelo's sexual transgression as the devious ruse by
which authority reproduces itself, cultural materialists are more
likely to see that transgression as revealing a potentially disabling
contradiction within power itself. Interestingly, Michel Foucault's
own reading of Shakespeare lends support to both positions.

Historicizing Dreams and Madness in *Macbeth*: Michel Foucault

The thought of Michel Foucault (1926–84) has left a deep imprint on
new historicist studies of Shakespeare, despite the fact that his most
influential works deal primarily with examples from eighteenth- and
nineteenth-century France. In studies like *The Birth of the Clinic*,
Discipline and Punish, and *The History of Sexuality*, Foucault considers

the discourses of the human sciences and how these were formalized in the wake of the French Revolution. None of these books makes reference to Shakespeare; yet they have all shaped studies of power, knowledge, deviance, and sexuality in his plays. Paradoxically, Shakespearians have ignored Foucault's earliest writings, in which Shakespeare makes repeated appearances. Foucault's first published essay—his extended introduction to Ludwig Binswanger's existentialist theory of dreams—and his first book, *Madness and Civilization*, repeatedly turn to *Macbeth*. In the process, he reads the play to formulate early versions of his critique of the autonomous individual and his theory of the epistemic shift from premodernity to modernity.

Throughout his career, Foucault was a fierce critic of psychoanalysis. In *The History of Sexuality*, he attacked Freud's 'repressive hypothesis', which in his reading reifies desire as pre-social. He also criticized psychoanalysis for bolstering a regime of power in which categories of normal and deviant sexuality are understood simply as objects of scientific knowledge rather than as historically contingent effects constructed within and by its discourse. As early as his essay on Binswanger, Foucault mounted a critique of psychoanalysis. Freud believed dreams to express desire and hence the inner truth of the subject. Foucault, paraphrasing Binswanger, argues that dreams are not so much expressions of inner truths as mediations of a world organized in time as well as space. That is why dreams are not just about repressed desires; they are also revelatory premonitions, directed towards a future shared by the dreamer and her world. To illustrate the point, Foucault cites Calpurnia's dream from *Julius Caesar*, which foretells the death of Caesar. But he also considers how Macbeth is said to murder sleep. If 'Sleep . . . knits up the ravelled sleave of care' (2.2.35), it does so by relieving us of the agonies of our worldly existence. By contrast, dreams reacquaint us with those agonies: 'it is the dream that makes sleep impossible by waking it to the light of death. The dream, as with Macbeth, murders sleep' (Foucault 1985, 54). Dreams thus confront us with death, which is a universal condition of existence rather than (as in Freud) the concealed object of the individual's repressed desire. Indeed, it is this existential aspect of dreams that Foucault sees as their real meaning. To illustrate the distinction between sleep and dreams, or between escape from life and submission to its complexity (including death), Foucault quotes Macduff's plea to Malcolm and Donalbain to 'Shake off this downy sleep, death's counterfeit, | And look on death itself!' (2.3.73–4). It's worth noting here how Foucault's existentialist dream analysis, a method that he was later to discard, is layered over a historicist impulse with which his name would later become synonymous. He turns to *Macbeth*, a work of fiction rather than an actual record of a dream, because it exemplifies an epoch in which the relations between the psyche and the world are understood differently from how they are in the age of psychoanalysis. Freud's methods are thus revealed to be not so much inaccurate as historically contingent.

Foucault was to develop this position in much greater detail with his first book, *Madness and Civilization*. Here, he argues that madness does not exist outside the forms of sensibility—the modes of knowledge—that identify and isolate it. From the Middle Ages up to the Renaissance, madness spoke the absurd truth of a world in which the omnipresence of epidemic disease and death exposed the vanity of human reason. But this understanding of madness underwent a shift that began with the confinement, in the seventeenth century, of insane people in buildings that had previously housed lepers at the outskirts of cities. Madness was thus increasingly marginalized and silenced. Once confined, it could become an object of psychiatric and psychoanalytic knowledge, a deviance spoken for by the language of reason. In the process, it lost the function of revelation that it had enjoyed in the age of Shakespeare. Here Foucault notes the instance of Lady Macbeth's supposed madness. She speaks a truth that cannot be assimilated to psychoanalytic explanation: 'Lady Macbeth's delirium reveals to those who "have known what they should not" words long uttered only to "dead pillows"' (Foucault 1973, 30). Her madness confounds the doctor's attempts to make sense of it, revealing the vanity of his science. As such, Lady Macbeth's madness speaks not only *to* but also *as* death—specifically, the death of reason represented by medicine or psychoanalysis.

For Foucault, the association of Lady Macbeth's madness with the absoluteness of death is brutally underlined by the '"cry of women" that announces through the corridors of Macbeth's castle that "the Queen is dead"' (Foucault 1973, 31). And this suggests for him a fundamental difference between our age and Shakespeare's:

In Shakespeare, madness is allied to death and murder...[he establishes] a link with a meaning about to be lost, and whose continuity will no longer survive except in darkness. But it is by comparing [his] work, and what it maintains, with the meanings that develop among [his] contemporaries or imitators, that we may decipher what is happening, at the beginning of the seventeenth century, in the literary experience of madness....In Shakespeare..., madness still occupies an extreme place, in that it is beyond appeal. Nothing ever restores it to truth or reason. It leads only to laceration and thence to death. Madness, in its vain words, is not vanity; the void that fills it is 'a disease beyond my practice', as the doctor says about Lady Macbeth; a madness that has no need of a physician, but only of divine mercy. (Foucault 1973, 31)

Foucault was evidently captivated by Lady Macbeth's madness. In an interview with *Le Monde* in 1961, he again cites her case as exemplary of a pre-modern form of knowledge different from modern psycho-analysis: 'Lady Macbeth begins to speak the truth when she becomes mad' (Miller 2000, 98). Foucault's various remarks about *Macbeth* point in two potentially different directions. On the one hand, he uses the play to advance a functionalist model of culture. He understands Shakespeare's thought to exemplify an epoch where the supremacy of reason and the sovereignty of the individual are con-tinually undermined by the existential reality of death; *Macbeth* thus differs from our modern *episteme*, in which dreams express the truth of the individual and madness no longer overturns but rather shores up the authority of reason. On the other hand, Foucault uses Lady Macbeth's insanity not just to contrast but also to reveal instabilities within modern representations of madness, instabilities that are revealed in a counter-tradition of mad lyrical protest from Nerval to Artaud (and in which his own somewhat mad prose takes its place). As we will see, the first, functionalist mode of interpretation distinguishes Stephen Greenblatt's new historicism. The second, dissident mode of interpretation anticipates Alan Sinfield's cultural materialism.

Subversion and Containment in *Henry IV Parts 1* and *2* and *Henry V*: Stephen Greenblatt

Stephen Greenblatt (1943–) is the leading exponent of new historicism, which in recent decades has become arguably the dominant critical practice in Shakespeare studies. Yet, as he writes in an early essay, 'my own work has always been done with a sense of just having to go about and do it, without first establishing exactly what my theoretical position is' (Greenblatt 1989, 1). Indeed, new historicism has often been faulted for its lack of theoretical rigour and self-reflection. Part of its appeal rests in this turn away from abstraction, a turn exemplified by a signature hallmark: an opening anecdote, usually concerning some shocking event that took place at the same time as the text under consideration was written. Anecdotes offer what Greenblatt calls a 'touch of the real', an escape from the Derridean motto that there is nothing outside the text. Yet, as Greenblatt reminds us, 'both the literary work and the anthropological (or historical) anecdote are texts...both are shaped by the imagination and by the available resources of narration' (Gallagher and Greenblatt 2001, 31). This underscores the new historicist insistence that distinctive strategies of representation are replicated across different domains of culture. Greenblatt thus subscribes to a variant of Althusser's model of structural causality. Unlike Althusser, however, Greenblatt presumes subjects who deliberately appropriate representational strategies from other domains of culture for use in their local institutional settings. He theorizes this process most fully in his influential chapter 'Invisible Bullets' (1988), which offers a parallel reading of Thomas Harriot's *Brief and True Report of the New Found Land of Virginia* (1588) and Shakespeare's second Henriad.

Typically, the essay starts with an anecdote. In 1593, the Elizabethan spy Richard Baines notified the authorities that the playwright Christopher Marlowe, Shakespeare's competitor, had declared 'Moses was but a Juggler, and that one Heriots...can do more than he' (Greenblatt 1988, 21). This 'Heriots' is Thomas Harriot, the mathematician and American colonist, who also had a reputation for atheism. Whether or not Harriot was actually an atheist is of little concern to Greenblatt. Rather, he is interested in how—as Baines's

libel suggests—Elizabethan authority 'confirms its power by disclos-
ing the threat of atheism' (Greenblatt 1988, 22). And Greenblatt
detects this strategy, whereby the possibility of subversive religious
doubt functions to reinforce rather than undermine authority, everywhere in Shakespeare's culture. Even as his account of subversion as
an effect of power bears the stamp of Foucault, Greenblatt couches it
in the terms of a Renaissance canard restated by Baines. The sixteenth-century Italian political theorist Niccolò Machiavelli was
(wrongly) accused of arguing that religion originated in a series
of tricks and illusions perpetrated by Moses upon the simple and
gullible Hebrews. In this argument, however, the cynical subversion
of religion becomes the basis of religious and civic power.

Greenblatt argues that Harriot tests the 'Machiavellian hypothesis'
in his encounter with Algonquian Indians in Virginia. Dazzled by
what Harriot supposes to be the vast European superiority in technology, the Indians speculate that the English colonists' gadgets and
books were made by gods; as a consequence, they begin to suspect that
religious truth 'was rather to be had from us, whom God so specially
loved than from a people that were so simple, as they found themselves to be in comparison to us' (Greenblatt 1988, 27). The colonists
are quite happy to foster this delusion, and Harriot thus subtly raises
the 'Machiavellian' possibility that religion is based on fraudulent
illusion and functions as a means of social control rather than as a
transcendental truth. But this is not the only subversive possibility
raised in Harriot's text. He repeatedly records the voices of the
Algonquians and, in the process, lends expression to Indian beliefs
that seem to subvert their European counterparts. For instance, once
the Indians start dying from epidemic disease, they surmise that the
colonists' dead ancestors have shot them with 'invisible bullets'
(Greenblatt 1988, 36)—a theory much closer to our modern micro-
biological conception of disease than to the dominant explanation of
Harriot's culture, according to which epidemic disease is a plague sent
by God. Equally subversive is Harriot's account of English explanations to the Indians of their behaviour. He notes how, when the
Indians ask the colonists to shoot these invisible bullets into their
tribal rivals as well, the English explain that to do so would be
ungodly. But such an explanation runs the risk of coming across as

sanctimonious humbug, especially in light of the 'Machiavellian' experiment conducted by the colonists.

Thus for Greenblatt, Harriot resorts to three potentially subversive strategies—*testing* a hypothesis of the real origins of religion, *recording* alien voices and theories, and *explaining* a course of action in a way that reveals the violence at the heart of the enterprise. Yet, Greenblatt asks, why 'should power record other voices, permit subversive inquiries, register at its very center the transgressions that will ultimately violate it?' In response, he offers his most explicit theorization of how power operates through the production and containment of subversion:

The answer may be in part that power, even in a colonial situation, is not monolithic and hence may encounter and record in one of its functions materials that can threaten another of its functions; in part that power thrives on vigilance, and human beings are vigilant if they sense a threat; in part that power defines itself in relation to such threats or simply to that which is not identical with it. Harriot's text suggests an intensification of these observations: English power in the first Virginia colony *depends* upon the registering and even the production of potentially unsettling perspectives. (Greenblatt 1988, 37)

Greenblatt starts here by acknowledging that power is not monolithic. Yet by the end of this excerpt, it seems to have become precisely that, inasmuch as subversion—that which would contest and fracture power—ends up being produced by and reproducing it. This functionalist turn also provides Greenblatt with the grounds for a more recognizably Foucaultian understanding of knowledge and power: 'The recording of alien voices, their preservation in Harriot's text, is part of the process whereby Indian culture is constituted as a culture and thus brought into the light for study, discipline, correction, transformation' (Greenblatt 1988, 37).

It is precisely this nexus of knowledge and power, Greenblatt argues, that characterizes Shakespeare's second Henriad. The first part of *Henry IV* uncannily resembles Harriot's seemingly subversive strategy of recording alien voices. The rakish Prince Hal's dalliances with London's criminal underworld and its midnight tavern haunts allows him to learn a language starkly opposed to that of English royal authority: 'I am so good a proficient in one quarter of an hour, that I can drink with any tinker in his own language during my life' (2.5.15–17). Yet just as Harriot records Algonquian voices in order ultimately to consolidate English colonial power, so does Hal's seeming receptiveness to criminal culture augment rather than undermine English royal power. As Warwick says in the second part of *Henry IV*:

> The Prince but studies his companions
> Like a strange tongue, wherein, to gain the language,
> 'Tis needful that the most immodest word
> Be looked upon and learnt, which once attained,
> Your Highness knows, comes to no further use
> But to be known and hated. So, like gross terms,
> The Prince will in the perfectness of time
> Cast off his followers, and their memory
> Shall as a pattern or a measure live,
> By which his Grace must mete the lives of other,
> Turning past evils to advantage.
>
> (4.3.68–78)

In *Henry V*—by the end of which the tavern characters Falstaff and Bardolph have not only been 'Cast off' but also died—King Harry's recording of alien voices and 'gross terms' sheds any pretence of subversion. He speaks French to his future bride, Princess Katherine, but in this instance his linguistic prowess is the explicit recognition of his political and sexual conquest of France. Likewise, Harry's unexpected declaration of kinship with the Welsh Captain Fluellen offers a faux pluralism; his claim that he too is Welsh represents not a subversive displacement of English power but rather a vision of pan-British brotherhood headed by a charismatic English king.

   If Shakespeare duplicates Harriot's strategy of recording, he also makes use of Harriot's strategy of explanation. At the beginning of *Henry IV Part 1*, Hal explains his scheme for redemption in language that simultaneously enhances his moral stature and exposes his Machiavellian talent for fraudulent illusion and manipulation: 'By how much better than my word I am', he announces, 'By so much shall I falsify men's hopes' (1.2.188–9). Shakespeare resorts also to Harriot's strategy of testing. Greenblatt argues that *Henry IV Part 2*, with its repeated displays of the illegitimacy of legitimate authority, 'seems to be testing and confirming a dark hypothesis about the nature of monarchical power in England: that its moral authority rests upon a hypocrisy so deep that the hypocrites themselves believe it' (Greenblatt 1988, 55). Yet once again, these 'subversive' strategies are never truly subversive. As Greenblatt says, no censor stopped the plays. And that is because their 'paradoxes, ambiguities, and tensions' parallel the 'poetics' of Elizabethan royal power in general (Greenblatt 1988, 65). Here Greenblatt commandeers Cleanth Brooks's critical vocabulary for a formalist vision of culture, in which power rather than the imagination transcends all conflicts. As Greenblatt argues, Elizabethan power—which, in an age before standing armies or developed bureaucracies, depended so much on the queen's visibility in public ceremonies—'is manifested to its subjects as in a theater, and the subjects are at once absorbed by the instructive, delightful, or terrible spectacles and forbidden intervention or deep intimacy'. Like the theatre, then, this royal form of power 'helps to contain the radical doubts it continually provokes' (Greenblatt 1988, 65).

Greenblatt's essay deftly traces two parallel movements of representational strategies from one domain of culture to another. Harriot appropriates the subversive 'Machiavellian hypothesis' of the origin of religion and tests it in a colonial setting; Shakespeare appropriates the charismatic forms of royal power and adapts these for the theatre. Taken together, these two appropriations demonstrate, not an intertextual relation (in which Shakespeare was influenced by Harriot), but rather a theory of structural causality—an omnipresent, virally proliferating logic of subversion contained—that holds as true for Greenblatt's time as for Shakespeare's: 'There is subversion, no end of subversion, only not for us' (Greenblatt 1988, 39, 65). Thus does Greenblatt's historicist reading of appropriation shade into a universalist claim about power.

Sexual Dissidence in *A Midsummer Night's Dream* and *The Two Noble Kinsmen*: Alan Sinfield

An early version of 'Invisible Bullets' appeared in a collection, *Political Shakespeare*, subtitled *New Essays in Cultural Materialism*. Yet Greenblatt's theorization of power was to become a significant bone of contention between the new historicism and its British counterpart. The co-editor of *Political Shakespeare*, Alan Sinfield (1941–), is the most prolific spokesperson for cultural materialism. He has theorized cultural materialist practice in a series of books that examine topics as diverse as Alfred Tennyson's poetry, Oscar Wilde's legacy, the post-war English novel, and the cultural politics of Shakespeare. The movement's name, however, derives from Raymond Williams. As Sinfield remarks in his essay, 'Unfinished Business: Problems in Cultural Materialism' (2006), Williams offers a theorization of power (or 'hegemony') that diverges sharply from that of Foucault:

> The contribution of Raymond Williams has been crucial, precisely because he argued...that hegemony is not unitary...We should expect the co-occurrence of subordinate, residual, emergent, alternative, and oppositional cultural forces alongside the dominant in varying relations of incorporation, negation, and resistance. The dominant may tolerate, repress, or incorporate subordinate formations, but that will be a continuous, urgent, and even strenuous project. This framework improves on Foucault's expectation of an even, staged development, whereby one model characterizes an epoch and is then superseded by another. (Sinfield 2006, 7)

Even if Williams departs from Foucault's theory of the episteme, he follows Foucault in embracing counter-hegemonic possibilities. For Sinfield, Williams's dialectical understanding of power enables the theorization of the 'sources of dissidence', which 'arise out of the conflict and contradiction (the faultlines) which the dominant, itself, produces' (Sinfield 2006, 10). In other words, power does not turn all subversion to account, as it does for Greenblatt. Instead, as in Dollimore's reading of the perverse dynamic, power also generates contradictions that produce dissent and radical social transformation. This means that a cultural materialist will historicize a text somewhat differently from a new historicist. Both might analyse, for example, 'the relations between King James and monarchs in Jacobean plays, and for this they are going to quote from diverse documents, noting connections and disjunctions'. But whereas a new historicist will tease out from these connections and disjunctions a larger, integrated configuration of power, a cultural materialist will 'regard the text and its context as a site of struggle—riven with conflict and contradiction, sustaining alternative as well as oppositional elements' (Sinfield 2006, 17).

This mode of reading distinguishes Sinfield's analysis of authority and sexuality in *A Midsummer Night's Dream* and *The Two Noble Kinsmen*, Shakespeare's late collaboration with John Fletcher. Sinfield teases out dissident same-sex possibilities glimpsed in yet repudiated by Shakespeare's earlier comedy. These possibilities are illuminated by the homosocial and often unabashedly homoerotic universe of *The Two Noble Kinsmen*, which replays the beginning of *A Midsummer Night's Dream* by, once again, interrupting the nuptials of Theseus and Hippolyta. Yet Sinfield's intertextual reading does not produce, in the manner of Greenblatt, an overarching cultural poetics of sexual normalcy and deviance. Rather, he reads the two plays for their contradictions. This entails a cultural materialist adaptation of deconstructive 'reading against the grain'. Sinfield, like Elaine Showalter, is suspicious of deconstruction's investment in undecidability and indeterminacy, which in his view affords the oppositional critic no grounds for resistance. Instead he stresses how a text, by gesturing to possibilities that contradict its overt statements, discloses fault lines that enable dissident readings.

For Sinfield, the opening interruption to Theseus and Hippolyta's nuptials in *A Midsummer Night's Dream* reveals, only to plaster over, one such fault line. Hermia loves Lysander; she refuses to marry her father's choice, Demetrius, and thus exposes a contradiction at the heart of patriarchal marriage—a daughter must comply with her father's choice of husband, yet she and her husband are expected to love each other. The play shows how the dual imperatives of paternal choice and companionate love are difficult to reconcile. Yet it stages a magical resolution that ensures 'Jack shall have Jill' and 'Naught shall go ill' (3.3.45–6). By contrast, the interruption to Theseus and Hippolyta's nuptials in *The Two Noble Kinsmen* opens up a fault line within marriage that the play never succeeds in papering over. Three queens importune Theseus to go to war with Creon, who has refused burial to their husbands. Hippolyta urges that Theseus defer their marriage and heed the queens' wish, as does her sister Emilia. This urging initiates the play's preoccupation with same-sex bonding, a preoccupation that both slips into homoeroticism and questions the inevitability of marriage and cross-gender relations. Theseus is said to share a 'knot of love' (1.3.41–4) with his warrior friend Pirithous; Emilia recalls her childhood friendship with Flavina, now dead, in even more erotic terms, saying that 'true love 'tween maid and maid may be | More than in sex dividual' (1.3.81–2); and after their imprisonment by Theseus, Arcite tells his kinsman Palamon that 'We are one another's wife, ever begetting | New births of love' (2.2.80–1). Such same-sex disturbances haunt the play's conclusion: Emilia's marriage to Palamon is overshadowed by Arcite's death and Palamon's lament, 'That we should things desire, which do cost us | The loss of our desire!' (5.6.110–11). Male–male 'desire' is here homologous with, and even supplants, male–female 'desire'.

Sinfield suggests that, by attending to *The Two Noble Kinsmen* and its unconventional same-sex relations, one might produce 'a less complacent reading of *A Midsummer Night's Dream*' (Sinfield 2006, 73). In the latter, Hippolyta is reduced to silence after Theseus orders Hermia to comply with her father's choice of husband. The female–female bonds of the *Two Noble Kinsmen* encourage an interpretation of Hippolyta's silence as a pointed act of solidarity with Hermia. One might develop this reading further: Hippolyta's silence stands as mute testimony to the violent suppression of same-sex possibilities by the institution of enforced marriage, hers as much as Hermia's. After all, Hippolyta—an Amazon from a single-sex community in which there are no men—has been forcibly captured and injured by Theseus. In his words, 'I wooed thee with my sword' (1.1.16). Likewise, Helena's reflection on her childhood friendship with Hermia also acquires a dissident potential in opposition to compulsory heterosexuality:

> So we grew together,
> Like to a double cherry: seeming parted,
> But yet an union in partition,
> Two lovely berries moulded on one stem.
>
> (3.2.209–12)

The later play thus enlarges the ideological environment of the earlier, undermining the apparently natural supremacy of marriage. Yet this does not make *A Midsummer Night's Dream* a radical text. Sinfield pairs the two plays not to use the one as leverage with which to articulate the radical potential of the other, but rather to show how *A Midsummer Night's Dream* actively suppresses the 'dissident interpersonal intensities' (Sinfield 2006, 73) to which *The Two Noble Kinsmen* gives fuller scope.

Sinfield considers in particular the vexed sexual politics of the fairy world in *A Midsummer Night's Dream*. The possibility of same-sex companionate love is glimpsed in Titania's devotion to a votaress (now dead) of her order. Titania's love acquires an Amazonian intensity: she refers nostalgically to the votaress's womb, 'rich with my young squire' (2.1.131), as if she and the votaress have managed to conceive without the aid of a man. Oberon's desire for the squire, an Indian 'changeling boy' (2.1.120) of unspecified age, seems to mirror Titania's same-sex infatuation. Yet as Sinfield reminds us, not all treatments of same-sex desire need be progressive. Oberon's desire for the boy comes across as the assertion of a *droit de seigneur*, a patriarchal claim to property. Given the play's references to India and merchant traders, Oberon's desire for the boy might be read also as a disturbing fantasy of European colonization of Asia and enslavement of its people. In terms of the play's formal resolution, however, Oberon acts within his rights: Titania's preference for female company is a transgression that must be punished. Patriarchal homosocial bonds thus work not only (as in Sedgwick) to shape marriage but also to erase the spectre of same-sex female passion.

Sinfield's intertextual reading of *The Two Noble Kinsmen* and *A Midsummer Night's Dream* may transform our perception of the latter, but it does not make the two plays interchangeable: 'The alternatives which [*A Midsummer Night's Dream*] *is not choosing* lurk at the boundaries of the text, but they do not *become* the text' (Sinfield 2006, 81). The play's unconventional possibilities are, for Sinfield, ultimately foreclosed by its conservative sexual ideology. Yet no matter how much we might idealize the refreshing array of same-sex relations in *The Two Noble Kinsmen*, it too upholds a conservative erotic norm: the ideal of the couple, whether heterosexual or same-sexed. Why, Sinfield asks, should the couple circumscribe the horizons of erotic possibility? He notes Emilia's radical thought that she might 'cry for both' Palamon and Arcite (4.2.54). Theseus forbids this possibility: 'They cannot both enjoy you' (3.6.275). Yet why not? Indeed, why cannot a character have *both* his Jack *and* his Jill? As Sinfield notes, there are diverse hints of this possibility throughout Shakespeare's drama: 'Achilles, Patroclus and Polyxena;

Portia, Bassanio and Antonio; Rosalind, Orlando and Celia; Romeo, Juliet and Mercutio' (Sinfield 2006, 84). Even the unpaired Puck, the agent of wayward desire, suggests another unorthodox erotic possibility—a queer singleness—beyond the enduring ideal of coupledom. The pressure Sinfield places on this ideal suggests how cultural materialist readings of normalcy and deviance in Shakespeare seek to illuminate the ideological formations not just of the past but also of the present. In other words, 'Reading against the grain may produce, not a more elaborate realization of the most favoured Shakespearian texts, but a critical perspective upon their ideological assumptions and, indeed, upon our own' (Sinfield 2006, 85).

For all the differences in their theorizations of culture and power, Sinfield's and Greenblatt's essays share a notable fascination: both read problems of authority and transgression within Shakespeare's plays in relation to fantasies of domination over non-European peoples. Real and fictive encounters with Indians—of the American West and the Asian East—provide Greenblatt and Sinfield with the grounds for theorizing, and critiquing, arrangements of power in Shakespeare's England. In Greenblatt's essay more than in Sinfield's, however, the Indians get to speak back, albeit in highly mediated fashion. The challenge of speaking back is the terrain of postcolonial theory, which we will explore in the next chapter.

12

Postcolonial Theory

Wole Soyinka, Edward Said, Sara Ahmed

> They shall be my East and West Indies, and I will trade to them both.
>
> *The Merry Wives of Windsor*, 1.3.61–2

Falstaff refers here to his would-be double sexual conquests, Mistress Ford and Mistress Page. Yet his remark speaks also to important developments that were to transform the world over the course of the fifteenth to the twentieth centuries. The discovery of new oceanic trade routes linking Europe to the East and the West Indies prompted European merchant venturing companies—hungry for direct access to profitable exotic commodities such as gems, spices, tobacco, silk, and calico—to set up outposts and factories in the Americas, Africa, and Asia. These laid the foundation for several violent centuries of colonialism and empire. Shakespeare was very much aware of Europe's rising global power. In *The Comedy of Errors*, 'America' pays tribute to Spain with 'rubies, carbuncles, sapphires' (3.2.131, 133); Antonio's fortune in *The Merchant of Venice* stems from his trade with 'the Indies', 'Tripolis' and 'Mexico' (1.3.16–17); and *A Midsummer Night's Dream* imagines trading ships 'rich with merchandise' sailing through the 'spicèd Indian air' (2.1.134, 124). Absent for the most part from these fantasies of global trade, however, are native Asians, Africans, and Americans, who are eclipsed by the commodities that their lands yield to European merchants. As Falstaff's remark suggests, however, the sexual conquest of women was easily understood on the model of European 'trade' with the East and West Indies. Troilus similarly sees Cressida as a 'pearl' in 'India', and himself as a 'merchant' venturing for her (1.1.96, 99). Yet in *The Merry Wives of Windsor*, the 'Indies' of East and West prove harder to master. The resistance of Mistress Ford and Mistress Page to Falstaff hardly constitutes a critique of the mercantile ventures that would pave the way for European colonialism and imperialism. But the play does suggest an imaginative space in which not only the (metaphorical) conquest of the Indies is doomed to fail but also its inhabitants volubly resist the man who would be their conqueror. This resistance is the theme of postcolonial theory.

'Postcolonial theory' is, in fact, the umbrella term for a cluster of very different theoretical tendencies concerned with the history and aftermath of European colonialism and empire. These tendencies can be grouped within three distinct phases. The first responded, in the decades after the Second World War, to the independence struggles of colonized nations in Africa and the West Indies. In this phase, postcolonial theory sought to liberate 'authentic' native voices that had been suppressed by colonial European hegemony. Writers from French colonies in the Caribbean and West Africa, including the Martiniquan poet Aimé Césaire, found solidarity in a common black identity and culture (or what they dubbed *négritude*) opposed to colonial racism. Influenced by Marxism and psychoanalysis, Frantz Fanon—Césaire's student—argued that the consciousness of colonized black subjects is not grounded in racial essence but in material conditions, including the European languages they are forced to learn. Decolonization therefore necessitates not only national independence but also repudiation of the world view implicit in colonial tongues. Fanon's influence led some anglophone African novelists and playwrights, such as the Kenyan Ngũgĩ wa Thiong'o, to reject English in favour of their native languages. Others, such as the Nigerian playwright, novelist, and poet Wole Soyinka, continued to write in English even as their work incorporated native African forms of narrative, ritual, and myth.

In its second phase, postcolonial theory entered into dialogue with the ideas of poststructuralist thinkers. Here the quest for native authenticity was superseded by a concern with problems of representation—epistemological, linguistic, political—as the grounds of both colonial hegemony and resistance. The defining work of this second phase was Edward Said's *Orientalism* (1978). Influenced in particular by Foucault's theory of power and knowledge, Said argued that European representations of the 'Orient' have repeatedly constructed Arabo-Islamic culture as an irrational feminine Other opposed to the rational masculine West. This manufactured difference, misrecognized as timeless and essential, confirms the supremacy of European identity as well as justifying colonialist intervention in the Arab world. Drawing on Derrida's critique of logocentrism, Gayatri Chakravorty Spivak theorized the complex relation of postcolonial subjects or 'subalterns' to representation in ways that go beyond Fanon's or Ngũgĩ's repudiation of colonial languages. In her influential essay 'Can the Subaltern Speak?' (1988), she argues that any attempt to advocate for Indian subalterns by granting them collective speech (in whatever tongue) makes a logocentric assumption of shared cultural identity amongst heterogeneous peoples, which serves to reproduce their subordinate position. And in his essay 'Of Mimicry and Man' (1994), Homi K. Bhabha, building on Lacan's notion of mimicry as a subversive camouflage, theorized the constitutive ambivalence of colonial discourse. Even as it insists that native subjects should reproduce European ideals of language, knowledge, and behaviour, colonial discourse is bedevilled by the spectre of native mimicry—an imperfect re-presentation that both reinforces the priority of the supposedly pure and authentic European ideal and discloses the lack that has always already haunted the latter.

In recent years, postcolonial theory has arguably embarked on a third phase. If the first was concerned with authenticity, and the second with representation, this new phase is preoccupied with movement: specifically, the movement of subaltern subjects and objects across borders of time as well as space. In this, it has suggestive affinities with rhizome and actor-network theory, inasmuch as it is interested in material objects, their migrations, and the assemblages they form with people. In *Provincializing Europe* (2000), Dipesh Chakrabarty explores how European conceptions of historiography and material culture have repeatedly presumed a linear conception of time that not only places the West at its cutting edge but also serves to strand non-European cultures in the 'waiting room of history (Chakrabarty 2000, 8). Chakrabarty theorizes what he terms subaltern 'time-knots'—entanglements of humans and things that, by tying together many times, suggest alternatives to Western linear chronology. And in *Queer Phenomenology* (2006), Sara Ahmed considers the question of 'orientation', whether to objects, sexual partners, or the Orient itself, and how postcolonial migrations can produce queer timelines and (dis)orientations.

Shakespeare's plays have been of recurrent interest to postcolonial writers, theorists and critics. Even if England was in Shakespeare's time not yet a global power, it had already succumbed to fantasies and practices that anticipate its later imperialist adventures. *Henry V* fantasizes the supposedly willing subjugation of Irish, Scottish, and Welsh subjects to English rule. Other plays refer to the English traffic not just in exotic commodities but also in alien people: we hear of how Englishmen will flock to see a 'dead Indian' (*The Tempest*, 2.2.31) and a 'strange Indian with the great tool' (*Henry VIII*, 5.3.32). And plays such as *Titus Andronicus* and *Othello* dramatize the European conquest and enslavement of African peoples. Shakespeare's drama does more, however, than simply stage the suppression of the subaltern: it also imagines colonial subjects speaking back to Europeans who would seek to (re)educate them. In *The Tempest*, the native islander Caliban tells his European enslavers: 'You taught me language, and my profit on't | Is I know how to curse' (1.2.366–7). As we will see, postcolonial writers have turned repeatedly to *The Tempest* to 'curse' Western tradition in its own language—a tradition that has often invoked Shakespeare's drama as the repository of supposedly universal truths and values. But *The Tempest* is not the only work by Shakespeare that postcolonial writers have used to displace European interpretive authority.

Antony and Cleopatra by Shayk al-Subair: Wole Soyinka

In his essay 'Shakespeare and the Living Dramatist' (1983), Wole Soyinka (1934–) notes how Shakespeare's drama very rarely captures the colourful details of its exotic locations. 'What country, friends, is this?' asks the newly shipwrecked Viola in *Twelfth Night* (1.2.1); the revelation that she is in Illyria is not especially consequential, because nothing in the play's language evokes the nation's physical or cultural distinctiveness. The Padua of *Taming of the Shrew*, the Vienna of *Measure for Measure*, and the Athens of *Midsummer Night's Dream*, *Two Noble Kinsmen*, and *Timon of Athens* are similarly exotic names rather than realistically evoked places. The Egypt of *Antony and Cleopatra*, however, stands as a notable exception. Think of Antony's verbal slideshow, on a Roman galley, about his Egyptian holiday:

> Thus do they, sir: they take the flow o' th' Nile
> By certain scale i' th' pyramid. They know
> By th' height, the lowness, or the mean, if dearth
> Or foison follow. The higher Nilus swells
> The more it promises; as it ebbs, the seedsman
> Upon the slime and ooze scatters his grain,
> And shortly comes to harvest.
>
> (2.7.16–22)

Or Cleopatra's outrage at the thought of being captured and killed by Caesar:

> Rather a ditch in Egypt
> Be gentle grave unto me; rather on Nilus' mud
> Lay me stark naked, and let the waterflies
> Blow me into abhorring; rather make
> My country's high pyramids my gibbet,
> And hang me up in chains.
>
> (5.2.57–62)

For many readers of the play, Shakespeare's Egypt exemplifies Edward Said's account of orientalism. Just as orientalist knowledge posits a sequence of related binary oppositions between a feminine, sensuous, irrational Orient and a masculine, sober, rational Europe, so too does *Antony and Cleopatra* assert a series of clear-cut distinctions between Egypt and Rome. The former is associated with the turbulent excesses of the Nile and Cleopatra; it is a feminine domain, given to hot sexual sport, and its element is fluidity. By contrast Rome is associated with the walled-in restraint of the Tiber and Caesar; it is a masculine realm, given to sobriety, and its element is marble. So is the Egyptian local colour noted by Soyinka simply Shakespeare's orientalist projection?

   To the contrary: Soyinka argues that Shakespeare has captured something authentic about Egypt beyond its pyramids, river, and waterflies. He notes that the play has held an enduring fascination for Arabic poets, playwrights, and readers. This is partly because of the singularities of the colonial situation in North Africa:

> The experience of colonized North Africa has been one of a cultural struggle between French and English cultures—beginning with their educational systems—wherein the literature is always centrally placed. Then there is the history of Arabic literature itself on which the Islamic culture placed a number of constraints from which the European culture became not merely a liberating but, in certain aspects, even a revolutionary force. At the heart of that literary culture—the European that is—stood Shakespeare, with his limitless universal themes, themes which were congenial to the Arabic epic—or narrative—tradition. (Soyinka 1983, 2–3)

However, Soyinka argues that the Arabic fascination with the play stems from more than the colonial legacy of European culture and the constraints of Islamic culture. The Egyptian playwright Ahmed Shawqi's drama *Masra'a Kliyupatra* (The Death of Cleopatra, 1929) may rewrite *Antony and Cleopatra* as an allegory of the Egyptian struggle for independence from the British, with Cleopatra recast as a woman torn between love for her country and love for Antony. But Shawqi's work had already been done for him by Shakespeare: if *Antony and Cleopatra*'s loving evocations of Egypt have repeatedly provoked in its Arabic-speaking readers, translators, and rewriters a nationalist nostalgia, that is because the nostalgia is already there in Shakespeare's play, desperate as it is to flee the 'holy, cold, and still conversation' (2.6.120) of northern lands for the profane warmth and vibrancy of Egypt. That is why, according to Soyinka, many in North Africa believe that Shakespeare 'must have sailed up the Nile and kicked up sands in the shadow of the pyramids to have etched the conflict of Rome on such a realistic canvas, evoking tones, textures, smells, and even tastes which were so alien to the wintry climes of Europe' (Soyinka 1983, 3). Some have even speculated that, to write *Antony and Cleopatra*, Shakespeare himself must have been an Arab. According to one Egyptian scholar, Shakespeare's real name, 'cleansed of its anglicized corruption, was Shayk al-Subair, which everyone knows of course is as dune-bred an Arabic name as any English poet can hope for' (Soyinka 1983, 2).

Soyinka is amused by the theory—so much so that he jokingly speculates that Shakespeare's wife was also an Arab named Hanna

Hathawa—but he also professes himself to be in sympathy with it. And this is not because he believes Shakespeare was familiar with the *specific* geographical terrain of Egypt. Rather, Shakespeare captures to perfection a *universal* mythopoetic domain figured by the divide between Rome and Egypt: 'It is not entirely by accident that the physical terrain in *Antony and Cleopatra* was the meeting point of the Orient and Occident—for Shakespeare, these had come to represent more than the mercantile or adventurers' stomping ground; they are absorbed into geographical equivalents of the turbulences which the poet observed in human nature' (Soyinka 1983, 4). The specific 'turbulence' that interests Soyinka is the conflict between life and death. We see this conflict in numerous other plays, but Shakespeare elsewhere never understands death the way he does in *Antony and Cleopatra*. In Soyinka's reading, the play repeatedly imagines death as a mythic phenomenon in a way that 'can only be fully absorbed by an Egyptian, or one steeped in the esoteric cults of Egypt and allied religions, including Islam' (Soyinka 1983, 6). He argues, for example, that Cleopatra channels the cult of Osiris when she asks 'is it sin | To rush into the secret house of death | Ere death come to us?' (4.16.82–4). Soyinka also contrasts Othello's death scene with that of Cleopatra. Whereas the Moor of Venice is suffused with a sense of loss for what he has thrown away in his life, the Egyptian queen—asp at her breast—heaps scorn on the mundane vanities of the world and embraces a transcendent death that, fully Egyptian, bears the hallmarks of the Isis cult. For Soyinka, Othello's death scene is obviously the work of William Shakespeare; Cleopatra's, by contrast, is the work of Shayk al-Subair, the man who understands the real Egypt.

Soyinka's tone is ironic throughout his essay even as he is serious in attributing to Shakespeare an understanding of death that explains his appeal to Arabic writers. However, if death is an 'undiscovered country' (*Hamlet*, 3.1.81) and in *Antony in Cleopatra* that country is Egypt, there is still something uncannily Anglo-Saxon about Soyinka's account of it. All death's trappings might be Egyptian: 'The unearthly moisture of suicide, the aspic's trail of slime on fig-leaves transports us to this totally alien earth, and I mean alien, not from the view of Shakespeare's culture alone'. But 'this totally alien earth' reconfigures itself into something familiar to us from Anglo-American critical tradition: 'This is yet another world opening inwards from the mundane one into which we have already been inducted by some of the most unnerving imageries in poetic drama: a yoking of approaching bodily corruption with the essence-draining paradox of birth and infancy closes the fatal cycle of the union of opposites that began with the aspic's slime' (Soyinka 1983, 7). The transcendent power of paradox: this is Cleanth Brooks's vision of the poetic imagination—albeit converted into the mythopoetic register that distinguishes the work of Soyinka's mentor at the University of Leeds, G. Wilson Knight, author of a study of mythic themes in Shakespeare. How 'authentic' is Shakespeare's 'Arab' vision when Shayk al-Subair starts sounding suspiciously like an American formalist or a British mythopoeticist? Little wonder, perhaps, that Soyinka has been repeatedly lambasted by African proponents of *négritude* and decolonization for 'importing imagery from alien environments' (Chinweizu, Jemie, and Madubuike 1983, 168).

Yet such a charge misses the effect of Soyinka's irony—which is not the same as saying that he doesn't mean a word of what he says. Soyinka might insist on the universal truth of Shakespeare's representation of death in *Antony and Cleopatra*. But in Soyinka's rendering, this is a counter-intuitively *local* universalism, born on African soil. Shakespeare's African universalism represents less a Brooksian paradox than an ironic decentring of European critical tradition. Here it might be useful to think of Soyinka's strategy in terms of Homi Bhabha's theory of colonial mimicry. Soyinka mimics—respectfully— the interpretive strategies of Brooks and Wilson Knight. Yet his mimicry foregrounds the cultural location of its instantiation: he performs mythic formalism with an African accent. Soyinka has elsewhere insisted that the critic is 'a socially situated producer', and laments the tendency for critics to universalize their contingent positions (Soyinka 1984, 29). He thus reads contingency—his African location—back into his version of the universal. Moreover, just as Bhabha argues that colonial mimicry reveals something impure in the origin that it copies, so too does Soyinka's African universalism expose the trace of the local in the universalist models it reproduces. He cites another well-known adapter of Shakespeare: 'The ideological interrogatories which a Marxist playwright like Brecht injects into his versions of Shakespeare, such as *Coriolanus*, are normal developments in European literary and dramatic sensibilities' (Soyinka 1983, 2).

For all that Brecht insists himself on the social situatedness of the critic and dramatist, his reinterpretation of *Coriolanus* has been recuperated as a 'normal development' of a literary and dramatic sensibility that is less European than universal, or rather, European *therefore* universal. Soyinka's reading of *Antony and Cleopatra*, with its jolting African universalism, implicitly asks us to recognize that the universalism of critics like Brooks and Wilson Knight, or of writers like Brecht (whose *Threepenny Opera* Soyinka adapted for an African setting), is every bit as locally situated as his own. Soyinka thus uses Shakespeare to rewrite the script of theory.

Caribbean *Tempests*: Edward Said

By contrast, as Edward Said (1935–2003) notes in *Culture and Imperialism*, other postcolonial writers use theory to rewrite the script of Shakespeare, specifically *The Tempest*. In *Orientalism*, Said presents Shakespeare largely as a precursor and instrument of orientalist knowledge. Shakespeare's drama uses the 'Orient' as a synonym for a homogeneously exotic East, and in ways that help constitute a Europe defined in opposition to it. This is the case in *Othello*, where 'the Orient and Islam are always represented as outsiders having a special role to play *inside* Europe' (Said 1978, 71). Said's subsequent project, *Culture and Imperialism* (1994), views Shakespeare's texts and their horizons of possibility somewhat differently. The book began as a sequel to *Orientalism*: Said sought to show that, just as Europe was in large part constituted by its orientalist knowledge about Arabo-Islamic cultures, so too did its self-definition depend on discourses about Africa, the Caribbean, and other non-European cultures. Yet the more Said read, the more he was struck by a phenomenon that he had largely neglected in *Orientalism*: 'Never was it the case that the imperial encounter pitted an active Western intruder against a supine or inert non-Western native; there was *always* some form of active resistance, and in the overwhelming majority of cases, the resistance finally won out' (Said 1994, p. xii). *Culture and Imperialism* is devoted to theorizing this resistance and its strategies. The main battle in imperialism, Said argues, is waged over land; yet issues of land ownership, settlement, work, and future development are always at root battles over narrative. Hence Said is interested in resistance narratives of culture and nation, and it is here that Shakespeare—specifically, Shakespeare's play *The Tempest*—has played a crucial role in anticolonial struggles.

In his chapter on 'Resistance and Opposition', Said considers how colonized cultures often rewrite key Western narratives and motifs about their territories. For example, aspects of Joseph Conrad's *Heart of Darkness* have been reworked by African writers, like Ngũgĩ, who lend an Afrocentric perspective to Conrad's tale of a nightmare voyage up the Congo river. Shakespeare's *The Tempest*, probably inspired by an account of an English shipwreck on Bermuda in 1608, has been similarly reclaimed by writers from the Caribbean. Perhaps the best known of these is Aimé Césaire's adaptation, *Une Tempête* (1968). According to Said, Césaire is motivated by 'an affectionate contention with Shakespeare for the right to represent the Caribbean' (Said 1994, 212–13). Shakespeare's Caliban, the half-African native inhabitant of the island, resists his European master Prospero; but his resistance—including his attempted rape of Prospero's daughter Miranda—is presented as evidence of his barbaric nature. In other words, Shakespeare's play does little to undermine Prospero's characterization of Caliban as 'A devil, a born devil, on whose nature | Nurture can never stick' (4.1.188–9). In Césaire's adaptation, by contrast, Caliban's resistance is the product of his keen knowledge of himself, Prospero, and Prospero's strategies of domination:

> Prospero, you are the master of illusion.
> Lying is your trademark.
> And you have lied so much to me
> (lied about the world, lied about me)
> that you have ended by imposing on me
> an image of myself.
> Underdeveloped, you brand me, inferior,
> That is the way you have forced me to see myself
> I detest that image! What's more, it's a lie!
> But now I know you, you old cancer,
> and I know myself as well.
>
> (Césaire 1990, 162)

Such a speech shows how Césaire's adaptation is, in Said's words, 'part of a grander effort to discover the bases of an integral identity different from the formerly dependent, derivative one' (Said 1994, 213).

That 'integral identity' represents, for Césaire, the timeless essence of *négritude*. But Said notes that Caliban's identity has also been reconceived in less essentialist, though equally exemplary, terms. In *The Pleasures of Exile*, the Barbados writer George Lamming argues that Caliban's identity should be seen as stemming not from his biology but from processes of history. Once Caliban can recognize himself as an independent historical agent rather than an instrument of others' development, he will acquire a capacity for growth to which only Europeans had previously been entitled. It is significant that in *The Tempest* Prospero's daughter, Miranda, is considered educable, whereas Caliban is not: he is an 'Abhorrèd slave, | Which any print of goodness wilt not take' (1.2.354–5). In other words, the play itself gives him an 'integral identity' that refuses improvement by European elements. But other Caribbean interventions in *The Tempest* take issue with any pure or essentialist conception of subaltern identity, noting that Caliban is, for all his refusal of European 'goodness' or civility, an irreducibly hybrid character who mingles African and European, human and beast. Writing in opposition to the Uruguayan essayist José Enrique Rodó, who had read the airy spirit Ariel as a figure for the pure Latin American and the mongrel Caliban as a figure for the oppressive Yankee imperialist, the Cuban philosopher and poet Roberto Fernández Retamar valorizes Caliban's hybridity, which, as Said suggests, is 'truer to the Creole, or *mestizo* composite of the new America' (Said 1994, 213).

Said sees Césaire's, Lamming's, Rodó's, and Retamar's interventions in *The Tempest* as staging different responses to the question: 'How does a culture seeking to become independent of imperialism imagine its own past?' (Said 1994, 214). All four responses entail a choice between the two native inhabitants of the island, Ariel and Caliban. Rodó advocates doing as Ariel does, willingly serving Prospero in order to gain his freedom and return to his native element—a strategy that resembles that of the bourgeois native who supports the colonists in the hope of gaining independence. Amongst those who reject Ariel, Lamming and Retamar tout an impure Caliban who looks to a new future; Césaire embraces a pure Caliban, who sheds his disfigurements in order to reclaim his essential, pre-colonial self. Said too is a Calibanist; but rather than pick one version of Caliban over the other, he argues that 'Both Calibans nourish and require each other' (Said 1994, 214). A sense of a pre-colonial self, Said maintains, is a foundational condition for anti-imperialist nationalism. Yet that decolonized self also has to recognize that nationalism can lead to violent chauvinism and that replacing white rulers with black ones does not necessarily guarantee liberation. Instead, Said argues, 'It is best when Caliban sees his own history as an aspect of the history of *all* subjugated men and women, and comprehends the complex truth of his own social and historical situation' (Said 1994, 214).

'*All* subjugated men and women': the universalism of Said's appeal is somewhat qualified, however, by the fact that his discussion of *The Tempest* and its rewritings offers only a circumscribed range of Shakespearian subject positions from which to resist colonialist hegemony. Other Caribbean rewriters of *The Tempest* have suggested intriguing alternatives to the straightforwardly masculine Ariel/Caliban choice considered by Said. For the Barbados poet Edward Kamau Brathwaite, Caliban's dead mother Sycorax is the computerized representative of a native writing that precedes yet also represents an innovative alternative to Prospero's; she thus provides a key with which to unlock and escape the prison-house of the Caribbean colonizer's language. The Jamaican-American novelist Michelle Cliff turns to *The Tempest* to imagine a more androgynous set of cross-identifications, seeing herself as an unstable aggregate of Caliban, Ariel, and Miranda. If the subaltern speaks in Cliff's work, it is not in a singular voice that presumes the logocentric homogeneity critiqued by Gayatri Spivak. And if we shift out of the Caribbean and consider an adaptation of *The Tempest* from another formerly colonized island—the Mauritian playwright Dev Virahsaw-my's *Toufann* (1991)—we might encounter another heterodox form of anti-colonialism. *Toufann* (Hindi and Urdu for 'Tempest') is set in a computer-generated harbour, home to Prospero and Kalibann. Yet Virahsawmy also provides a queer plotline in the form of a relationship between Ferdjinan and Aryel, whose shared bathtub provides an unexpected site of queer resistance to Prospero's hetero-normative and racist schemes.

Shakespeare's Subcontinental Books: Sara Ahmed

A queer postcolonial Shakespeare is imagined also by the British theorist Sara Ahmed (1969–). In a series of studies that includes *Difference That Matters: Feminist Theory and Postmodernism* (1998) and *Strange Encounters: Embodied Others in Post-Coloniality* (2000), Ahmed examines the experiences of non-normative bodies and subjectivities. Her emphasis on embodied experience draws on and critiques the philosophical method called phenomenology, associated primarily with the German thinker Edmund Husserl, who argued that consciousness is always consciousness of an object—albeit inflected by experience of one's body. Near the end of her book *The Cultural Politics of Emotion* (2004), which considers issues of embodiment and emotion in the spheres of terrorism, migration, and political asylum, Ahmed poses the possibility of a 'queer phenomenology'. This, she suggests, 'might offer an approach to "sexual orientation" by rethinking the place of the object in sexual desire, attending to how bodily directions "toward" some objects and not others affects how bodies inhabit spaces, and spaces inhabit bodies' (Ahmed 2004, 166). Ahmed expands this provisional definition in her study *Queer Phenomenology* (2006). Throughout the book, she demonstrates how our orientation to objects depends on our embodied position in relation to the world. We know things only inasmuch as we perceive them along the 'line' of our orientation. The line we follow, however, prevents us from other possible orientations. Ahmed writes: 'The lines that allow us to find our way, those that are "in front" of us also make certain things, and not others, available. . . . When we follow specific lines, some things become reachable and others remain or even become out of reach' (Ahmed 2006, 14). Ahmed considers normative lines—heterosexual family lines, white racial lines—which, in their reiteration, shape the orientations of bodies towards their objects. But she also theorizes queer or oblique lines, which deviate from convention by orientating themselves towards unexpected objects. These queer lines resemble Gilles Deleuze's theory of lines of flight, abstract lines that transform or deterritorialize a multiplicity by connecting it to other multiplicities.

Crucially, Ahmed's analysis thinks through the relation between orientation and the Orient. The latter is not only a direction that shapes embodied experience (everyone stands in relation to an east as well as a west). It is also a reified space that presumes normative lines of orientation—that is, Western subjects oriented both *towards* a homogeneous non-Europe and *around* their whiteness. Building on the work of Frantz Fanon, Ahmed applies a queer phenomenology to questions of orientalism and race. Fanon had argued that European colonialism forces non-white bodies to assume white orientations. As a result, colonial subjects are alienated from themselves: 'Racism ensures that the black gaze returns to the black body, which is not a loving return but rather follows the line of the hostile white gaze. The disorientation affected by racism diminishes capacities for action' (Ahmed 2006, 111). Here Ahmed considers the etymology of 'direction', whose meaning is linked to straightening or correction (making *recto* or right). An orientation is a direction, inasmuch as it both points a certain way and serves as a straightening device. Yet in their oblique orientations, certain bodies deviate from the straight lines of normative direction. For example, colonial and postcolonial migrations have resulted in mixed-race bodies that refuse the purity of racial and familial lines. From the perspective of a queer phenomenology, however, mixed-race bodies foreground how such lines were never pure to begin with. Despite the matronymic suppressions conventionally performed in the name of the father, the family is never a singular line; it consists of multiple oblique lines that are nominally parenthesized in favour of one parent. Mixed-race bodies can thus remind us how hybridity is not a deviation from a prior purity but the very condition of existence: every subject and object has a mixed genealogy. Direction in its literal etymological sense, however, is the means by which that mixture is suppressed.

It is in this context that Ahmed recounts a memory of a beloved object from her childhood. The object is easily pressured into tracing a singular line of normative whiteness as well as familial inheritance. Yet its unusual history of migration also discloses a mixed genealogy that prompts Ahmed to tease out oblique lines of orientation:

The object from Pakistan that made the greatest impression on me was an old, battered set of Shakespeare's plays. How I loved those books, with their ripped covers and failed bindings. My love came in part from the story around them. During partition my family left India to become citizens of the newly formed Pakistan. It was an imperial journey, and a hard and painful one. How I liked to hear about this journey, as if I could follow the line, as if my life did follow the line they took. After their arrival in Model Town, Lahore, they found the books—left in the house by those who had left in a hurry. The books were given to my father by his father, who found them in the house that received him, which had taken him in. How off that these objects, reachable at home for me as the objects that arrived from Pakistan, should be the works of Shakespeare. They pointed to England, and one could say that I followed the point. Back to English words, English culture, English history. (Ahmed 2006, 151–2)

In Ahmed's autobiographical tale, the Shakespeare books trace normative colonial and familial lines. The books are patrilineal talismans, handed down from father to son; they also direct Ahmed towards England. Yet there is something odd, something queer, about the books' trajectories. For, as Ahmed notes, 'even if the books seemed to direct me to England and to another space, they also always took me back to another time, a time in which my family made the long journey to Lahore. Although the books of Shakespeare might have seemed to lead me to England, in some ways they took me back to Lahore. After all, I never developed an interest in Shakespeare' (Ahmed 2006, 152). Shakespeare's books thus acquire, like Ahmed herself, a mixed English and Pakistani ancestry. And even their Pakistani genealogy is not singular. It is complicated by the dislocations of Partition that saw the books migrate (without physically moving) from a presumably Hindu family in British India to a Muslim family in post-independence Pakistan.

The migration of Shakespeare's books through space and time points to the histories of colonialism in the Indian subcontinent. Yet if the printed matter of these books was once pressed into serving British colonial hegemony—as an instrument of English language instruction in order to disseminate supposedly enduring English truths and values—the books as objects are, as Ahmed's story shows, not quite so straightforwardly Anglocentric. They become the latter only when reified as tokens of imperialism, when their orientation follows normative white directions. Yet they point also in oblique directions, making connections with unexpected times and places. The books are a spatially and temporally multiple assemblage, or what Dipesh Chakrabarty calls *shomoy-granthi*—his Bengali term for the subaltern time-knot that disorients the linear timelines of European historiography (Chakrabarty 2000, 112).

Ahmed's disoriented Shakespeare reappears in the index to her book. Look there for Shakespeare, and you may not find him. For his name is out of order, coming not immediately before 'Shame', as one would expect. Instead, it follows 'Skeggs, Beverly'. In *Queer Phenomenology*, then, Shakespeare is disoriented—or, rather, reoriented. Ahmed's Shakespeare traces oblique lines that deviate from the orderly directions of alphabetization and white Englishness. This is a suggestive metaphor for how postcolonial theory gets to work on Shakespeare. The African universalism of Soyinka's reading of *Antony and Cleopatra* and the Caribbean rewritings of *The Tempest* theorized by Said also transform Shakespeare's orientations. Postcolonial theory disorients both Shakespeare's cultural lines and our understanding of his written lines: that is, it finds in those lines mixed genealogies that do not simply reproduce the authority of England or Europe.

Ahmed's disoriented books also provide a powerful illustration of how Shakespeare functions in relation to theory. The theorists I have examined throughout this book each transform and reconfigure Shakespeare, dispatching his writings—and us—in new directions. Our theoretical migrations with Shakespeare's books may recall the adventures of Prospero's books, which accompany him in his exile from Europe. Under the aegis of theory, Shakespeare's books are likewise exiled from their original settings, dispatched to exotic locales, and challenged by dissident Calibans. Ahmed, like so many of the theorists I have considered here, shows how Shakespeare's books have no singular place; instead they materialize diverse orientations and disorientations. Theory too is both orientation and disorientation, a way of getting one's bearings but also of creatively losing them and finding oneself in unexpected locations. But it is not as if theory makes Shakespeare move to places where he wouldn't otherwise be found. His writing, in its complex movements and its moving contemplations, is not just theory's object but also one of its enabling horizons of possibility. For if theory performs a disorientation that is simultaneously a reorientation, Shakespeare's writing has been doing something similar all along. Polonius might observe, in *Hamlet*, that 'we of wisdom and of reach...by indirections find directions out' (2.1.63, 65). But Polonius, typically, gets things back to front. For if, as Ahmed says, 'direction' is etymologically related to 'straightening', then Shakespeare's writing has proved to be such an enduring theoretical resource precisely because it can continue to make us turn from the straight and narrow path of what we think we know, who we think we are, and how we think we should act. That is, Shakespeare's books—and Shakespeare's bookish theoric—can help us to 'by directions find indirections out'.

General introductions to 'Shakespearian theory' are hard to come by. Books on the subject tend to be either highly specialized studies of a few select theorists, or exercises in Iagoist debunking of 'bookish theoric'. For the former, see Stephen Bretzius's *Shakespeare in Theory* (Bretzius 1997), which has chapters on de Man and Greenblatt; for the latter, see Brian Vickers's *Appropriating Shakespeare* (Vickers 1993) and Graham Bradshaw's *Misrepresentations* (Bradshaw 1993), which take aim at poststructuralist and materialist literary theory respectively. A notable exception is Richard Wilson's book *Shakespeare in French Theory* (Wilson 2007); its discussions of Cixous, Deleuze, Derrida, Foucault, and Girard (amongst other theorists) are repeatedly fair and insightful.

Readers interested in specific theoretical movements and their engagement of Shakespeare will find the pantry rather less bare. A useful general survey of formalism and Shakespeare is offered in the second chapter of Michael Taylor's *Shakespeare Criticism and the Twentieth Century* (Taylor 2001). Lars Engle provides a particularly illuminating overview of 'William Empson and the Sonnets' (Engle 2007). Although there is little available material on Shakespeare and structuralism, there is a profusion of studies of poststructuralist approaches to Shakespeare: for helpful introductions, see Christopher Norris's essay in *Alternative Shakespeares* (Norris 1985) and the edited collection *Shakespeare and Deconstruction* (Atkins and Bergeron 1988). David Schalkwyk's *Literature and the Touch of the Real* (Schalkwyk 2004) offers an outstandingly clear and thought-provoking discussion of Derrida's essay on *Romeo and Juliet*. Not much has yet been written on Shakespeare and rhizome or actor-network theory. So-called 'transversal theory', a largely Shakespearian field of performance studies, draws much of its impetus from the work of Deleuze and Guattari; see *Performing Transversally* (Reynolds 2003). My own book, *Untimely Matter in the Time of Shakespeare* (Harris 2008), reads Serres's theorization of time as a crumpled handkerchief in relation to Shakespeare. And Julian Yates's essay 'Accidental Shakespeare' provides an excellent introduction to actor-network theory and Shakespeare studies (Yates 2006). None of these discussions, however, considers how Deleuze, Serres, and Latour themselves read (or act with) Shakespeare.

There are a number of very good books on Shakespeare's constitutive role in psychoanalysis. Philip Armstrong's *Shakespeare in Psychoanalysis*

(Armstrong 2001) is an excellent introduction to the uncanny affinities between Freud, Lacan, and Shakespeare. For the more advanced reader, Julia Reinhard Lupton and Kenneth Reinhard's *After Oedipus* (Lupton and Reinhard 1993) works with Freud's essay on 'The Theme of the Three Caskets' to offer sophisticated yet clear readings of *Hamlet*, *King Lear*, and Lacan's seminar on the ethics of psychoanalysis. For a history of feminist criticism of Shakespeare, see the first section of *The Feminist Companion to Shakespeare* (Callaghan 2000). Surprisingly little has been written about Cixous's theoretical writing on Shakespeare; Lynn Penrod's book on Cixous, however, notes her references to *Hamlet*, *Julius Caesar*, and other plays (Penrod 1996). The Shakespearian component of queer theory has been less remarked upon, but Madhavi Menon's extraordinary edited collection *Shakesqueer* (Menon 2010)—which includes essays on every one of Shakespeare's plays and narrative poems by contemporary queer theorists (including Lee Edelman's reading of *Hamlet*)—more than remedies that deficit.

There have been numerous studies of Marxist criticism of Shakespeare, but far less on how Marxist theorists—including Marx himself—read Shakespeare. Gabriel Egan's *Shakespeare and Marx* (Egan 2004) considers Marx's reading of *Timon of Athens*; also well worth consulting is Peter Stallybrass's essay on Marx's haunting by Shakespeare in Jean Howard and Scott Cutler Shershow's edited collection, *Marxist Shakespeares* (Stallybrass 2001). The same volume contains Richard Halpern's intelligent critical response to Derrida's reading of *Hamlet* and Marx (Halpern 2001). For a particularly illuminating discussion of how Brecht read Shakespeare, see Margot Heinemann's contribution to *Political Shakespeare* (Heinemann 1985). Because new historicism's and cultural materialism's leading practitioners are themselves Shakespearians, there is no dearth of critical literature on how each movement reads Shakespeare. An excellent overview is John Brannigan's book, *New Historicism and Cultural Materialism* (Brannigan 1998). For discussions of how postcolonial theory thinks with Shakespeare, readers will find much to ponder in Fredric Jameson's introduction to the English translation of Roberto Fernández Retamar's *Caliban and Other Essays* (Retamar 1989). Jonathan Goldberg provides an excellent summary of Caribbean rewritings and theorizations of *The Tempest* in *Tempest in the Caribbean* (Goldberg 2003). But it is hard to improve on Chantal Zabus's *Tempests after Shakespeare* (Zabus 2002), which provides an extensive discussion of postcolonial, postpatriarchal, and postmodern rewritings of the play from around the world.

Finally, I must recommend one study in particular, to which this book is greatly indebted. Any reader interested in how Shakespeare continues to haunt modern and postmodern culture, including theory, will learn much from the work of Marjorie Garber. Her book *Shakespeare's Ghost Writers* (Garber 1986) remains the most thoughtful and thought-provoking account of Shakespeare's 'uncanny causality'—the ways in which theorists, even when they criticize canonical authority, repeatedly turn to Shakespeare to lend authority to their critique. *Shakespeare's Ghost Writers* was the first sustained study of 'Shakespearian theory'; it remains the best.

Works Cited

Adorno, Theodor W. (1984). *Aesthetic Theory*. Trans. C. Lenhardt. Ed. Gretel Adorno and Rolf Tiedemann. London: Routledge

Ahmed, Sara (2004). *The Cultural Politics of Emotion*. New York: Routledge

—— (2006). *Queer Phenomenology: Orientations, Objects, Others*. Durham, NC: Duke University Press

Armstrong, Philip (2001). *Shakespeare in Psychoanalysis*. London: Routledge

Atkins, G. Douglas and David M. Bergeron (1988). Eds. *Shakespeare and Deconstruction*. New York: Peter Lang

Bakhtin, Mikhail (1981). *Rabelais and His World*. Trans. Hélène Iswolsky. Bloomington, Ind.: Indiana University Press

—— (1984). *Problems of Dostoyevsky's Poetics*. Trans. Caryl Emerson. Minneapolis: University of Minnesota Press

Barnfield, Richard (1598). *Poems: In Divers Humors*. London

Barthes, Roland (1972). *Mythologies*. Trans. Annette Lavers. New York: Hill and Wang

Benjamin, Walter (1969). *Illuminations*. Trans. Harry Zohn. Ed. Hannah Arendt. New York: Schocken

Bloom, Harold (1999). *Shakespeare: The Invention of the Human*. New York: Riverhead

Bradshaw, Graham (1993). *Misrepresentations: Shakespeare and the Materialists*. Ithaca, NY: Cornell University Press

Brannigan, John (1998). *New Historicism and Cultural Materialism*. New York: St Martin's Press

Brecht, Bertolt (1992). *Brecht on Theatre: The Development of an Aesthetic*. Ed. John Willet. New York: Hill and Wang

Bretzius, Stephen (1997). *Shakespeare in Theory: The Postmodern Academy and the Early Modern Theatre*. Ann Arbor: University of Michigan Press

Brooks, Cleanth (1947). *The Well-Wrought Urn: Studies in the Structure of Poetry*. New York: Reynal & Hitchcock

Callaghan, Dympna C. (2000). Ed. *A Feminist Companion to Shakespeare*. Oxford: Blackwell

Césaire, Aimé (1990). *Lyric and Dramatic Poetry 1946–82*. Trans. Clayton Eshleman and Annette Smith. Charlottesville: University of Virginia Press

Chakrabarty, Dipesh (2000). *Provincializing Europe: Postcolonial Thought and Historical Difference*. Princeton: Princeton University Press

Chinweizu, Onwuchekwa Jemie, and Ihechukwu Madubuike (1983). *Toward the Decolonization of African Literature, Volume I: African Fiction and Poetry and Their Critics*. Washington, DC: Howard University Press

Cixous, Hélène (1976). 'Laugh of the Medusa'. Trans. K. Cohen and P. Cohen. *Signs: Journal of Women in Culture and Society* 1 (1976): 875–94

—— (1986). 'Sorties: Ways Out/Attacks/ Forays'. Hélène Cixous and Catherine Clément, *The Newly Born Woman*. Trans. Betsy Wing. Minneapolis: University of Minnesota Press. 63–132

Deleuze, Gilles (1997). 'One Less Manifesto'. Timothy Murray. Ed. *Mimesis, Masochism, and Mime*. Ann Arbor: University of Michigan Press. 239–58

—— (2004). *Difference and Repetition*. Trans. Paul Patton. London: Continuum

Deleuze, Gilles and Félix Guattari (1987). *A Thousand Plateaus: Capitalism and Schizophrenia*. Trans. Brian Massumi. Minneapolis: University of Minnesota Press

de Man, Paul (1983). *Blindness and Insight: Essays in the Rhetoric of Contemporary Criticism*. 2nd edn. Minneapolis: University of Minnesota Press

—— (1984). *The Rhetoric of Romanticism*. New York: Columbia University Press

Derrida, Jacques (1967). *De la grammatologie*. Paris: Minuit

—— (1992). *Acts of Literature*. Ed. Derek Attridge. New York and London: Routledge

—— (1994). *Specters of Marx: The State of the Debt, the Work of Mourning, and the New International*. Trans. Peggy Kamuf. New York and London: Routledge

—— (1998). *Archive Fever: A Freudian Impression*. Trans. Eric Prenowitz. Chicago: University of Chicago Press

—— (2005). *Apprendre à vivre enfin: Entretien avec Jean Birnbaum*. Paris: Galilée

Dollimore, Jonathan (1991). *Sexual Dissidence: Augustine to Wilde, Freud to Foucault*. Oxford: Clarendon Press

Eagleton, Terry (1986). *William Shakespeare*. Oxford: Basil Blackwell

—— (1999). 'Marxism Without Marxism'. Michael Sprinker. Ed. *Ghostly Demarcations: A Symposium on Jacques Derrida's Spectres of Marx*. London: Verso. 83–7

Edelman, Lee (2004). *No Future: Queer Theory and the Death Drive*. Durham, NC: Duke University Press

—— (2010). 'Hamlet's Wounded Name'. Madhavi Menon. Ed. *Shakesqueer* Durham, NC: Duke University Press

Egan, Gabriel (2004). *Shakespeare and Marx*. Oxford: Oxford University Press

Empson, William (1963). *Seven Types of Ambiguity*. 3rd edn. London: Chatto and Windus

—— (1967). *The Structure of Complex Words*. Ann Arbor: University of Michigan Press

Engle, Lars (2007). 'William Empson and the Sonnets'. Michael Schoenfeldt. Ed. *A Companion to Shakespeare's Sonnets*. Oxford: Blackwell. 163–82

Foucault, Michel (1973). *Madness and Civilization: A History of Insanity in the Age of Reason*. Trans. Richard Howard. New York: Vintage

—— (1978). *The History of Sexuality: An Introduction*, vol. i. Trans. Robert Hurley. New York: Pantheon

—— (1979). *Power/Knowledge: Selected Interviews and Other Writings, 1972–1977*. Ed. Colin Gordon. New York: Pantheon

—— (1985). 'Dream, Imagination, and Existence'. Michel Foucault and Ludwig Biswanger. *Dream and Existence*. Trans. Forrest Williams and Jacob Needleman. Ed. Keith Hoeller. Seattle, Wash.: Review of Existential Psychology and Psychiatry. 29–78

Freud, Sigmund (1966). *The Complete Psychological Works of Sigmund Freud*. Trans. James Strachey. London: Hogarth

—— (1997). *Writings on Art and Literature*. Stanford, Calif.: Stanford University Press

—— (2000). *Three Essays on the Theory of Sexuality*. Trans. James Strachey. New York: Basic Books

Gallagher, Catherine and Stephen Greenblatt (2001). *Practicing New Historicism*. Chicago: University of Chicago Press

Garber, Marjorie (1986). *Shakespeare's Ghost Writers: Literature as Uncanny Causality*. London: Methuen

Girard, René (1978). *'To double business bound': Essays on Literature, Mimesis, and Anthropology*. Baltimore: Johns Hopkins University Press

Godzich, Wlad (1986). 'Foreword: The Tiger on the Paper Mat'. Paul de Man. *The Resistance to Theory*. Minneapolis: University of Minnesota Press. pp. ix–xviii

Goldberg, Jonathan (2003). *Tempest in the Caribbean*. Minneapolis: University of Minnesota Press

Greenblatt, Stephen (1988). *Shakespearean Negotiations: The Circulation of Social Energy in Renaissance England*. Berkeley and Los Angeles: University of California Press

—— (1989). 'Towards a Poetics of Culture'. H. Aram Veeser. Ed. *The New Historicism*. Berkeley and Los Angeles: University of California Press

Halpern, Richard (2001). 'An Impure History of Ghosts: Derrida, Marx, Shakespeare'. Jean E. Howard and Scott Cutler Shershow. Eds. *Marxist Shakespeares*. London: Routledge. 31–52

Harris, Jonathan Gil (2008). *Untimely Matter in the Time of Shakespeare*. Philadelphia: University of Pennsylvania Press

Heinemann, Margot (1985). 'How Brecht Read Shakespeare'. Jonathan Dollimore and Alan Sinfield. Eds. *Political Shakespeare: New Essays in Cultural Materialism*. Manchester: Manchester University Press. 226–54

Holderness, Graham (1988). Ed. *The Shakespeare Myth*. Manchester: Manchester University Press

Jakobson, Roman (1987). *Language in Literature*. Ed. Krystyna Pomorska and Stephen Rudy. Cambridge, Mass.: Harvard University Press

Jameson, Fredric (1981). *The Political Unconscious: Narrative As A Socially Symbolic Act*. Ithaca, NY: Cornell University Press

—— (1995). 'Radicalizing Radical Shakespeare: The Permanent Revolution in Shakespeare Studies'. Ivo Kamps. Ed. *Materialist Shakespeare: A History*. London: Verso. 320–8

—— (1999). 'Marx's Purloined Letter'. Michael Sprinker. Ed. *Ghostly Demarcations: A Symposium on Jacques Derrida's Spectres of Marx*. London: Verso. 26–67

Johnson, Samuel (1969). *Johnson on Shakespeare*. Ed. Arthur Sherbo. New Haven: Yale University Press

Jones, Ernest (1954). *Hamlet and Oedipus: A Classic Study in the Psychoanalysis of Literature*. New York: Doubleday

Klein, Melanie (1957). *Envy and Gratitude: A Study of Unconscious Sources*. London: Tavistock

Kristeva, Julia (1982). *Powers of Horror: An Essay on Abjection*. Trans. Leon S. Roudiez. New York: Columbia University Press

—— (1987). *Tales of Love*. Trans. Leon S. Roudiez. New York: Columbia University Press

Lacan, Jacques (1977). *Écrits*. Trans. Alan Sheridan. New York: Norton

—— (1982). 'Desire and the Interpretation of Desire in *Hamlet*'. Shoshana Felman. Ed. *Literature and Psychoanalysis*. Baltimore: Johns Hopkins University Press. 11–52

Latour, Bruno (1993). *We Have Never Been Modern*. Trans. Catherine Porter. Cambridge, Mass.: Harvard University Press

—— (2008). 'From Realpolitik to Dingpolitik, Or How To Make Things Public'. Bruno Latour and Peter Weibel. Eds. *Making Things Public: Atmospheres of Democracy*. Cambridge, Mass.: MIT Press. 14–41

Lévi-Strauss, Claude (1958). 'La Structure des mythes'. *Anthropologie structurale*. Paris: Plon

Lukács, Georg (1983). *The Historical Novel*. Trans. Hannah Mitchell and Stanley Mitchell. Lincoln, Nebr.: University of Nebraska Press

Lupton, Julia Reinhard, and Kenneth Reinhard (1993). *After Oedipus: Shakespeare in Psychoanalysis*. Ithaca, NY: Cornell University Press

Macray, William Dunn (1886). *The Pilgrimage to Parnassus: With the Two Parts of The Return from Parnassus*. Oxford: Clarendon Press

Marx, Karl (1975). *The Marx-Engels Reader*. Ed. Robert C. Tucker. 2nd edn. New York: Norton

Marx, Karl and Friedrich Engels (1975) 'The Manifesto of the Communist Party'. *The Marx-Engels Reader*. Robert C. Tucker. Ed. 2nd edn. New York: Norton. 469–500

Menon, Madhavi (2010). Ed. *Shakesqueer: The Queer Companion to Shakespeare*. Ralegh, NC: Duke University Press

Meres, Francis (1598). *Palladis Tamia: Wit's Treasury*. London

Miller, J. Hillis (1986). 'Ariachne's Broken Woof'. Laurie Lanzen Harris and Mark W. Scott. Eds. *Shakespearean Criticism: Excerpts from the Criticism of William Shakespeare's Plays and Poetry, from the First Published Appraisals to Current Evaluations*. Detroit, Mich.: Gale Research Company. 635–8

Miller, James (2000). *The Passion of Michel Foucault*. Cambridge, Mass.: Harvard University Press

Norris, Christopher (1985). 'Post-Structuralist Shakespeare: Text and Ideology'. John Drakakis. Ed. *Alternative Shakespeares*. London: Methuen. 47–66

Penrod, Lynn (1996). *Hélène Cixous*. New York: Twayne Publishing

Ransom, John Crowe (1938). 'Shakespeare at Sonnets'. *Southern Review* 3. 531–53

Retamar, Roberto Fernández (1989). *Caliban and Other Essays*. Trans. Edward Baker. Minneapolis: University of Minnesota Press

Reynolds, Bryan (2003). *Performing Transversally: Reimagining Shakespeare and the Critical Future*. New York: Palgrave Macmillan

Rubin, Gayle (1975). 'The Traffic in Women: Notes on the "Political Economy" of Sex'. Rayna Reiter. Ed. *Toward an Anthropology of Women*. New York: Monthly Review Press. 157–210

Said, Edward (1978). *Orientalism*. New York: Pantheon

—— (1994). *Culture and Imperialism*. New York: Knopf

Saussure, Ferdinand de (1983). *Course in General Linguistics*. Trans. Roy Harris. London: Duckworth

Schalkwyk, David (2004). *Literature and the Touch of the Real*. Wilmington, Dela.: University of Delaware Press

Sedgwick, Eve Kosofsky (1985). *Between Men: English Literature and Male Homosocial Desire*. New York: Columbia University Press

Serres, Michel (1982). *Hermes: Literature, Science, Philosophy*. Ed. Josué V. Harari and David F. Bell. Baltimore: Johns Hopkins University Press

—— (1995). *Genesis*. Trans. Geneviève James and James Nielson. Ann Arbor: University of Michigan Press

Serres, Michel and Bruno Latour (1995). *Conversations on Science, Culture and Time*. Trans. Roxanne Lapidus. Ann Arbor: University of Michigan Press

Showalter, Elaine (1994). 'Representing Ophelia: Women, Madness, and the Responsibilities of Feminist Criticism'. Susanne L. Wofford. Ed. *Hamlet*. Boston: Bedford. 220–40

Sinfield, Alan (2006). *Shakespeare, Authority, Sexuality: Unfinished Business in Cultural Materialism*. London: Routledge

Soyinka, Wole (1983). 'Shakespeare and the Living Dramatist'. *Shakespeare Survey* 36 (1983): 1–10

—— (1984). 'The Critic and Society: Barthes, Leftocracy, and Other Mythologies'. Henry Louis Gates Jr.. Ed. *Black Literature and Literary Theory*. New York: Methuen. 27–58

Stallybrass, Peter (2001). ' "Well grubbed, old mole": Marx, *Hamlet*, and the (Un)Fixing of Representation'. Jean E. Howard and Scott Cutler Shershow. Eds. *Marxist Shakespeares*. London: Routledge. 16–30

Taylor, Michael (2001). *Shakespeare Criticism in the Twentieth Century*. Oxford: Oxford University Press

Vickers, Brian (1993). *Appropriating Shakespeare: Contemporary Critical Quarrels*. New Haven and London: Yale University Press

Wilson, Richard (2007). *Shakespeare in French Theory*. London: Routledge

Wimsatt, William K. and Monroe C. Beardsley (1946). 'The Intentional Fallacy'. *Sewanee Review* 54 (1946): 468–88

Woolf, Virginia (1929). *A Room of One's Own*. London: Harcourt Brace Jovanovich

Yates, Julian (2006). 'Accidental Shakespeare'. *Shakespeare Studies* 34. 90–122

Zabus, Chantal (2002). *Tempests after Shakespeare*. New York and Houndmills, Basingstoke: Palgrave

Žižek, Slavoj (1991). *Looking Awry: An Introduction to Jacques Lacan through Popular Culture*. Cambridge, Mass.: MIT Press

—— (1997). *The Plague of Fantasies*. London: Verso

—— (2007). *How to Read Lacan*. New York: Norton

Index

(bold typeface indicates a sustained discussion of a theorist or shakespeare text)